AF473747

Bill Jacklin
Monotypes

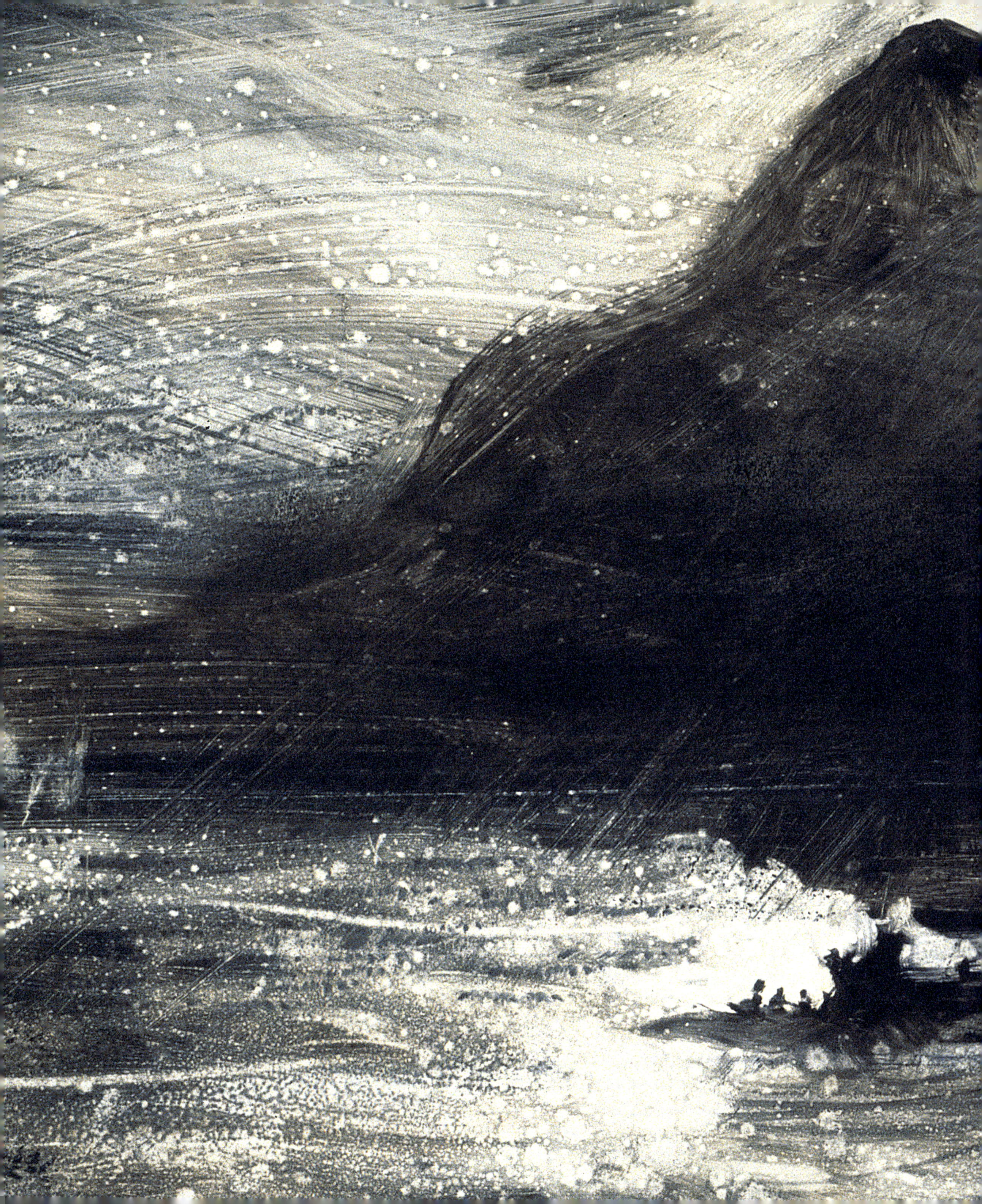

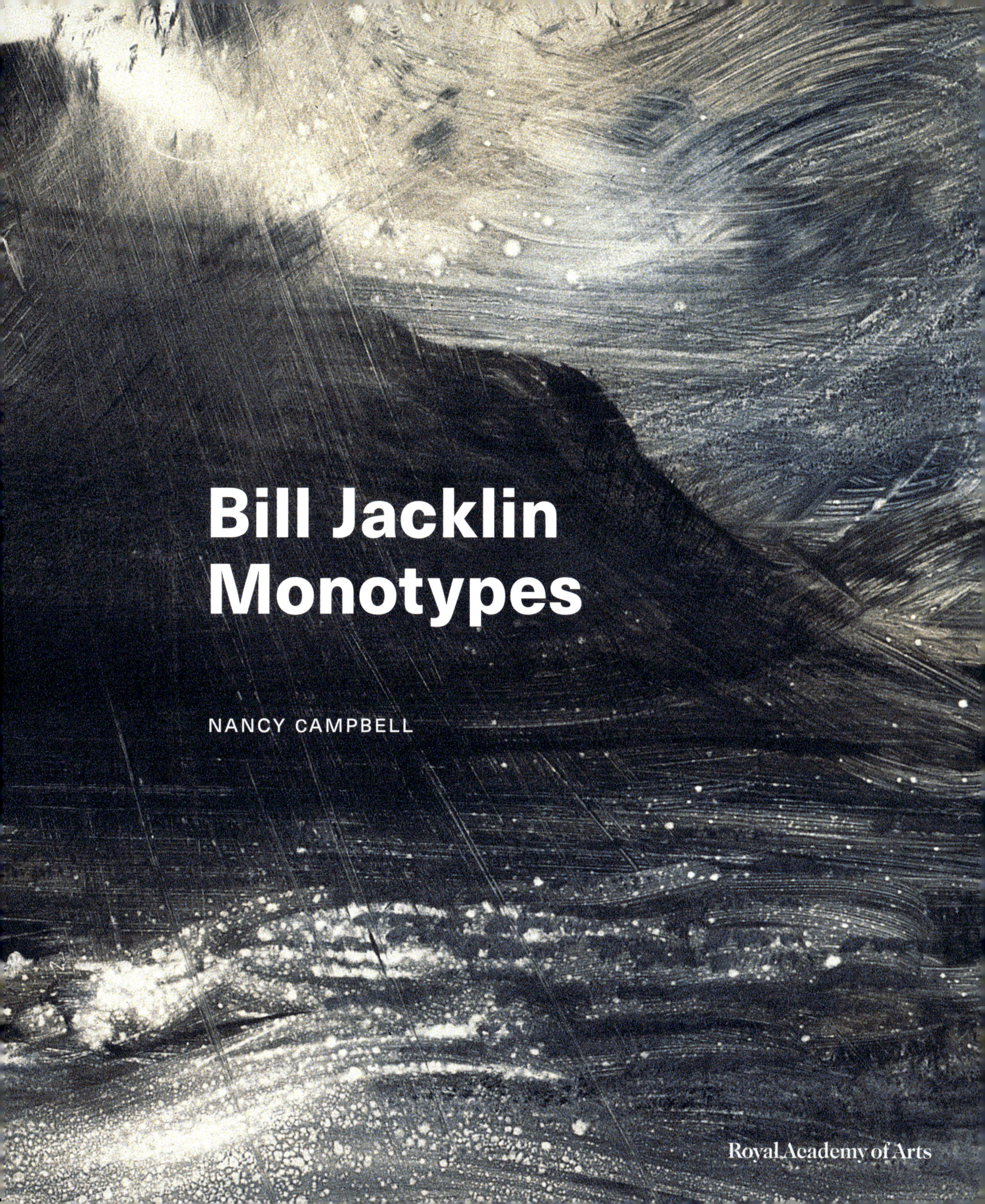

Bill Jacklin Monotypes

NANCY CAMPBELL

Royal Academy of Arts

Acknowledgements
I am extremely grateful to the following individuals for their invaluable assistance in the making of this book:

Nancy Campbell, Kate Chipperfield, Florence Dassonville, John Erle-Drax, Abe Frajndlich, Janet Russo Jacklin, Kathrin Jacobsen, Matt Kirkum, Carola Krueger, Susannah Lawson, Linda Manchester, Frankie Rossi and Peter Sawbridge.

Bill Jacklin RA

Royal Academy Publications
Florence Dassonville, Production and Distribution Co-ordinator
Carola Krueger, Production and Distribution Manager
Peter Sawbridge, Head of Publishing and Editorial Director

Copy-editing and proofreading: Susannah Lawson
Design: Kathrin Jacobsen
Colour origination and print: Gomer Press, Wales

British Library Cataloguing-in-Publication Data
A catalogue record for this book is available from the British Library

ISBN 978-1-915815-06-4

Distributed outside the United States and Canada by ACC Art Books Ltd, Riverside House, Dock Lane, Melton, Woodbridge, IP12 1PE

Distributed in the United States and Canada by ARTBOOK | D.A.P., 75 Broad Street, Suite 630, New York, NY 10004

Editorial Note
All works illustrated are by Bill Jacklin RA unless otherwise stated.

Dimensions of works of art are given in inches and centimetres, height before width.

Illustrations
Cover: detail of no. 60
Pages 2–3: detail of no. 47
Pages 16–17: detail of no. 64
Pages 104–5: detail of no. 54

Contents

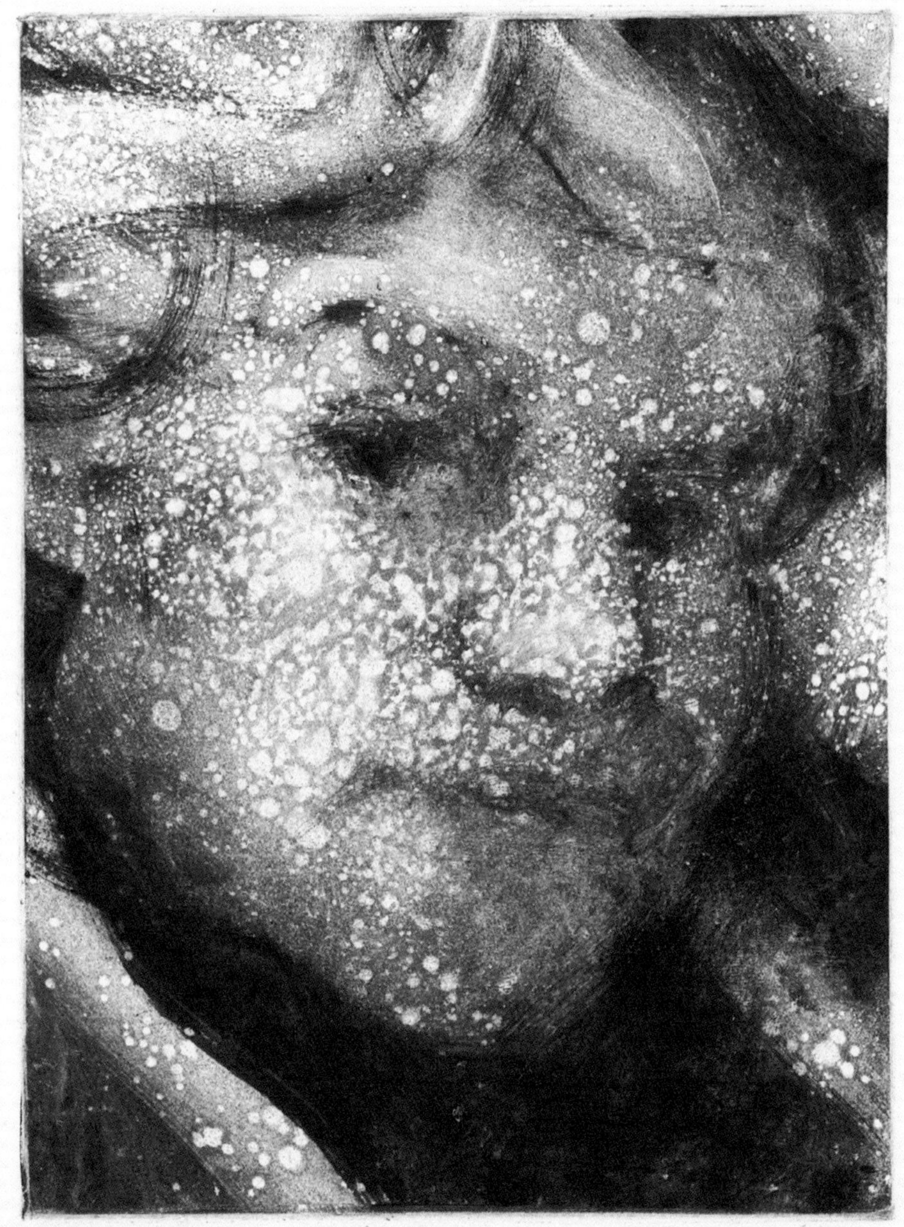

monotype *Portrait of Youth.* *Jachlei '08.*

'Form is the temptation of love and its peril... to round off a situation, to sum up a character. But the difference is that art has got to have form, whereas life need not.'
IRIS MURDOCH[1]

Materialise Like Magic: Bill Jacklin's Monotypes

NANCY CAMPBELL

FIG. 1 *Portrait of Youth*, 2008. Monotype, 11¾ × 9 inches (29.8 × 22.9 cm)

The nights are growing longer in Rhode Island. Halloween decorations glow lurid orange in front gardens in the early dusk. The Federal architecture is softened by the fading pompoms of Peegee hydrangea, turning from lime green to pink, and Michaelmas daisies growing from cracks in stone steps.

Bill Jacklin lives down by the Atlantic shore. As we drive to his studio from his home in Bristol, we go through the woods and pass Longfield, the Gothic Revival home of Charles Dana Gibson, grandfather of the famous artist of the same name who became so renowned for his idealised depictions of fashionable, young American women, the famous 'Gibson Girls'.

Jacklin loves the woods. He tells me that he has kept as many trees as possible on his property and planted more. He was advised to fell a rather grand cypress for a better view of the ocean at the end of the road, but decided not to, preferring the tree to be a home for the many creatures that visit his porch all year round. Here in Rhode Island there are none of the low walls and privet hedges to be found in the East End of London, where Jacklin grew up after the Second World War. Instead, well-kept lawns meet the pavements without any barrier. Our conversation, similarly, revolves around the marginal ground between printmaking techniques, crossing borders between places, between wildness and discipline, the seeping of light into darkness and of shadows into light, consciousness and dream, and the ocean Jacklin traverses with increasing frequency, lured back to his city of origin, to fulfil his duties at the Royal Academy and – often the same thing – to see his friends.

His studio, which he describes as 'my little place', is rented, a corner of an old brick building, its windows facing north and east over the town green.

BILL JACKLIN I've always rented spaces – that's my nomad thing. I've always liked walking away, disappearing. I keep starting over. But I've schlepped the same press around forever, about twenty years now. It's a good one, an Intaglio Etching Press built by Charles Brand of 84 East 10th Street, New York City. I bought it; I think it came out of an art school. It works well. These zinc plates, the ones I make my monotypes on, have a slight burr on them, which holds the ink. I think they were Robert Motherwell's plates. Catherine Mosley, his printer and later mine, gave them to me. Now I make the monos on this press.

NANCY CAMPBELL Interesting to think of you working on Motherwell's plates.

BJ Yes, a historical layering. My studio is in some disarray, I'm afraid.

NC A sign of work in progress.

BJ Do you know the ballet dancer Wayne Sleep?
NC I do, actually; I used to know him quite well. We shared an office in Covent Garden. He kept all his costumes, drag and panto, on racks among our books.
BJ What a coincidence! Well, Wayne and his partner came to my London studio in the 1970s, just after my show at Nigel Greenwood's gallery in Chelsea. I think they were a bit disappointed because everything was so tidy. At the time I was going through a period of reduction, I was doing those tight little drawings. It was just before I started going back into figuration. Wayne asked anxiously, 'Why is it so tidy?'
NC Yes, I can imagine. But now everything of yours is freer. With monotypes, you have no opportunity for the layering that occurs in a painting. The image relies on a swift gesture, even erasure. Perhaps we should just clarify exactly what monoprints and monotypes are, by quoting from Mychael Barratt's glossary in the Royal Academy's 2016 book on your graphics:

Although most printmaking techniques produce multiple editions, monoprints and monotypes are unique, one-off prints. There is an infinite range of techniques available to the ***monoprint*** *artist and not all of them involve a printing press. Techniques that do involve a press include the expressive and unique inking of plates or blocks made using other techniques such as etching or woodcut; the inking and printing of various overlaid objects and elements; or the inking up of a plate in a painterly manner to be transferred to paper. An example of a monoprint that does not involve a press is when a drawing is done on the back of a piece of paper that has been laid onto a surface rolled with ink, thus transferring a mirror image of the drawing on the reverse. A* ***monotype*** *is a monoprint in which no reusable element (such as an etching plate, woodblock or stencil) has been employed. Examples include printing from plates that have been inked up in a painterly manner, and creating an image by removing ink from a completely inked surface with rags or brushes or by spraying on solvents such as white spirit or lighter fluid. As unique pieces, the monoprint and monotype hold a status somewhere between the editioned print and a drawing or painting.*[2]

Did your monotypes emerge from your move to America in the mid-1980s, do you think? Was that where their freedom came from?
BJ Well, that's an interesting question. Yes, I think so. One of my earliest monoprints, *Woman in a Chair Rising* (no. 2), came out of a group of paintings, a series called *The Argument*, showing a woman getting up to walk away. I remember I had a model posing for a painting in London. I looked at her and said, 'You're pregnant!' Apparently, she'd been pregnant for a week or two. She got really mad at me, jumped up out of the chair and left. I'm an artist, I tend to see things.
NC You'd seen too much that time! The monotype is a response to the energetic force of her exit, although it hadn't been an argument as such.
BJ Right, yes, I think it must be tied to my own departure from England for America in 1985. I was working on these with Stanley Jones on a big press at Curwen Studios in London, an offset press. I was working on the roller and doing it every which way. I don't know what you'd call these because I was messing with everything, standing on the press bed, painting the press, painting the paper, and ending up with all these different images. All came from the same beginning. Then I added colour. One of the first monotypes I made was *Sheep Meadow*. Black and white. Then *Sunbather I* (no. 3). I was experimenting, seeing if I could make an image that was simple. They were one-offs. Then I did this series of the sea at Coney Island (nos 5–6).
NC I'm interested in this move you made, not only between places, but between this one figure in the chair or the sunbather, and then multiple figures. As soon as there are multiple forms or figures at play, you can see back to your earlier work again. In *Coney Island* (nos 5–6), for example, there's that reference to earlier works in your *oeuvre*. It feels like you're rediscovering something that has preoccupied you for a while.
BJ Well, those figures did come out of the subject too. When you go to Coney Island there are so many people there, it's crazy (fig. 2). You get imbued with it. I'd sit on the beach and do endless drawings and then bring them back and make things from the experience. I'd go with my photographer friend Abe Frajndlich. He and I had a close association. Like me, Abe never subscribed to doing only one thing. He always wanted to do what he wanted to do. We'd take the D train to Coney Island and walk down from the fairground towards Brighton Beach. We'd hang out; he'd photograph, I'd do endless drawings. We also went to 42nd Street in the early 1980s. It was wild, a crazy place; we often got chased out of clubs by the huge bouncers. I would distract people while he took photos (fig. 3), and then he would talk to them to get their attention while I was drawing. We got some good images out of that. The dark as well as the sweet moments in life.
NC Turning art into a crime – by sleight of hand! Tell me more about your process: you make a sketch, you return with your sketchbook to the studio and it becomes another image?
BJ I don't tend to copy, it comes from an internal energy and I *find* the shapes. When I started doing the black-and-white monotypes, I would paint the whole plate up with black ink and then I'd find the light, and out of finding the light I'd find the shapes. In other words, the subject is revealed by the way the light hits the shapes: I often didn't know what the subject was at the beginning. But I'd always find it.
NC Like Michelangelo seeing the form emerge from the marble?
BJ Maybe, yes. It's all about working backwards. Because I'm somewhat dyslexic I can think backwards.

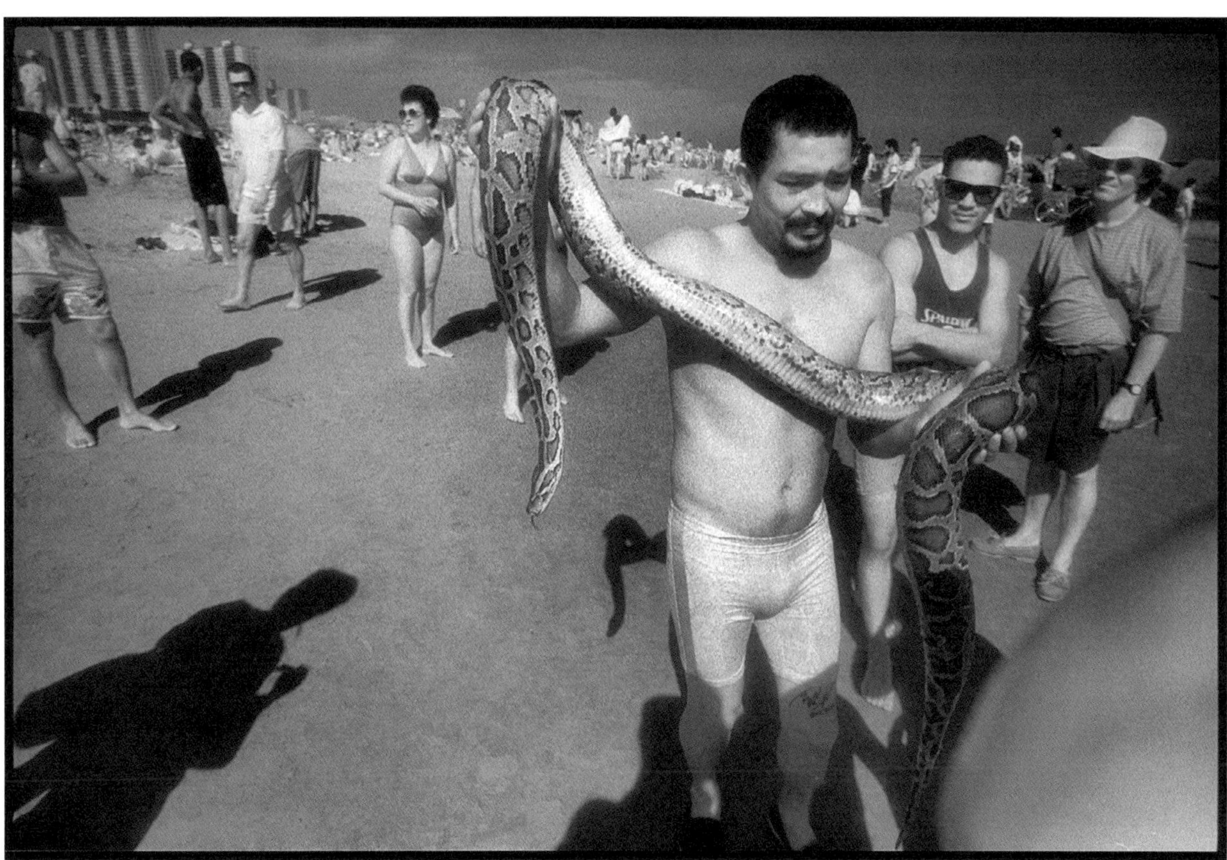

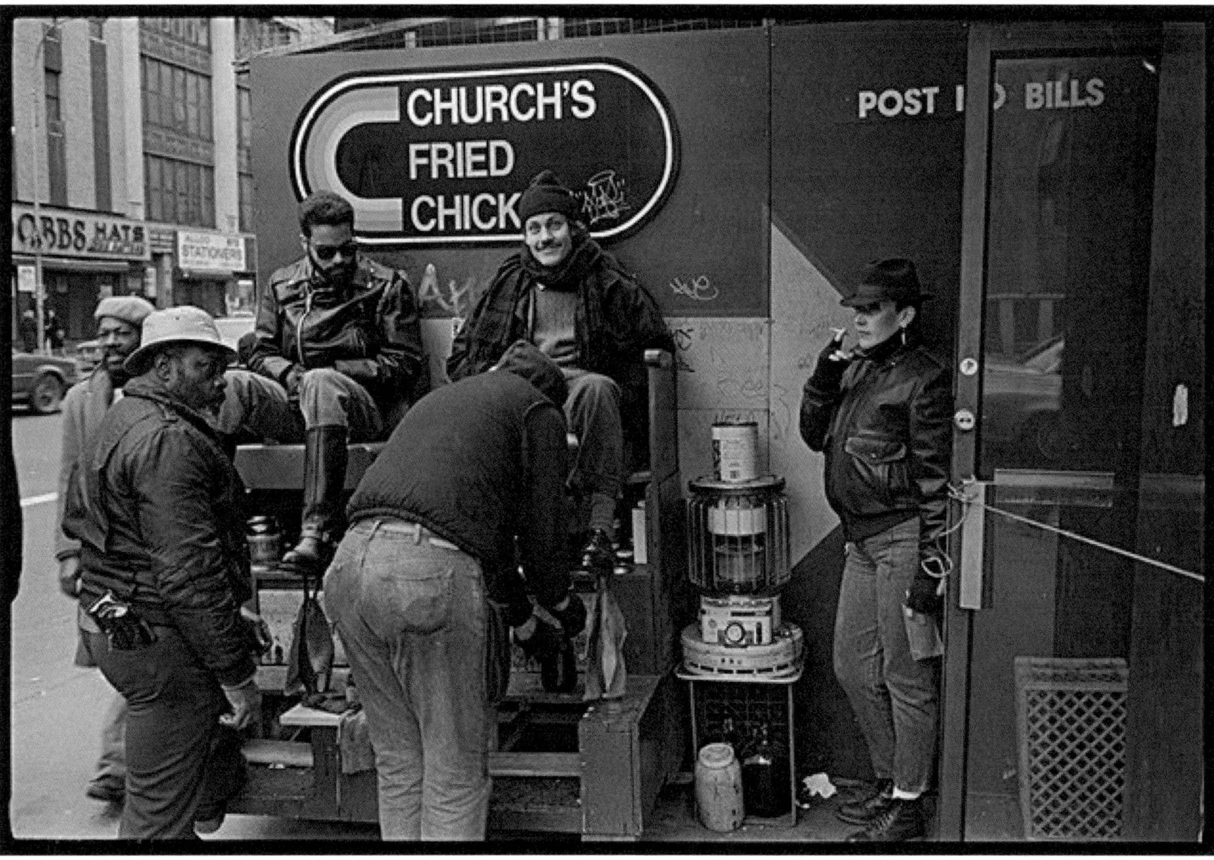

FIG. 2 Coney Island snakeman, 1991.
Photograph by Abe Frajndlich

FIG. 3 42nd Street, 1986.
Photograph by Abe Frajndlich

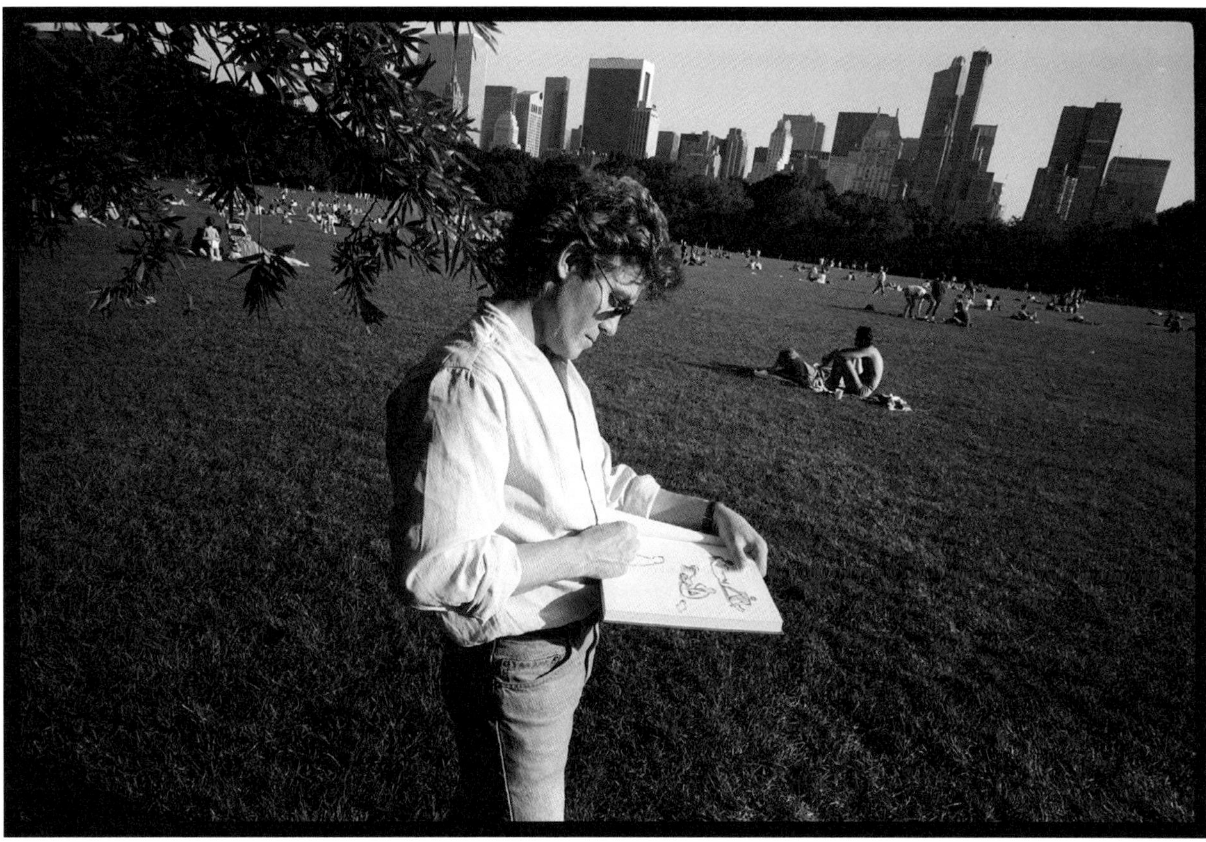

FIG. 4 Bill drawing in Central Park, 1990.
Photograph by Abe Frajndlich

NC I see. The blackness of the ink has such an emotional quality; its depth of tone can be very resonant. As a poet it interests me that the white is an absence, it signifies what has been wiped away. The hopeful act is a very conscious act.

BJ By disposition I am a hopeful person, although I get depression as much as anyone, and that can show in my work. In the portraits I made of my father when he was dying, for example, I attempted a self-portrait. I've got a few wrinkles – something the pen can catch on to. I might attempt a self-portrait again soon.

With regard to other monotypes, such as my *Literature Walk* series (no. 13), which I have continued to make since I left London for New York City in 1985, the silhouettes and shadows create the structure. I'd adhere to what I'd originally seen, the sun hitting the figures from over there, just as I saw it in Central Park (fig. 4). I'd be playing. And then there are my sketches of the Wollman Rink (nos 8–9) – each one is different. In some, the figures of the ice skaters are more defined.

NC Sometimes in the *Skaters* series there's a highlight of colour, a dash of red for instance. Its repetition seems to suggest a journey that is experienced over and over as the skater circles the rink. It hints at time having a circularity, with events that recur eternally, rather than the linear conception of Western thought. This is an idea one can see in other of your works too.

BJ Here's *Roseland II*; it was in New York, where my wife Janet and I met on a blind date set up by mutual friends. I was sketching people swirling and whirling around. Then *Park with Shadows*; I saw that image in the south of France 50 years ago, driving through those French lanes. It's classic isn't it, once you've seen it you can't forget it.

NC You're driving towards a vanishing point, I can almost hear John Coltrane on the radio.

BJ You can. That reminds me, I was walking down the street the other day and I saw two people kissing, and as I walked on – it was kind of cool – I saw their shadows, the shadow of their embrace on the road. I don't make anything up. I have to have been there, I have to have a sense of the experience. It's not a concoction. I must have the experience, even if I deviate from it. To have a sense of being with someone, somewhere, and only then can I deviate or re-create. But I have to know where I was in the first place, not just make it up from scratch, as some other artists might. There has to be an emotional context for me.

NC I wonder whether sometimes that comes about of its own accord? If a work has its own powerful will?

BJ Yes, the work emerges through the process. You do that too, surely, in your writing. All you've got to do is to be there.

Iris Murdoch taught me when I was a student at the Royal College. I knew her later too, in Oxford. When

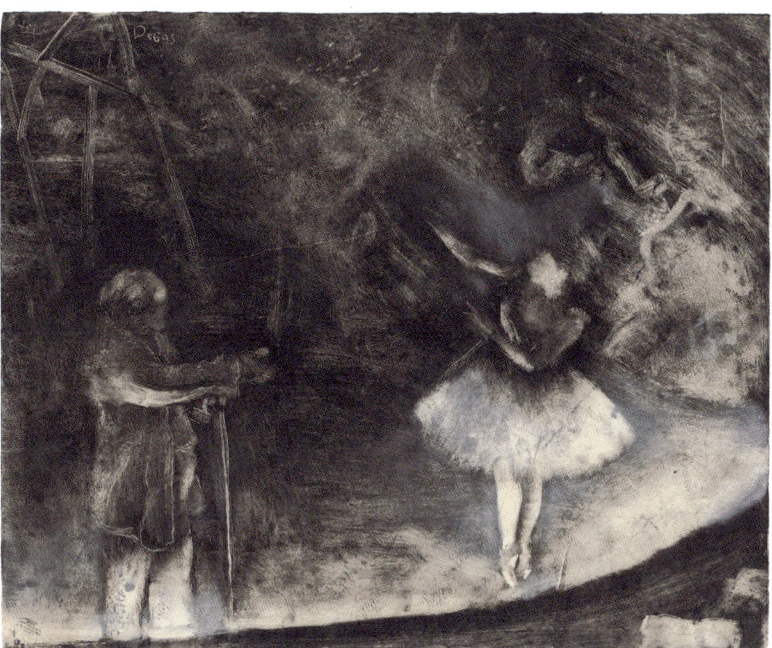

FIG. 5 Edgar Degas, *The Ballet Master*, *c.* 1876. Monotype, white chalk or wash on laid paper, sheet $24^{7}/_{16} \times 33^{7}/_{16}$ inches (62 × 85 cm). National Gallery of Art, Washington

I was a student I had to write an essay for her on Kant's *Metaphysics*, on morals and humanism. I worked all night on it, helped by a girlfriend, the artist Margaret Priest, who was smarter than me. Iris sent the essay back: 'You have a good understanding of the *Metaphysics*, but what about love, Mr Jacklin?' That question threw me. It opened up so much. She meant it in the broadest way, of course, philosophically.

NC Love, yes. Murdoch was preoccupied by love throughout her creative work, in her novels too – she had a fascination with people's messy lives. But your work at that stage was far from messy; it was highly controlled. Tell me, if Iris Murdoch found something lacking in your appreciation of Kant, was there perhaps a philosopher whose world view you found more sympathetic, as a young man? Or even now?

BJ Probably the existentialists, Sartre. I've always shared that angst, having been a war baby. However, I had a need to go beyond that for myself.

NC I see. Do you look at other artists' monotypes?

BJ I'm sure I must have. For me, monotypes just come out of my paintings. It's a process, a working towards something. I also use pastels. I pastel over the monotype, it's a classic thing. If you go to the National Gallery of Art in Washington you can see Degas drawing with pastel on top of a 'ghost' (fig. 5). He is an influence, and so is Daumier. Ghosts are, you know, a second impression taken after the first, when nearly all the ink or paint has already been absorbed. Degas would take the reverse of one of his ballet dancers and it would give him a faint impression of the image, then he'd work up a pastel on top.

Sometimes I work on a piece of Mylar. I'll make a black-and-white print, then work with colour – greens and blues – on the hand painting of the plate. A variation on something. That fascinates me: when does something become something else? When does a monotype become not a monotype? When does the graphic work actually become a painting? These are grey areas. People always want to know what it is, and you say, 'Well, it's a bit of this and a bit of that.' How to categorise it? Well, my gallery does that for me. There can be criticism, sometimes, if you cross a boundary and people don't know exactly what something is. I don't care about all that. The ongoing stages of a process that an artist takes an idea through are what matter to me.

NC After all, if you did this on the press, wouldn't it be more like a monoprint?

BJ Well yes, if there was an image on the plate, I *could* do it on the press too. I might also look at a monotype and feel it lacks density so I might put another wash on a plate and put the paper precisely over the second plate and run it. It'd still be a monotype, even with two plates, although the usual idea of a monotype is of a one-off action. I like to play around the edges. I could give you an argument to demolish any definition of a monotype! I can stand on the press and call it something else; I can print it several times, I can add things, you know. Sometimes my monotypes turn into pastels, sometimes paintings – an oil painting on top of a monoprint, an oil painting on paper.

NC Bill Jacklin rocking and rolling again, breaking the rules!

BJ Yes, breaking the rules! Degas did it all the time.

NC Well, printmakers are often the revolutionaries.

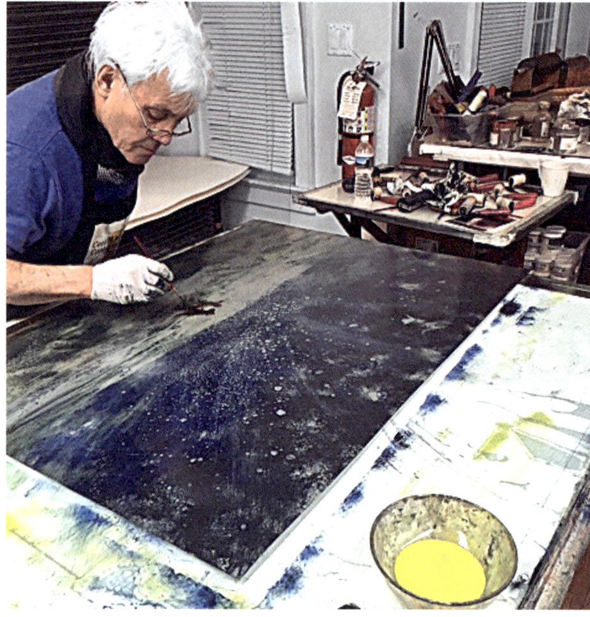

FIG. 6 Bill in the studio at Contemporary Print Center, Connecticut, 2016. Photograph by Paul DeRuvo

But here, in the monotypes, you're almost having a conversation with your own work. An image spoke to you, it may already be represented in other monotypes, and here you are, determined to enter that space again. How does this work, in relation to your process as a painter?

BJ Expressing an idea quickly, that's my motivation with monotypes. You can get stuck in a painting for years. With a monotype you've either got it or you haven't. Take a painting like this, which shows a large group of people forming a queue. It's very loose and abstracted. I'll develop this, I'll continue to layer and define it, some areas will be more representative, others looser, and so on. The key decision is when to stop. Do you make something in ten minutes, or take ten years over it?

You're right though. It is a dialogue with the work itself. Often, as I work on things, the subject matter changes entirely as I progress. A sea painting could become a sunlit field: the work demands what it wants to become. I participate, obviously – I watch it changing.

NC When did you begin to see water and the sea as subjects in themselves, without the figures of swimmers?

BJ When we moved to Rhode Island. Since I left New York City and its influences I have been preoccupied with making images that I see around me. The fields, the sea and the night sky have become my subject for now. My most recent monotypes are explorations of deep emotive spaces portraying the sea and the night sky (nos 60 and 65–68). They are on the edge of abstraction, but remain within the realm of what I can see here from my studio by the sea. The crowds have disappeared. You work from where you are. It sounds like you do too. Some people stay in one spot their whole lives and that's great, that's their experience – right? That hasn't been my life. Sometimes I wish I'd had a space of my own, just mine. But if I'd had more stability I'd have done a different kind of work and been a different kind of person and had different relationships, right?

NC Yes, our backgrounds push us forwards. And isn't human nature essentially torn – between the settled, who long to be nomadic, and the nomads, who long for a home?

BJ Yes, I think so. I was born during the war. We moved five times because of the war before I went to school. I was a London boy. You got kicked out of one place and then it got bombed. Many people have lived their entire lives in one place. I have no comprehension of that.

NC Yes, indeed. What is this lovely image?

BJ My *Poodles* came out of a series for Westminster Dog Show. I could do a little book of dog shows with all the images I have. My bestselling postcard is *Shooting Star II* (fig. 7).

NC Like William Blake's wonderful etching of a man reaching for the crescent moon. Humans need that cosmic stuff. But I do like this image, the puff of the poodle's tail – like those hydrangeas outside – there's such a sense of celebration and a joy to it. And the joy in your work, we mustn't lose sight of that.

BJ I'm always looking for the light. When I was in hospital recently I did feel something swirling around me. I wasn't frightened, I felt I was part of it, and then it left me. It was like a state of dreaming, and yet not. It was unlike any experience I had had before.

NC I do think once you experience severe ill health you begin to see the body almost as an ecosystem.

BJ Yes, everything's connected.

NC *Early One Morning* (nos 19–24), your sequence of eight monotypes, has a strong historical context. You

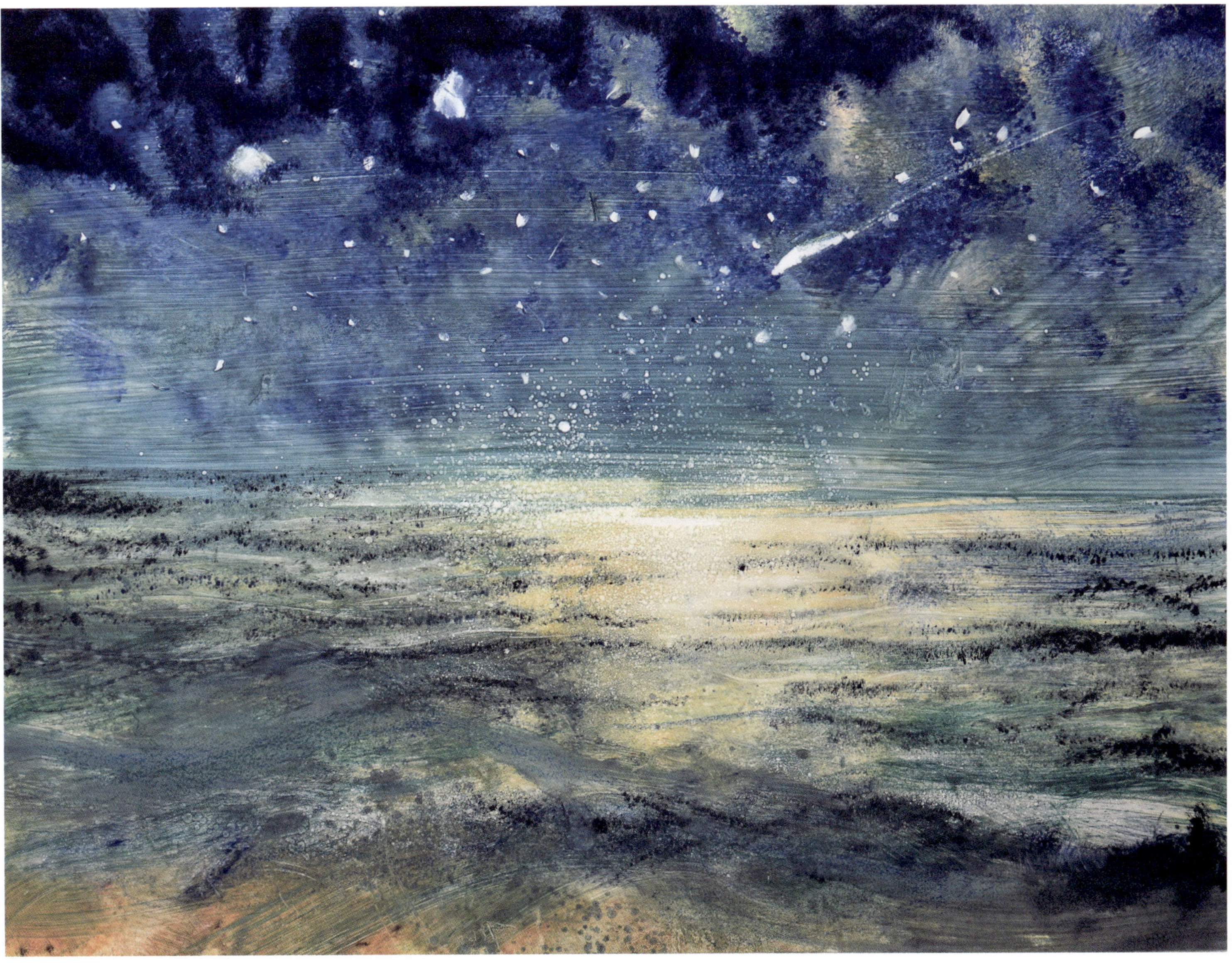

FIG. 7 *Shooting Star II*, 2016. Monotype, 29½ × 39½ inches (74.9 × 100.3 cm). Private collection

show an empty park in New York City and crowds forming beneath gathering clouds throughout the day. The crowds are still so pertinent to the current news. There's pleasure, there's life, there's vivacity, enjoyment of water. But crowds can be terrifying; they can turn so quickly. Here's the gesture of smoke coming across. The *New York Harbour* series (no. 36), they also reference 9/11 don't they? That iconic view. The changing weather relates to that sense of brooding climate elsewhere in your work – the rain, the snow. The images in the series capture moments of change.

BJ The changing weather has always preoccupied me, whether sun, rain or snow, but my concern remains the constant atmospheric flux and an acceptance of that. Monotypes allow me to follow those changing processes and to enjoy what they might bring.

Some critics have mentioned a filmic sensibility in my work. You know, double images. Time lapse. I made many of these images before 9/11, that series beneath the Twin Towers, they actually gave me a sense of foreboding. I called it *Before the Event, Great Lawn I* and *After the Event, Great Lawn I* (no. 16). I made *After the Event* in both monotypes and paintings. I wanted to describe New York in celebratory mood and at other times to show something much darker. That appeared to be the nature of the city to me. Things can turn dark very quickly. It's done with chemicals, water and oil, turpentine; it breaks things up, it creates a look. There is that duality of being an artist: you've got to transport the painting to something that is possibly something else. If you're creating a figurative image, those dots become rain or snow, so I have to find a way of doing it, for it to become that by

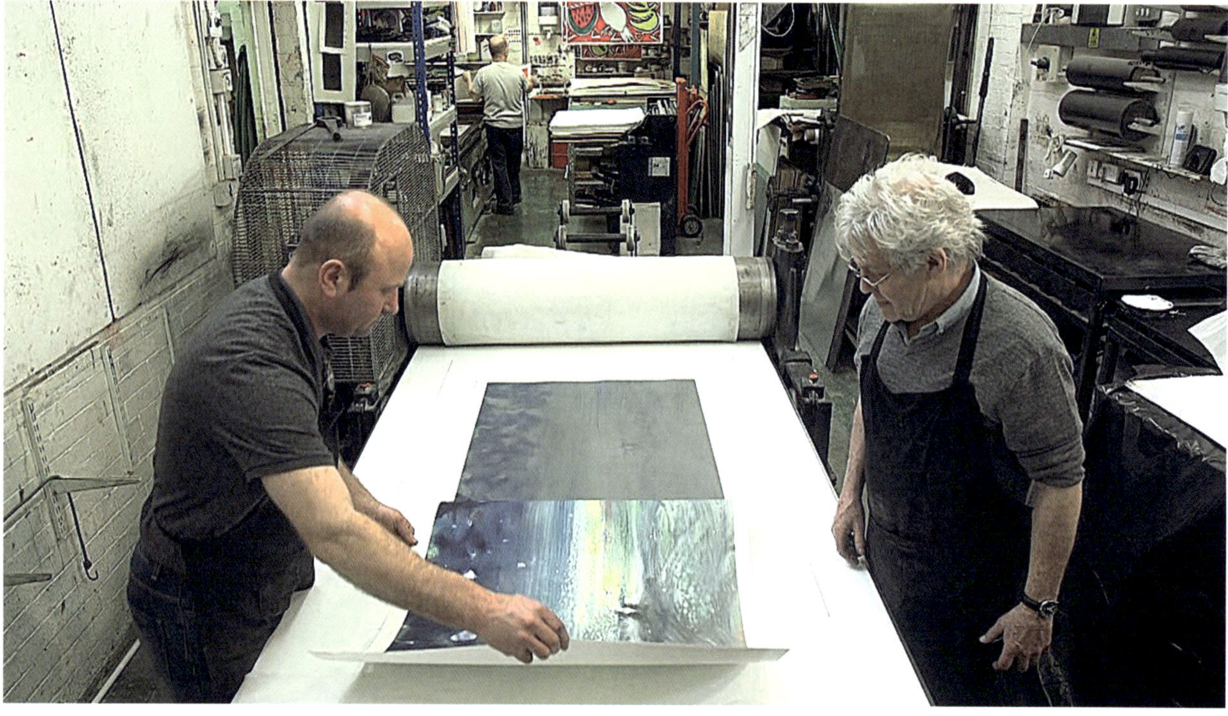

FIG. 8 Bill with Simon Marsh at Paupers Press, London, 2015. Photograph by Michael Taylor

association. One of these monotype images, *Great Lawn Event II* (no. 15), eventually developed into an etching that was commissioned by the Print Club of New York in 2000.

NC And so, would you say, in *After the Event*, that you're flicking the chemical, the turps, or spraying it onto the matrix?

BJ Trial and error. Making a throwaway gesture. Sometimes I flick with an old toothbrush. You can *pound* things. You have to imagine what the image will be transmuted into once it's been through the press. Just as with watercolour, if you're working wet on wet, you've got to anticipate how it will dry, not how it looks now. Some people are too timid when doing a watercolour, but if you're bold it dries down to what you want.

NC Look at this splodge in *After the Event*, there's a lot of action going on there.

BJ I like the word splodge! I just work completely instinctively – I might take a really big brush, and then splatter it, and wipe it. With monotypes you've got to be prepared to risk everything. You have to let go, whatever it is.

Michael Taylor of Paupers Press in London invited me to work at the Scuola Internazionale di Grafica in Venice in 2003 and I made many monotypes of the crowds, bridges and canals I witnessed there (nos 33–34). It rained a great deal so my use of the monotype with liquid solvents was a perfect conduit for what I was seeing and feeling. Venice is glorious and romantic, of course, but for me, there's a sense of foreboding there too.

NC They're made almost more out of energy than subject. It's a very different process to painting, or even carving soldiers out of balsa wood, as you did in *Invitation Card* (fig. 9), your student piece that was recently acquired by the National Army Museum in London. Such a small amount of pigment can be so eloquent.

BJ Making a monotype – well, it's either there or not there. A monotype will materialise like magic. Suddenly they're in the world, they weren't there a minute ago, whereas paintings can take a long time.

NC Nimbleness is the quality these works demonstrate to me. Gracefulness. Being able to move according to the demands of a situation. What about the time constraints the press and the ink exert on you?

BJ Not so much, because I tend to work in oils, they are quite pliable for some time. A lot of people don't do that now because of its potential toxicity. But it would have got me a long time ago if it were going to!

NC May I ask, where are you with the spiritual?

BJ Well, I was involved in the Gurdjieff Society for fifteen years in London. That's quite a long time for anything. I used to go to meditation meetings two or three times a week.

NC It's apparent in your work, the movement of forms.

BJ I did a bit of that swirling and whirling, dervish dancing. I found it hard, it takes a lot of practice. Some of the exercises are very difficult, very complicated. They illustrate the cosmos in different ways. In demonstrations they sometimes put me in the front row, and mostly I had no idea what I was doing. Because usually you tend to follow the person in front of you.

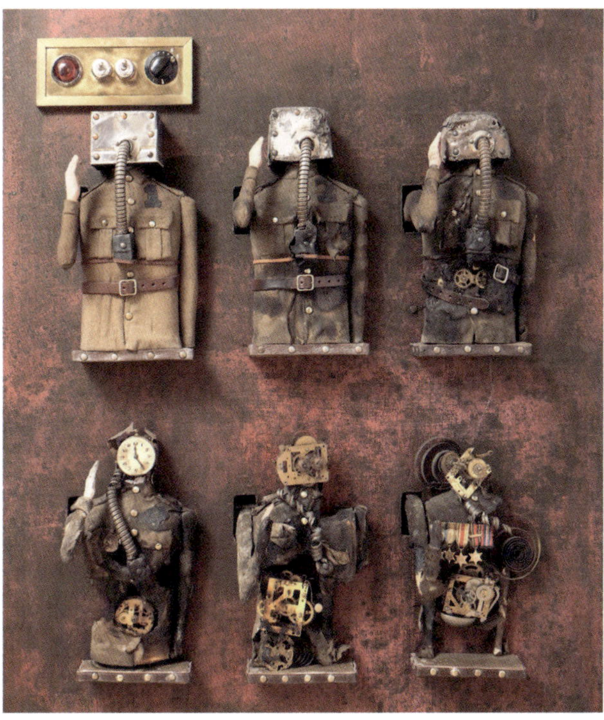

FIG. 9 *Invitation Card*, 1963. Mixed media, 50½ × 37½ × 10 inches (128.2 × 95.3 × 25.4 cm). National Army Museum, London

NC We can get through a lot of life without fully realising what we don't know. We're not aware of what we don't know until we have to initiate.

BJ Exactly so. In fact I'm glad I have occasionally been put in an uncomfortable spot. Yes, I learnt a lot from Gurdjieff's ideas. But then I learnt I had to leave it. I can still go to a place inside myself where I have a degree of freedom. I learnt how to do that. It's great. Takes a bit of work, like any meditative practice. All of us artists, we're so eager, we think we've got a view on the world, and yet with that practice you have to put your ego aside, or leave it at the doorstep at least. I don't regret that, but following a practice like the Fourth Way often began to make me cast doubt on what I was doing as an artist. Holding two ideas in your head at the same time can be challenging.

NC I've been doing Jungian work recently, and I'm intrigued by the synchronicities and the collective unconscious: symbols, archetypes. Why, for example, do people respond so deeply to bodies of water? When I began therapy, I was concerned it would resolve too much, destroy the grit in the oyster that forms the pearl. But it's been very interesting for my work as a poet, especially the sessions that explore dreams.

BJ I can understand that, Nancy. I have a lot of recurring dreams. Always the same feeling, not the same place, but anonymous cities that seem familiar. One way is down to the sea, one is to the bright lights. Classic dream of thinking you're somewhere but you're not, you don't know which way to go. Drawn to the dark water, yet you want the bright lights – but you can't quite get there. Anxiety. I have the same dream over and over again. It's always twilight. Existential angst. The darkness always looming. Look behind you and there it is. However, I've had many flying dreams too, looking down on oceans and cities in the hope of a clearer view. So I continue to make my work. And I think that's why I like planting trees; they're always looking for the light.

***

As we leave the studio, rain is spitting. 'Winter,' Bill shudders. 'Apparently there's going to be a lot of snow this winter.'

This conversation took place on 16 October 2023.

1 Iris Murdoch, *Existentialists and Mystics: Writings on Philosophy and Literature*, London, 1997, p. 285.

2 Mychael Barratt, 'Glossary of Bill Jacklin's Printmaking Techniques', in *Bill Jacklin: Graphics*, Royal Academy of Arts, London, 2016, p. 155.

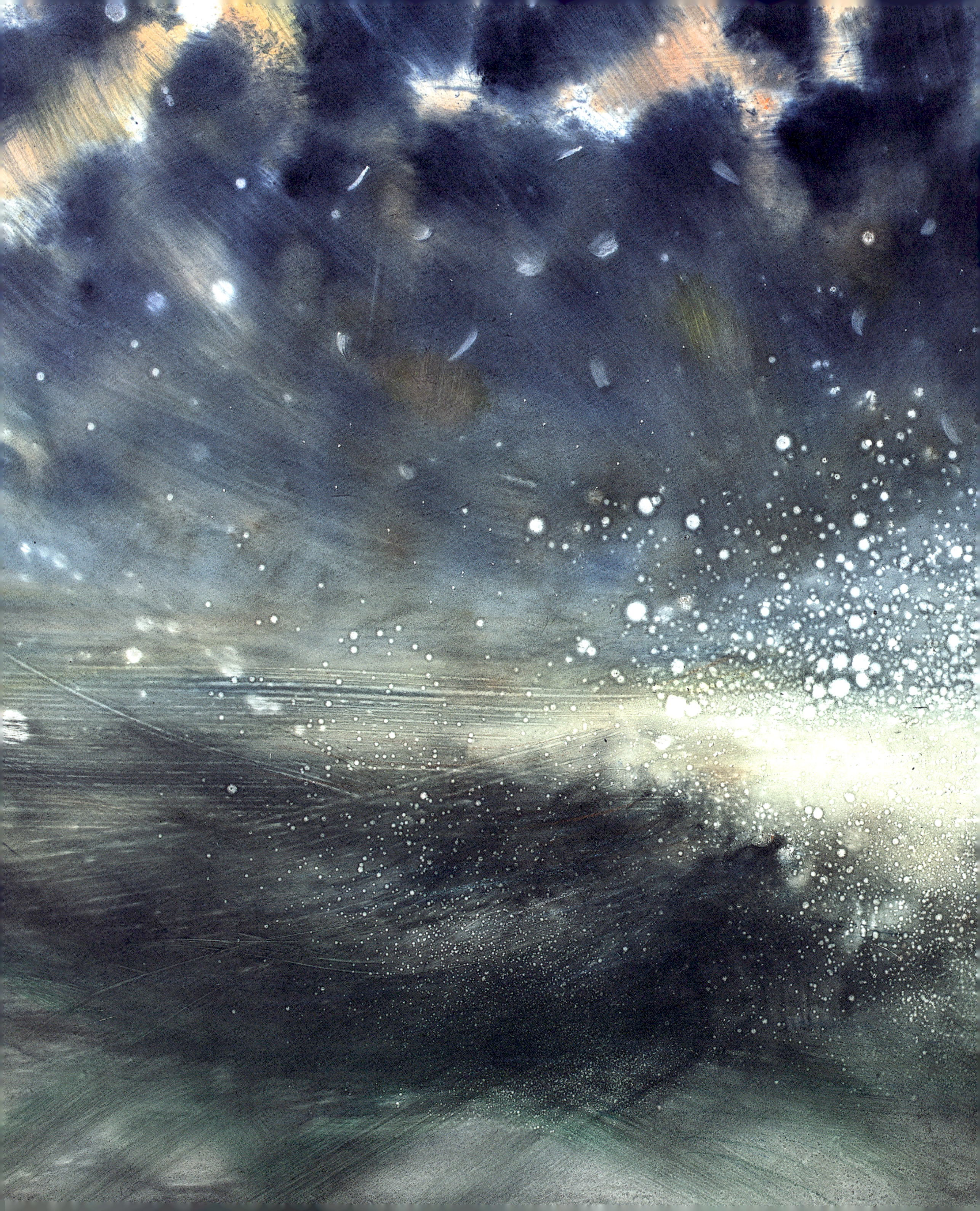

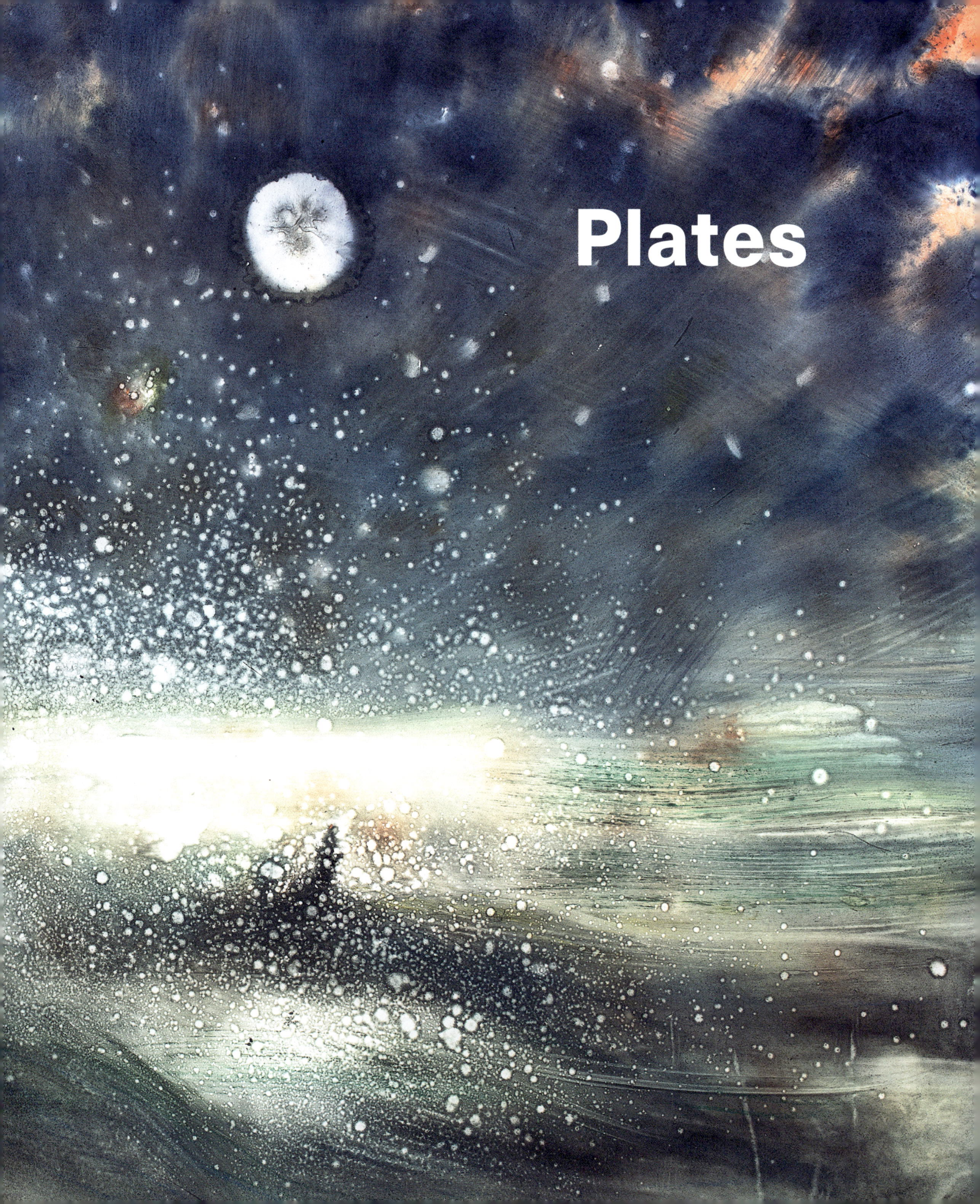

Plates

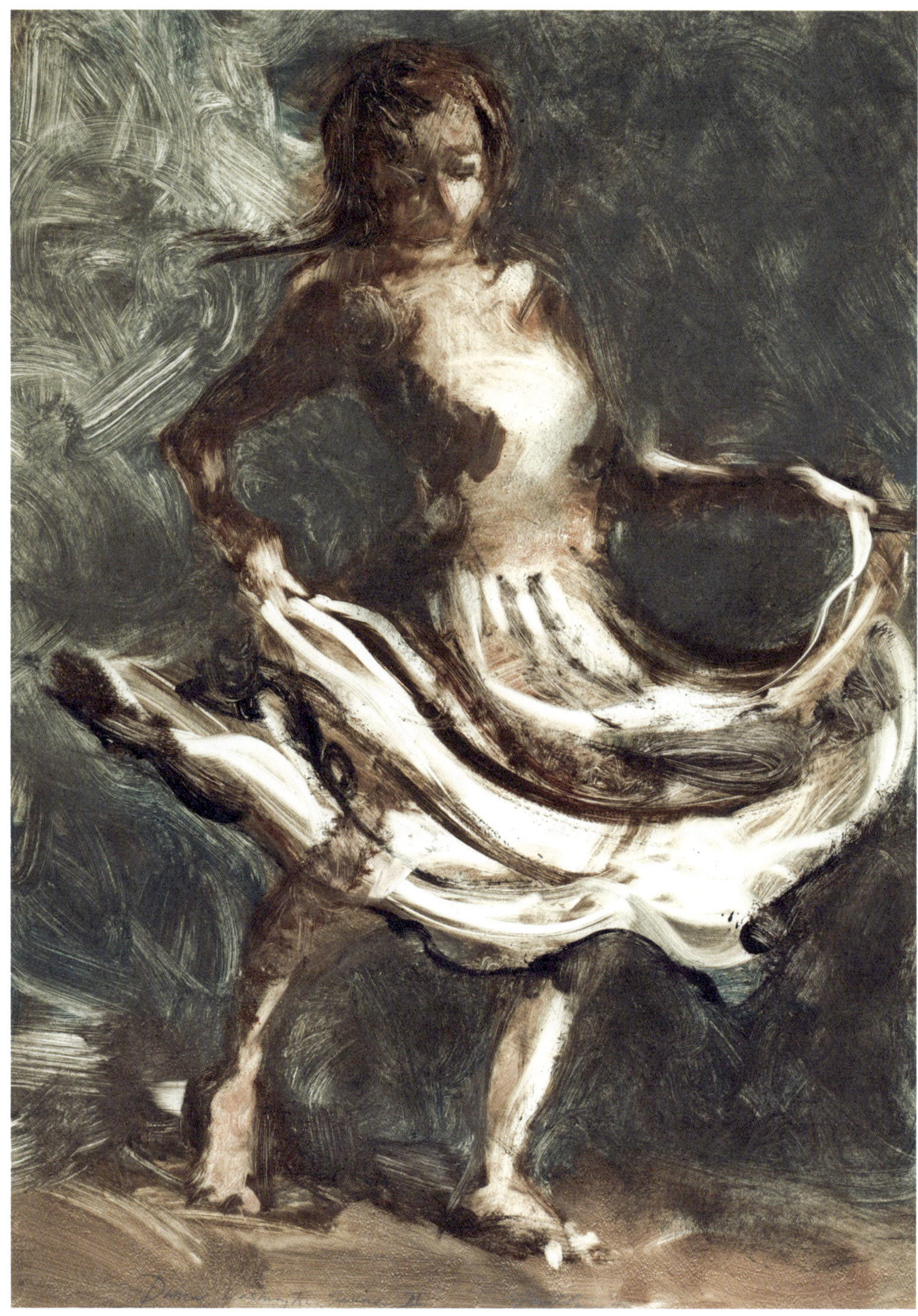

1
Dancer, Washington Square III, 1999
Monotype, 31 × 22¾ inches
(79 × 56.7 cm)

2
Woman in a Chair Rising, 1984
Monotype, 47 × 34 inches
(119.4 × 86.4 cm)

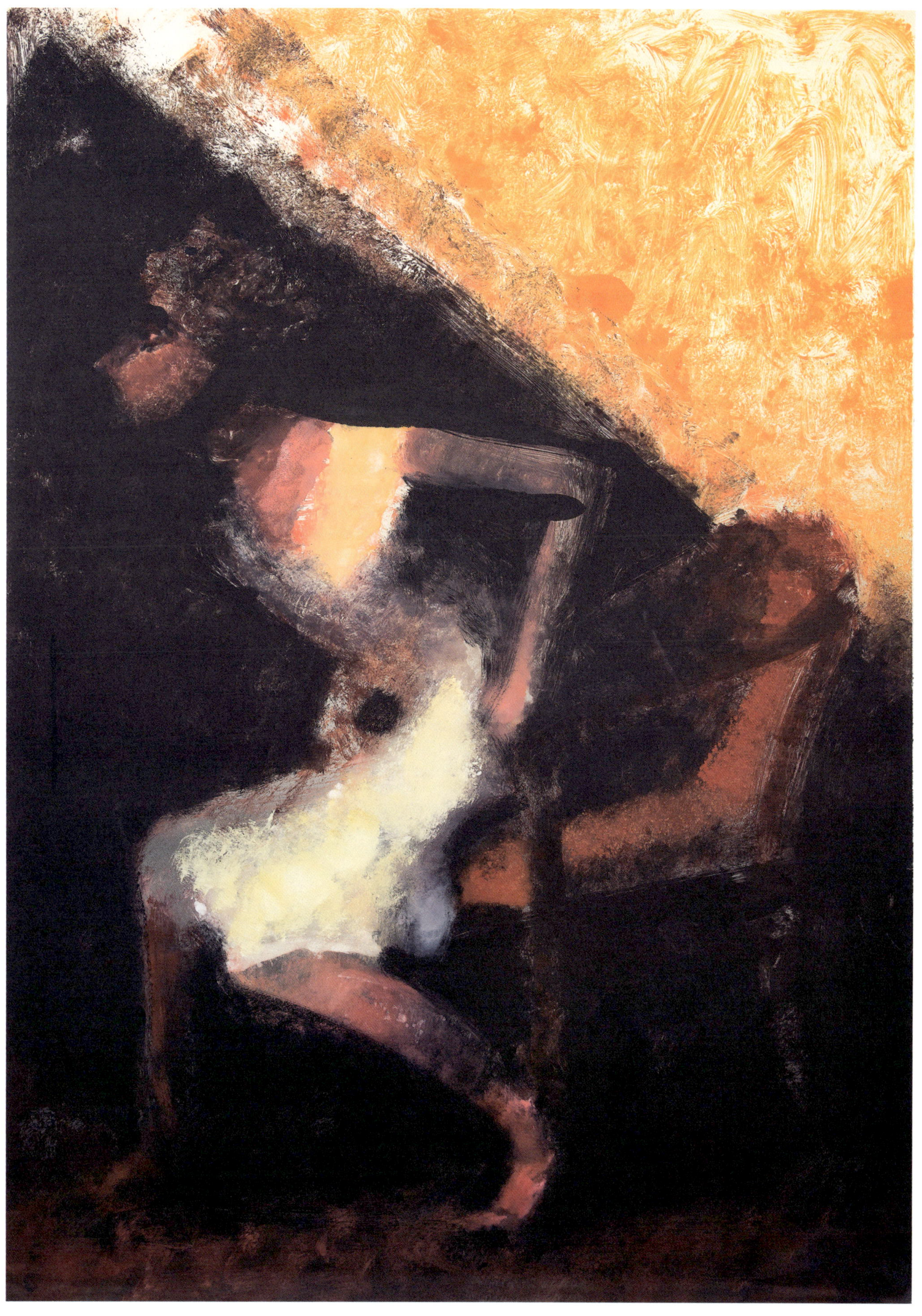

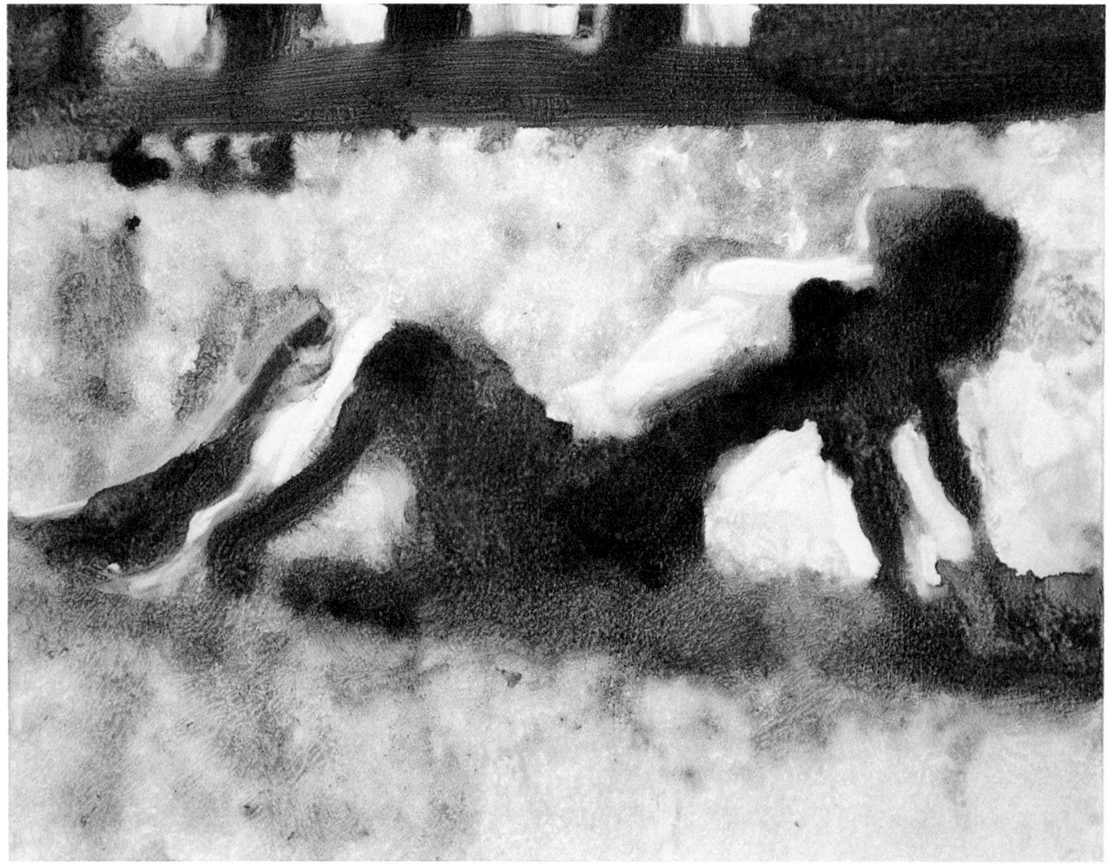

3
Sunbather I, 1991
Monotype, 9 × 11¾ inches
(22.9 × 29.9 cm)

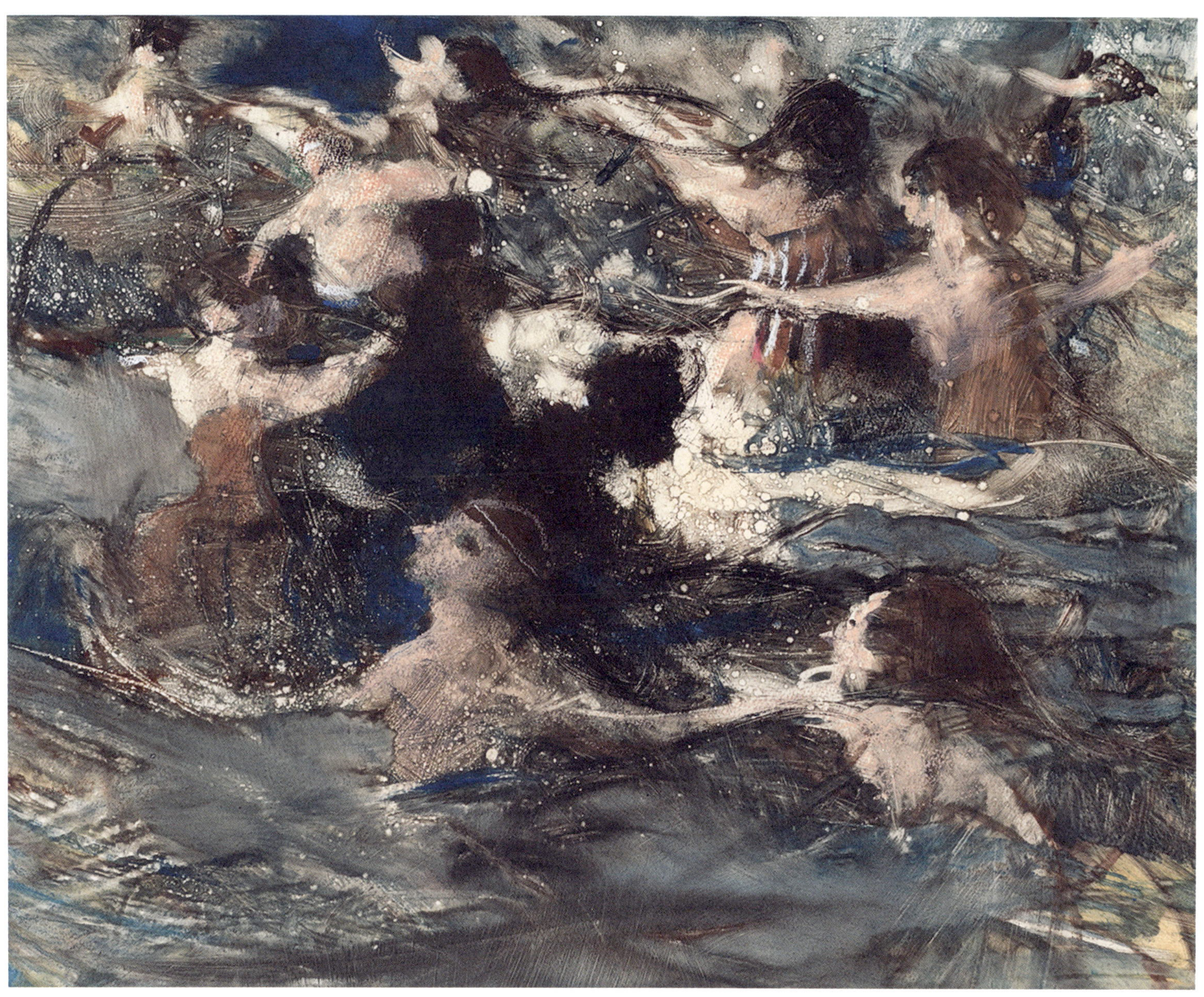

4
Into the Sea XI, 2007
Pastel monotype, 16 × 20 inches
(40.6 × 50.8 cm)

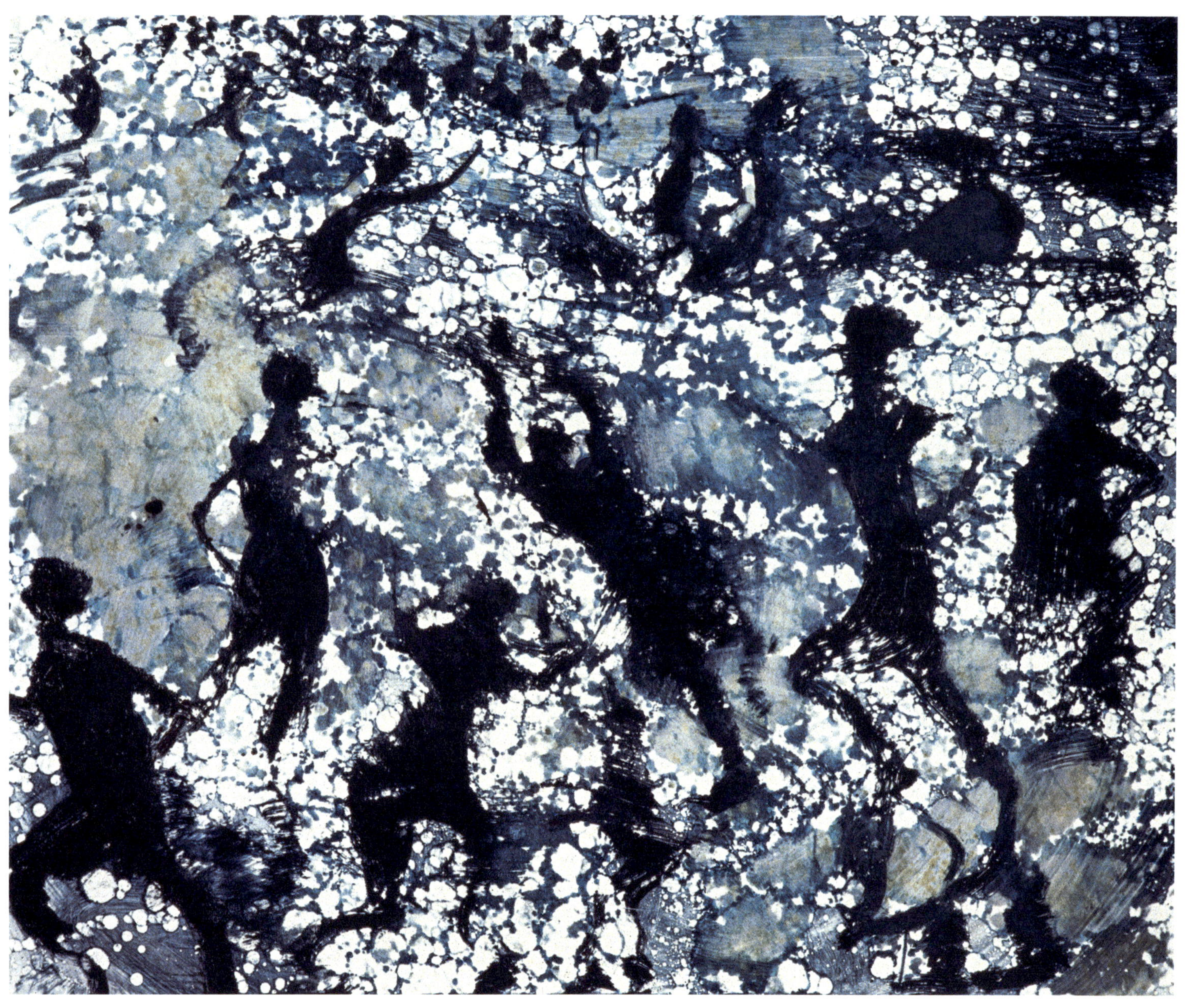

5
Coney Island, 1992
Monoprint, 35 × 43 inches
88.9 × 109.2 cm

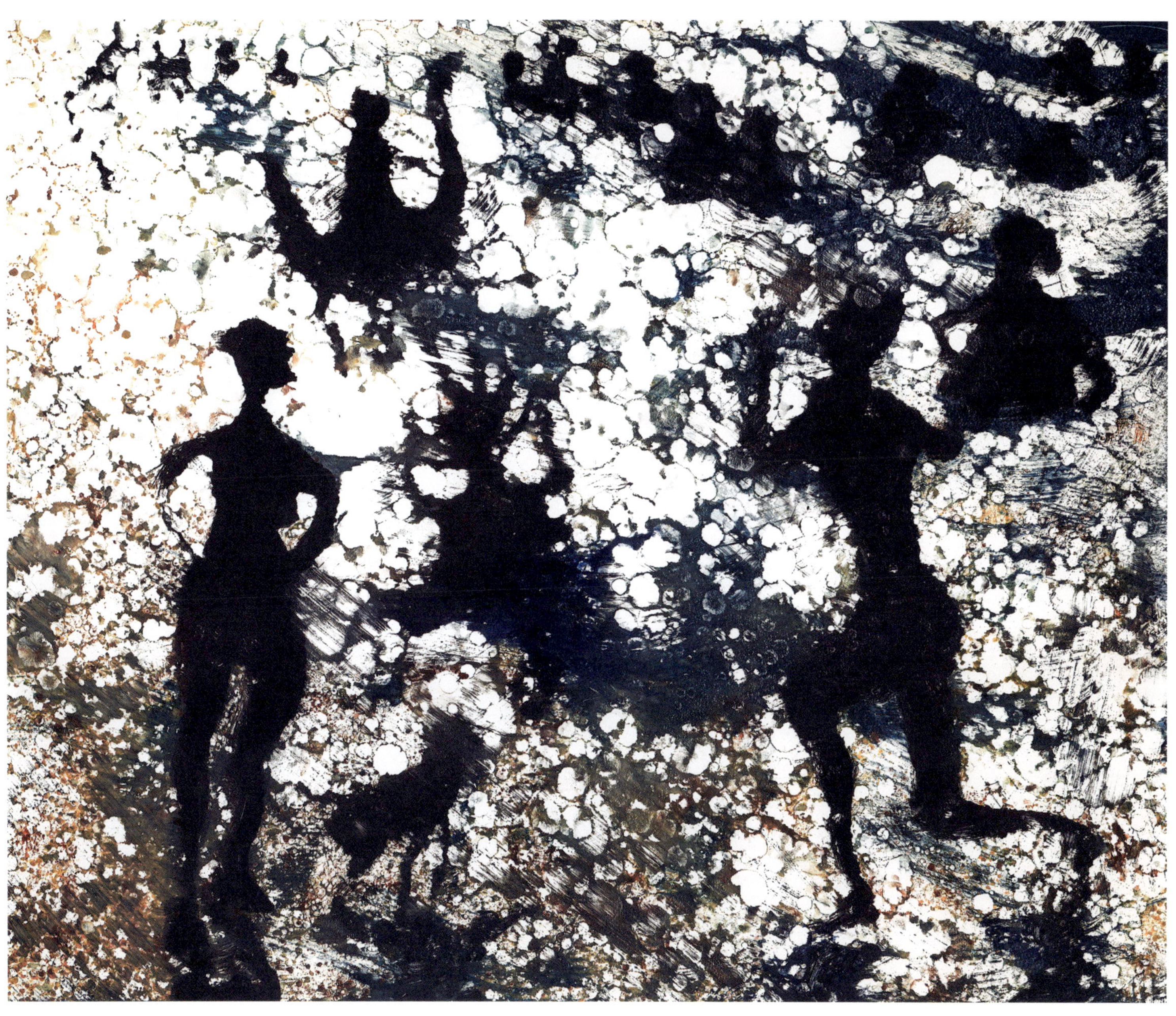

6
Coney Island, 1993
Monoprint, 34 × 47 inches
(86.4 × 119.4 cm)

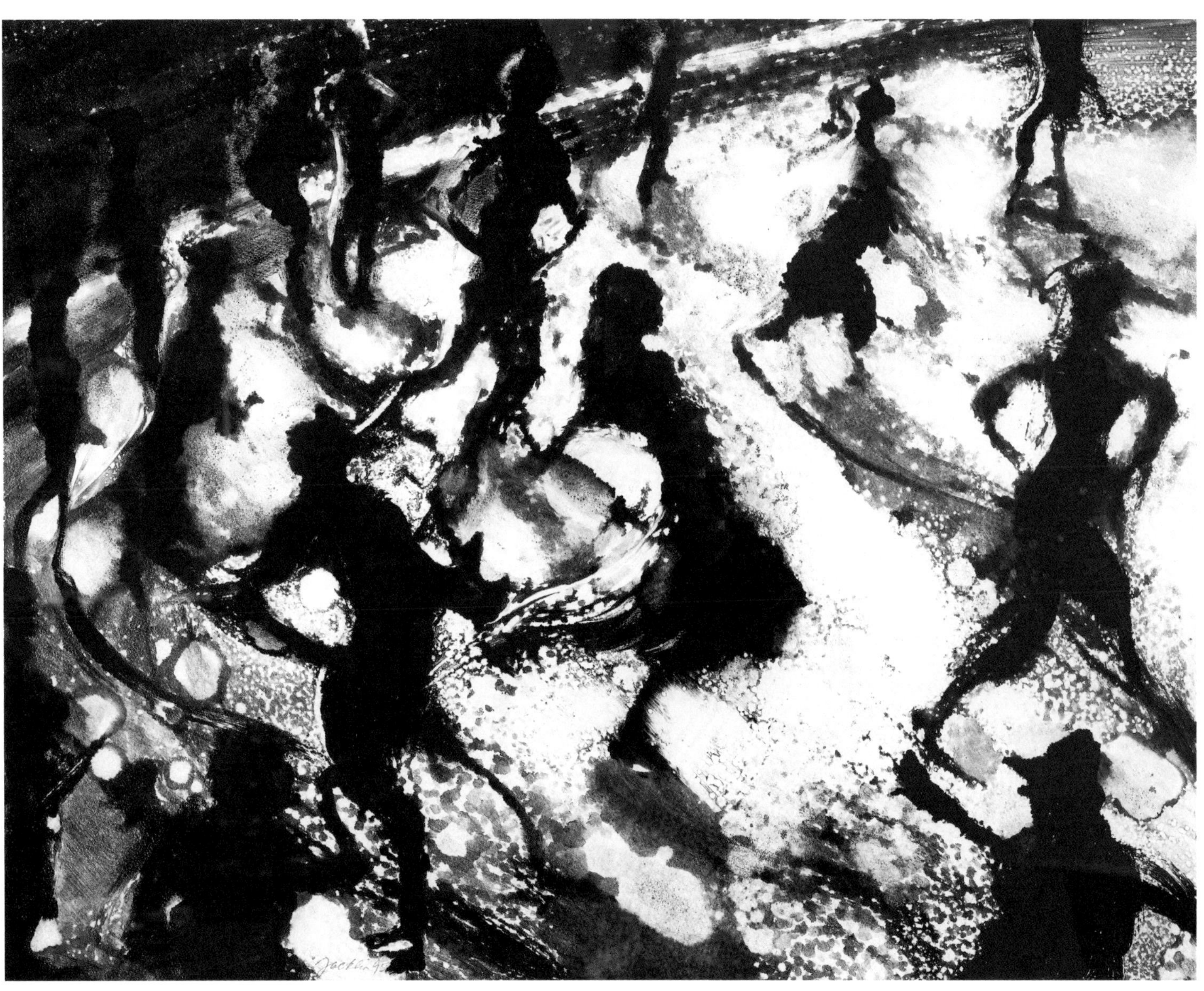

7
Skaters, 1995
Monotype, 27 × 34½ inches
(68.6 × 87.6 cm)

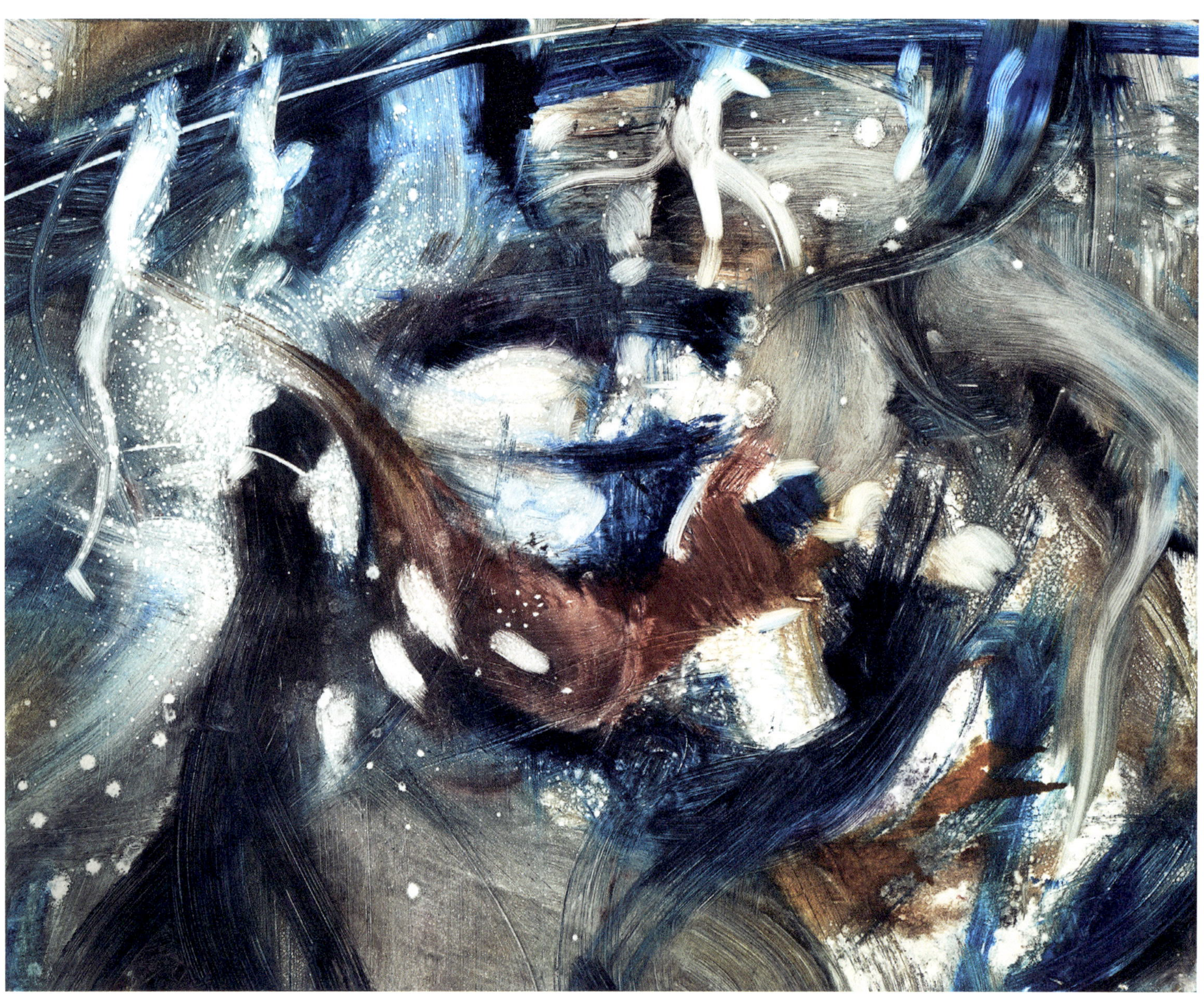

8
Wollman Rink IV, 2012
Monotype, 16 × 20 inches
(40.6 × 50.8 cm)

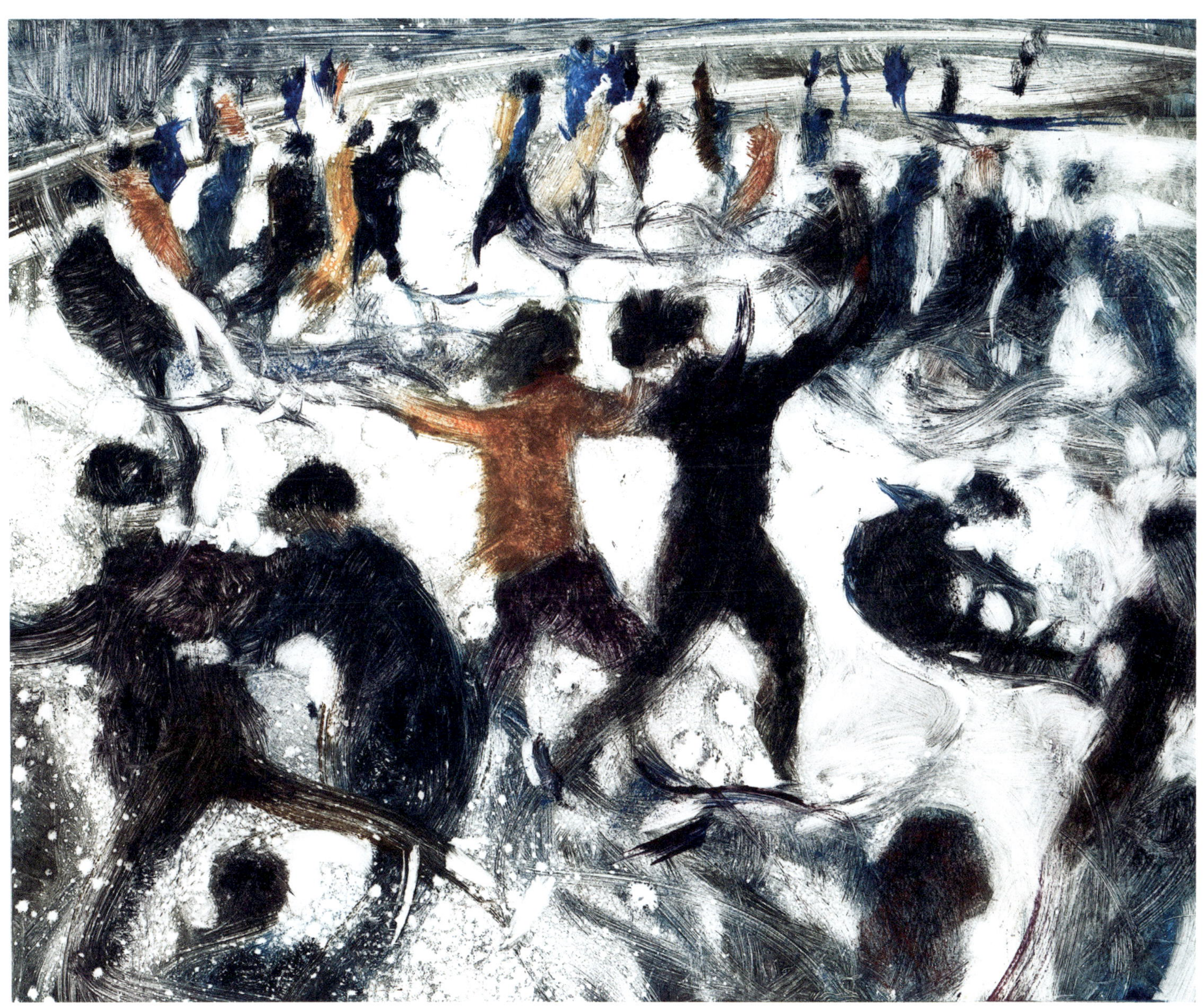

9
Wollman Rink III, 2012
Monotype, 16 × 20 inches
(40.6 × 50.8 cm)

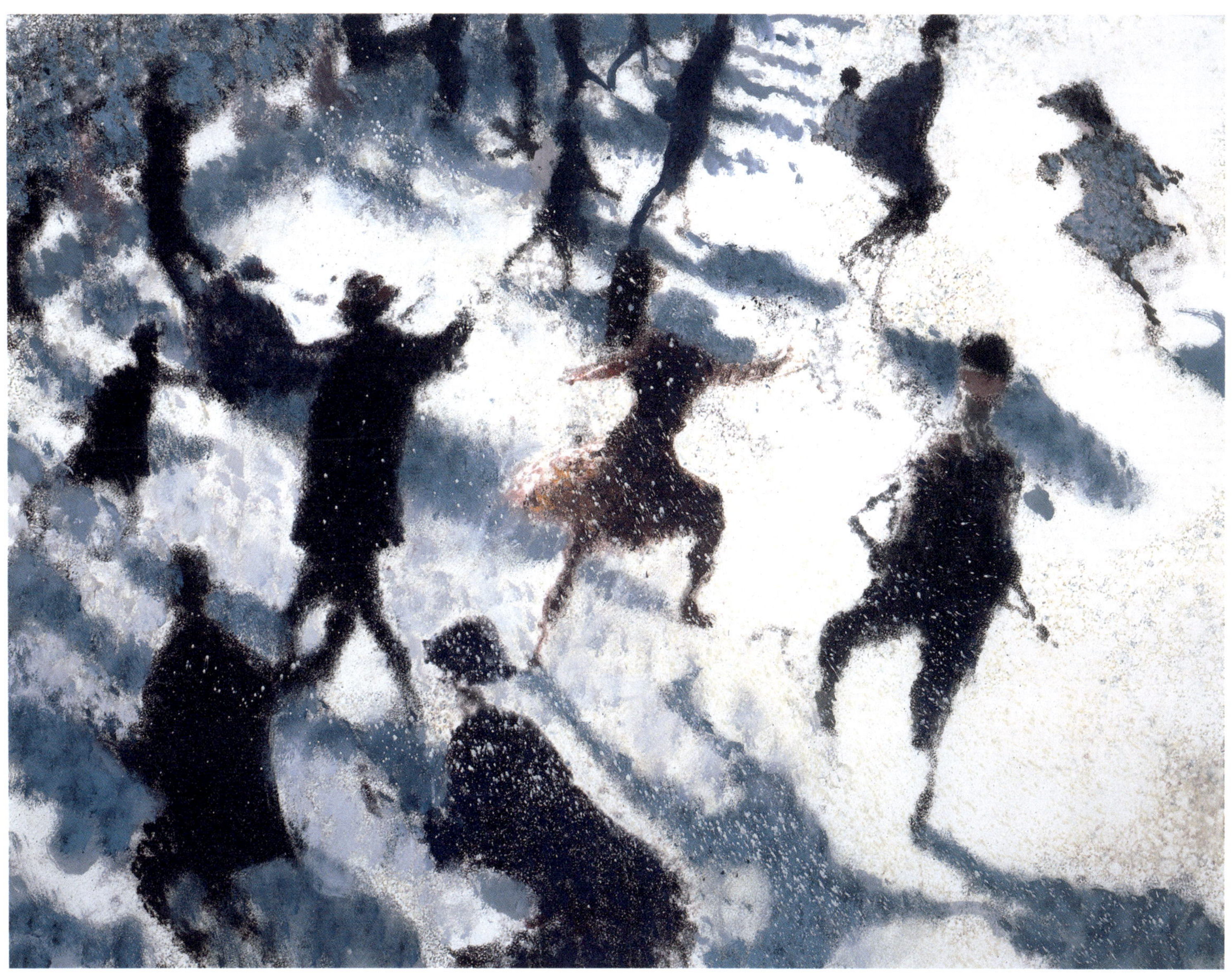

10
Skaters, 1996
Oil on monoprint, 27½ × 35¾ inches
(69.9 × 90.8 cm)

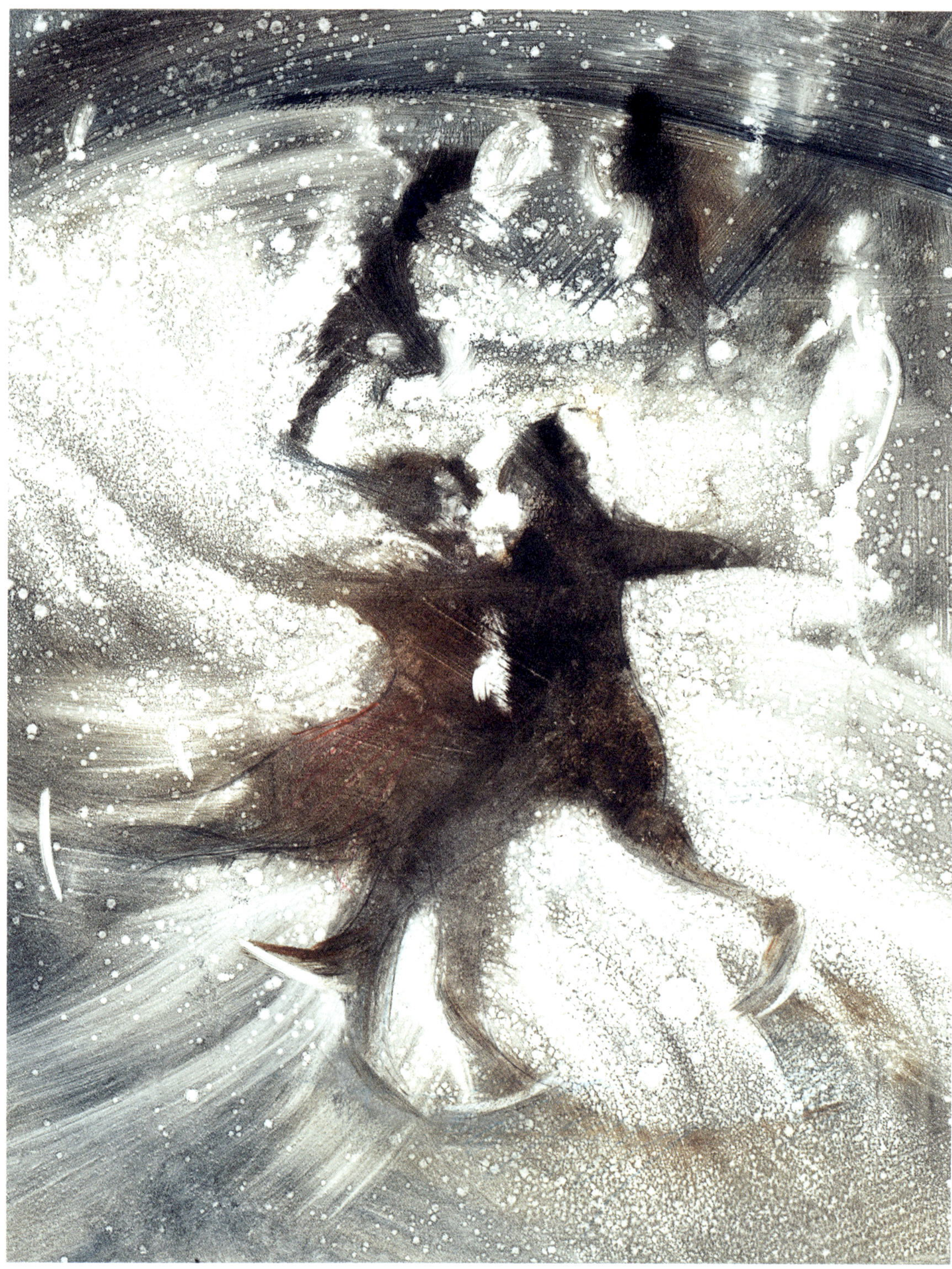

11
Twirling and Swirling II, 2012
Monotype, 20 × 16 inches
(50.8 × 40.6 cm)

12
Skaters, 2009
Pastel over monotype, 27 × 22 inches
(68.6 × 55.9 cm)

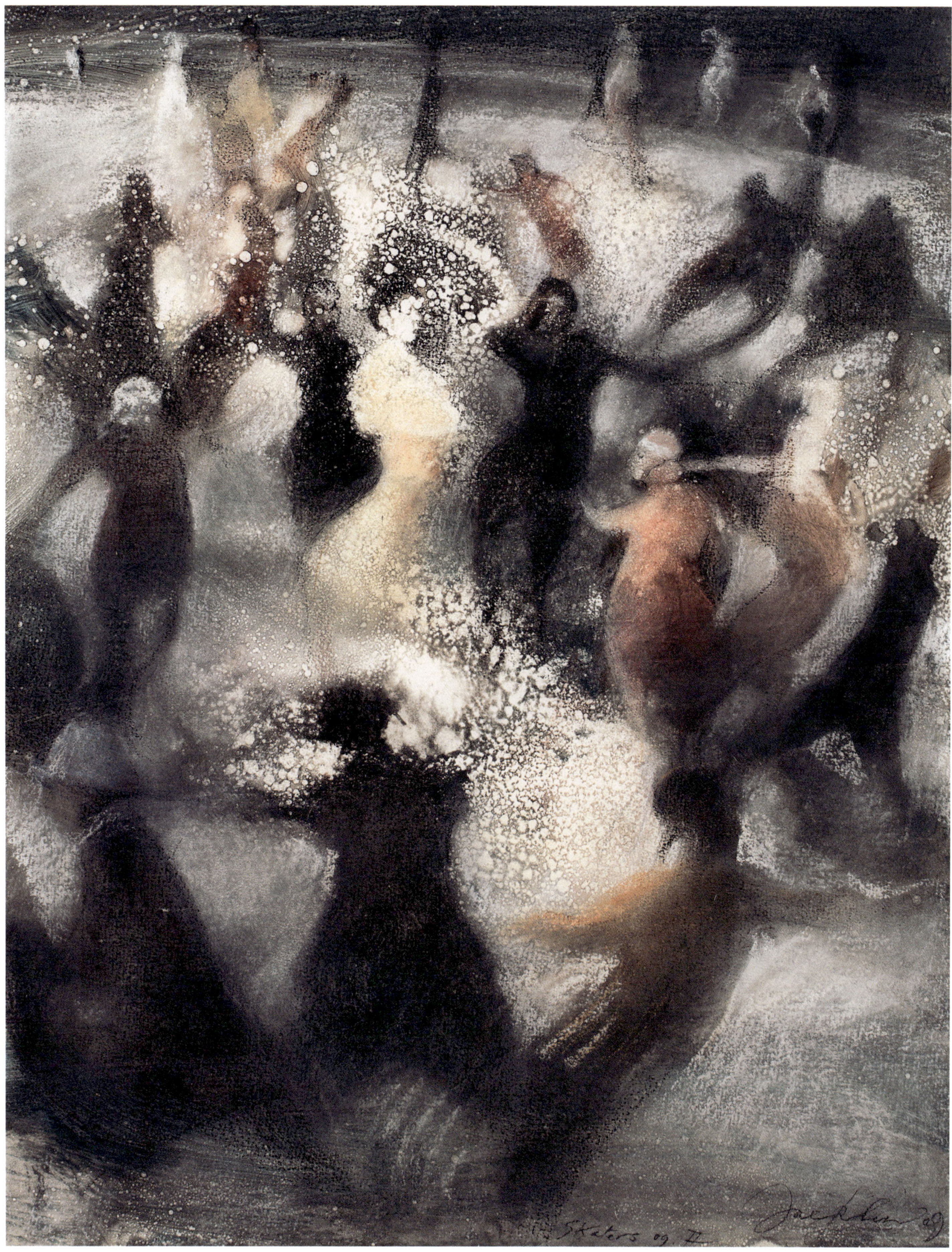
Skaters 09. II

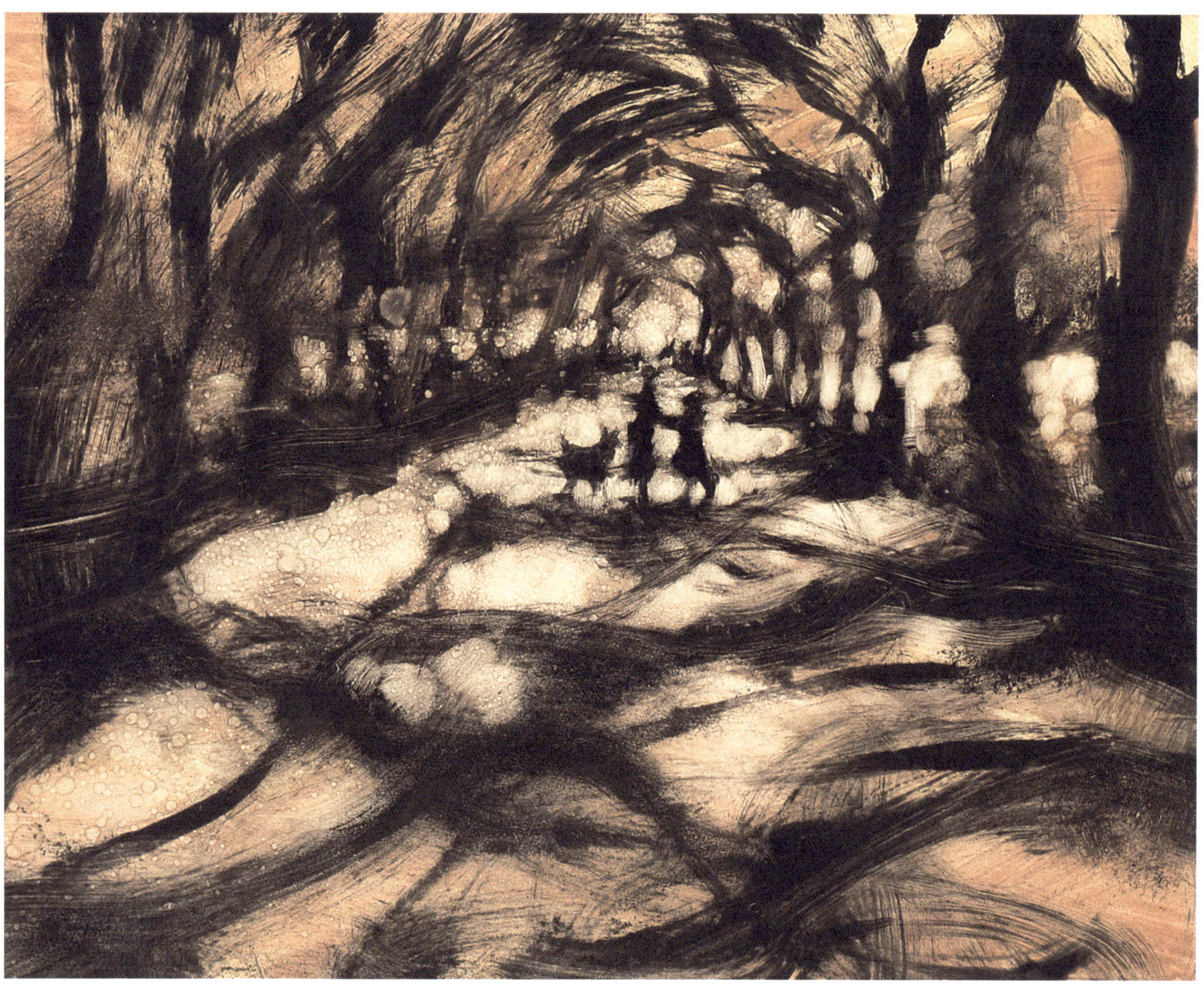

13
Central Park Mall to Literature Walk, 2001
Monotype, 21¾ × 26 inches
(55.3 × 66 cm)

14
Beneath the Towers IV, 2000
Monotype, 27 × 22½ inches
(68.6 × 57.2 cm)

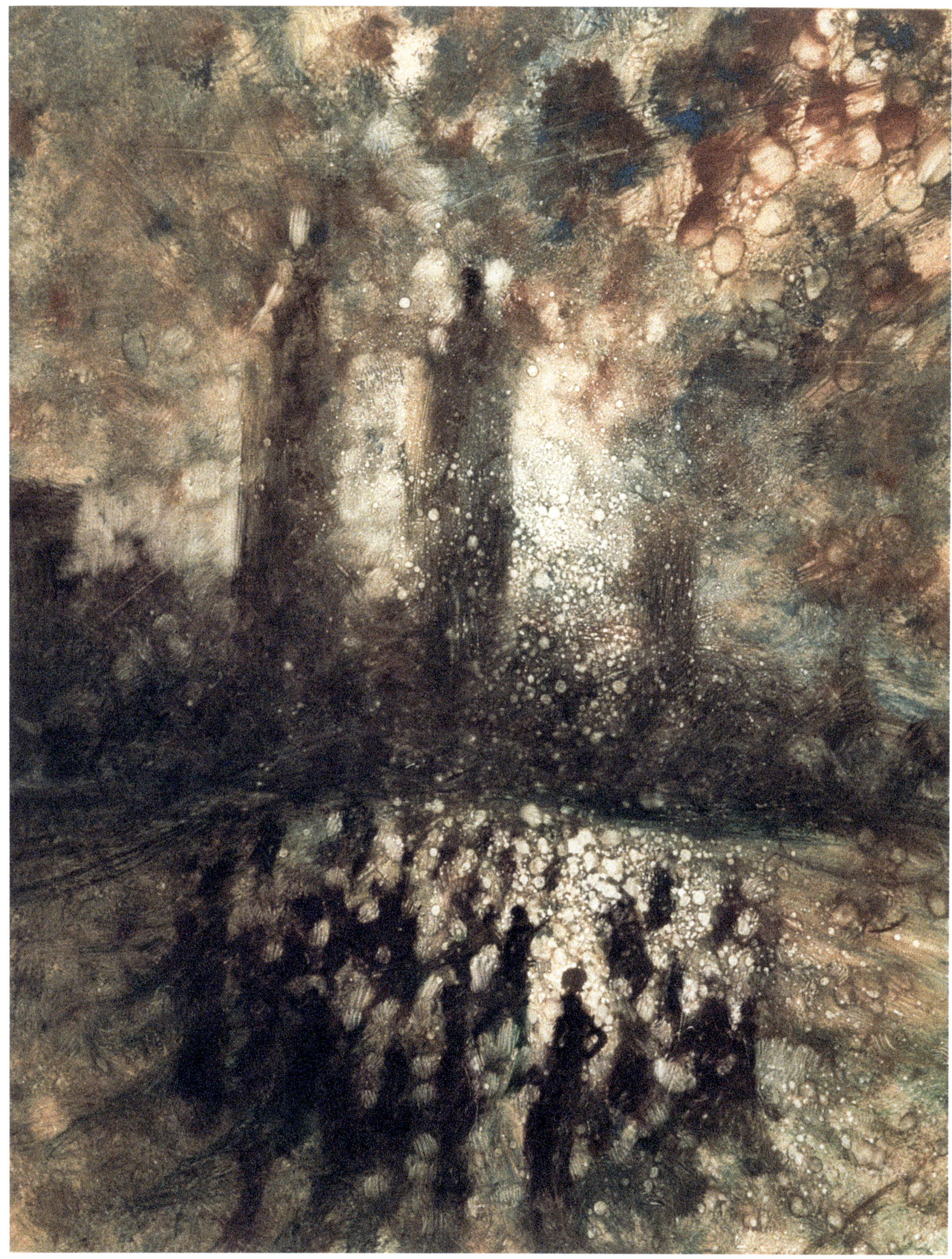

15
Great Lawn Event II, 2000
Monotype, 20 × 16 inches
(50.8 × 40.6 cm)

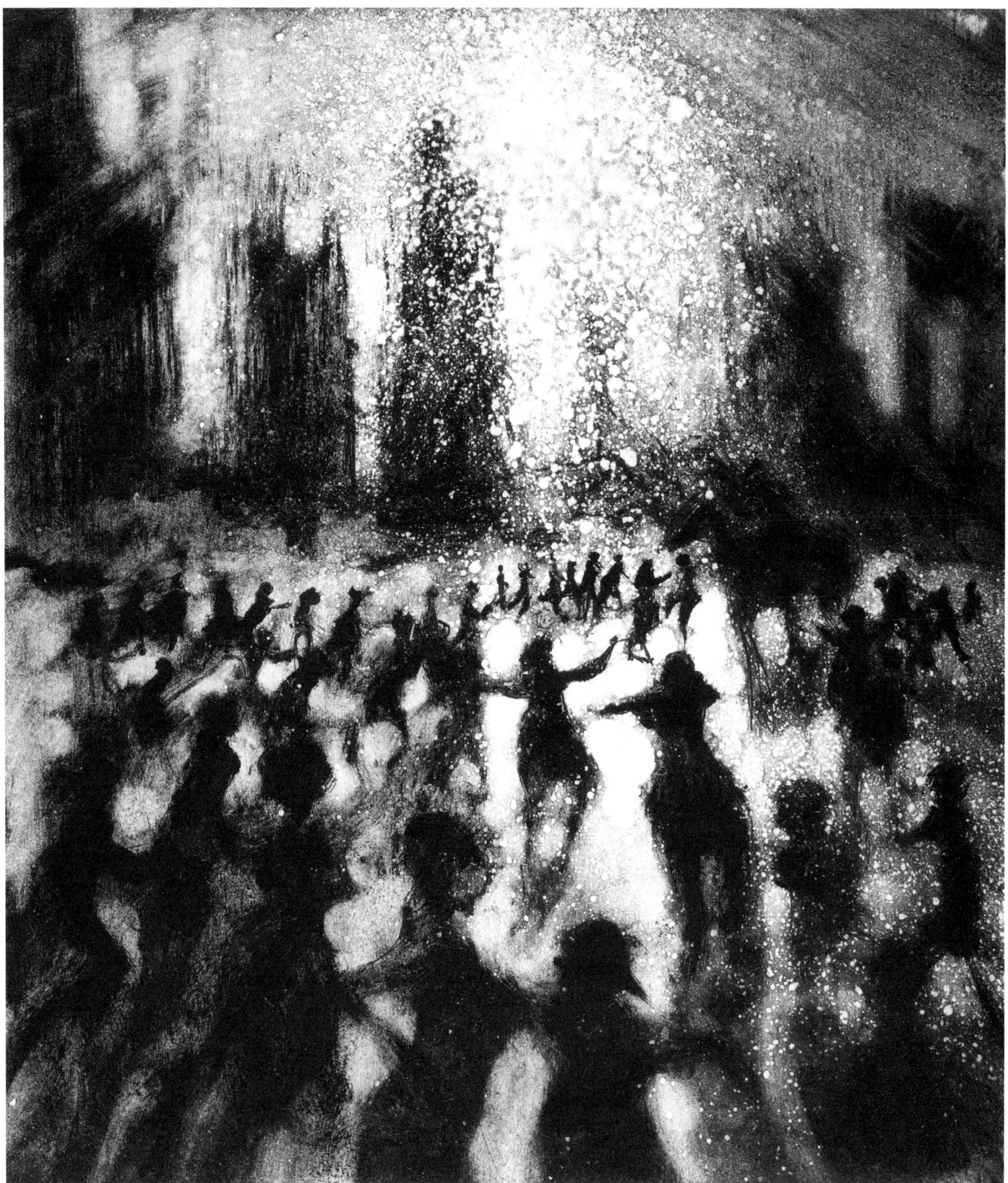

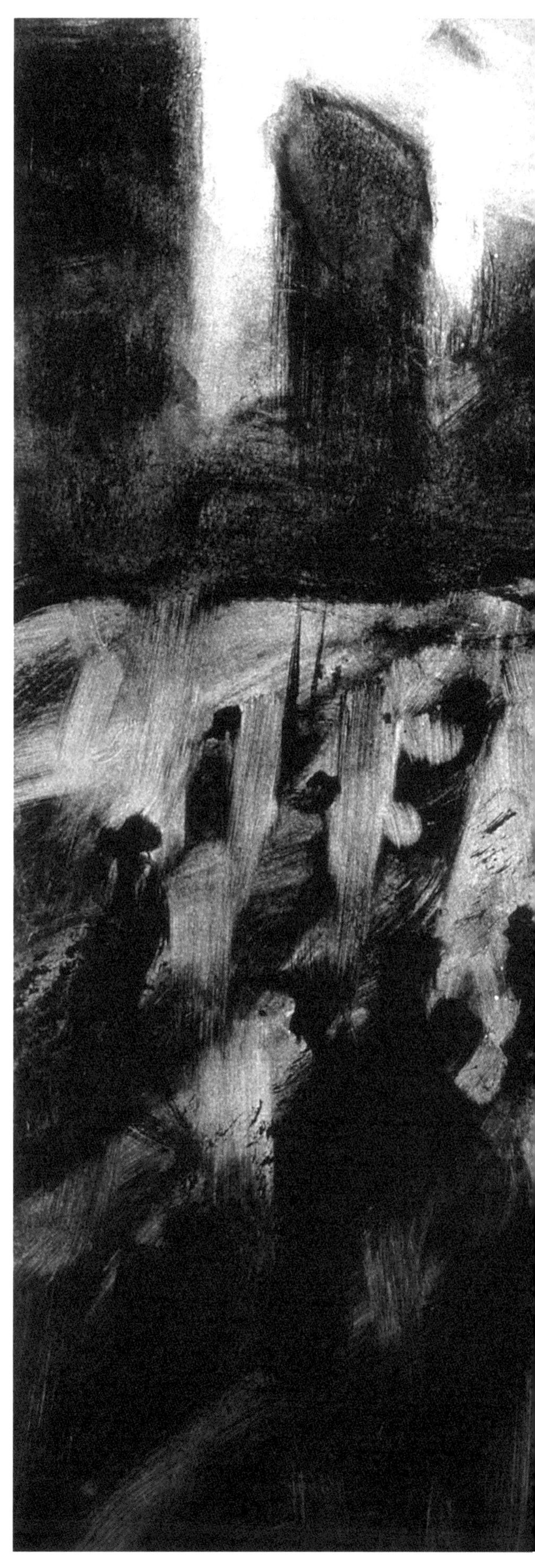

16
After the Event, Great Lawn I, 2000
Monotype, 25½ × 29 inches
(64.8 × 73.7 cm)

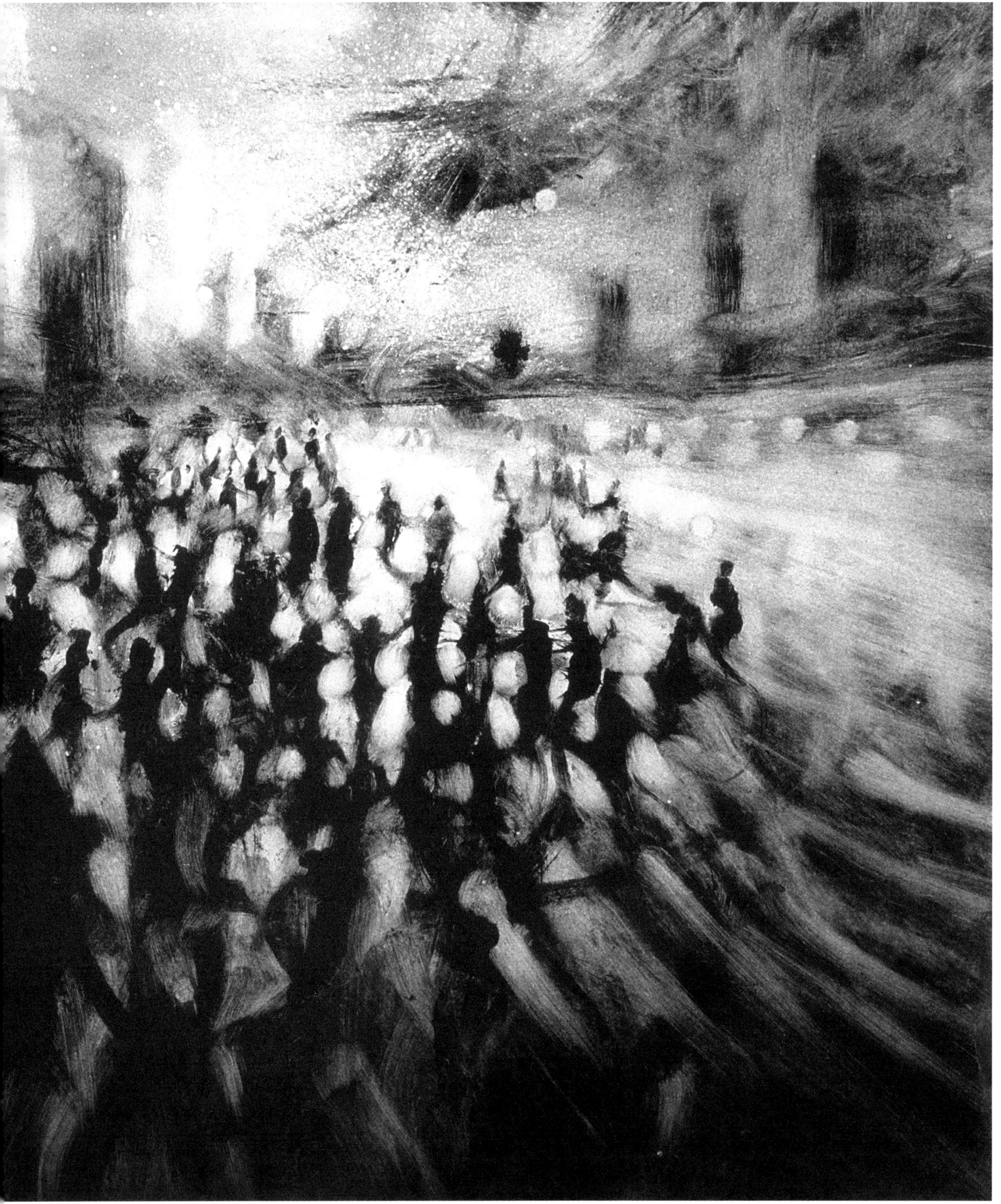

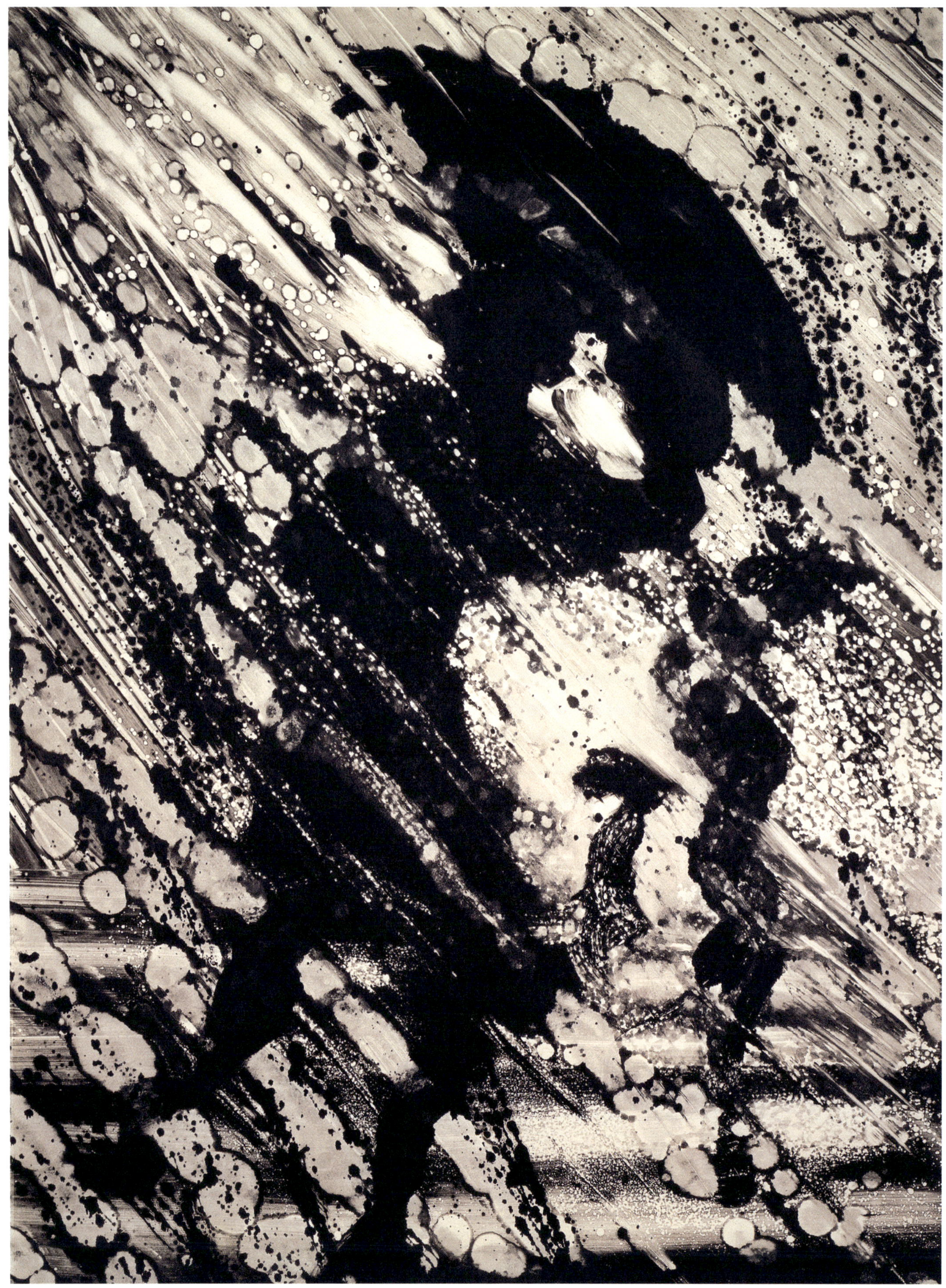

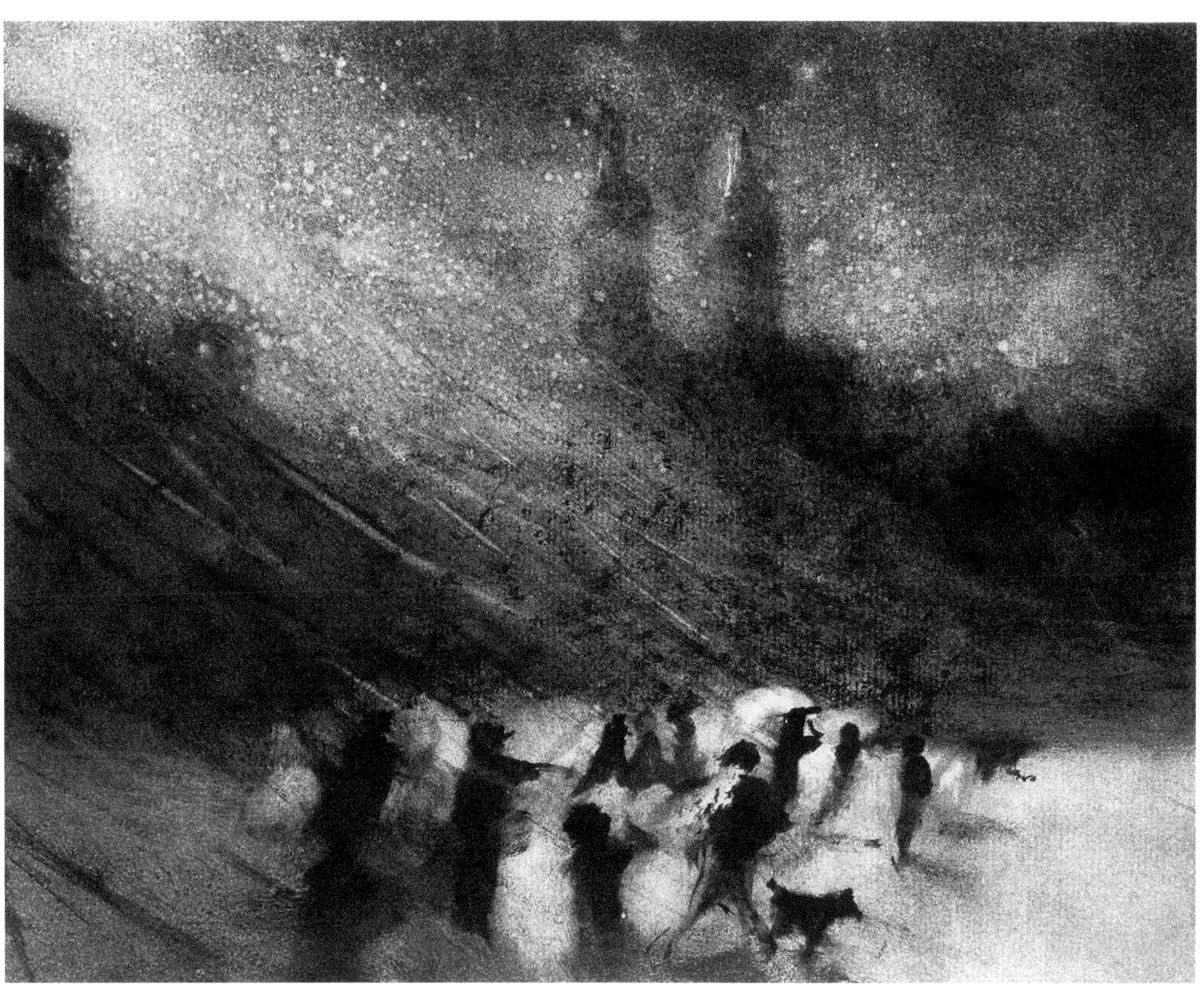

17
Crossing the Street in the Rain I, 1996
Monotype, 27½ × 22¼ inches
(69.9 × 56.6 cm)

18
Increase II, 2001
Monotype, 17½ × 19 inches
(44.5 × 48.3 cm)

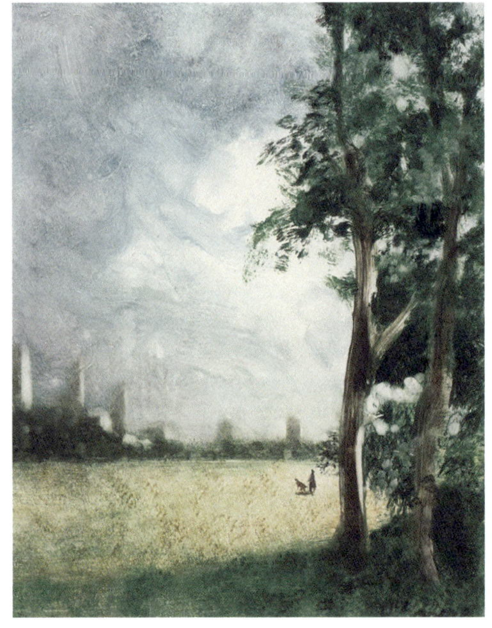

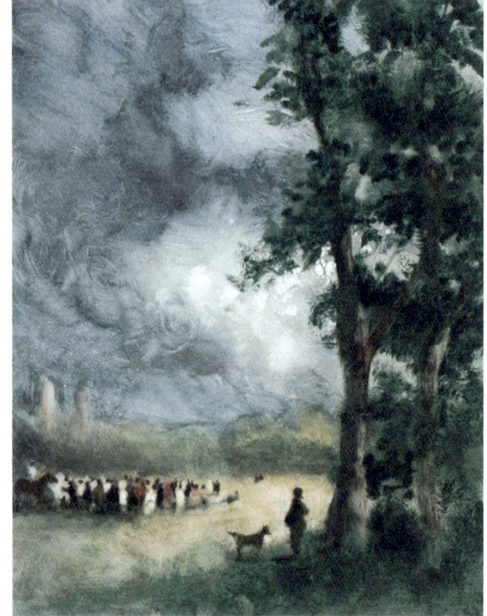

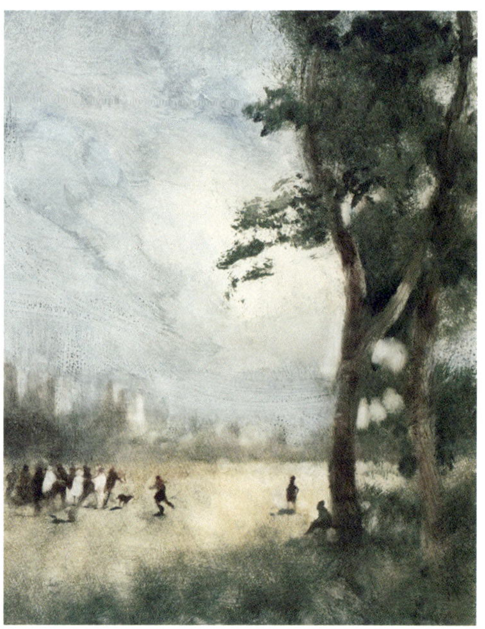

19
Early One Morning NYC I, 2001
Monotype, 36 × 29½ inches
(91.4 × 74.9 cm)

20
Early One Morning NYC IV, 2001
Monotype, 36 × 29½ inches
(91.4 × 74.9 cm)

21
Early One Morning NYC V, 2001
Monotype, 36 × 29½ inches
(91.4 × 74.9 cm)

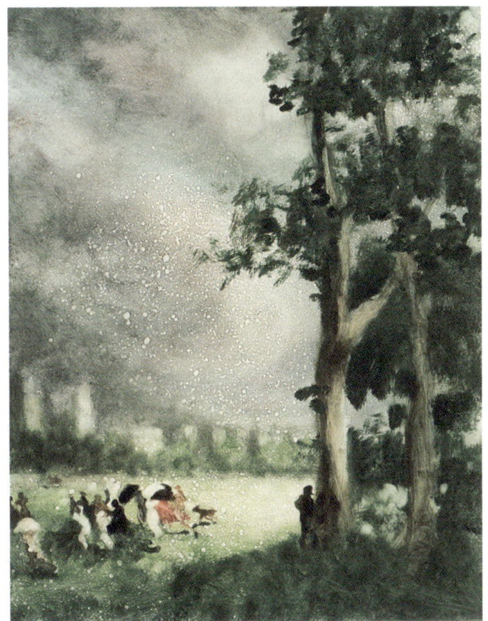

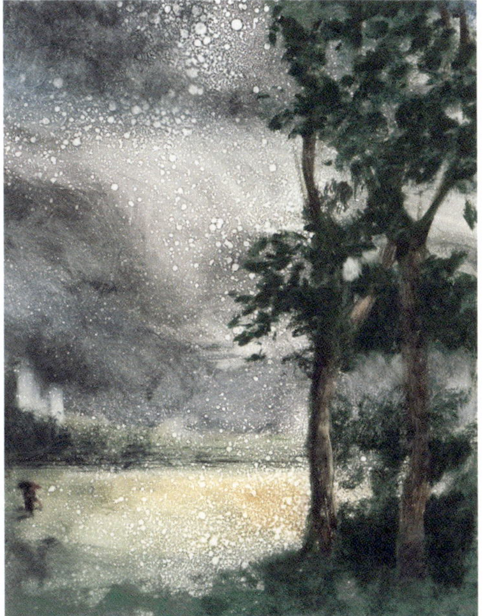

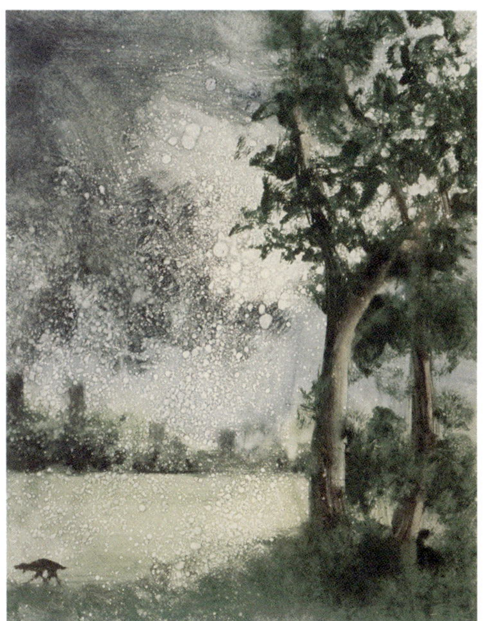

22
Early One Morning NYC VI, 2001
Monotype, 36 × 29½ inches
(91.4 × 74.9 cm)

23
Early One Morning NYC VII, 2001
Monotype, 36 × 29½ inches
(91.4 × 74.9 cm)

24
Early One Morning NYC VIII, 2001
Monotype, 36 × 29½ inches
(91.4 × 74.9 cm)

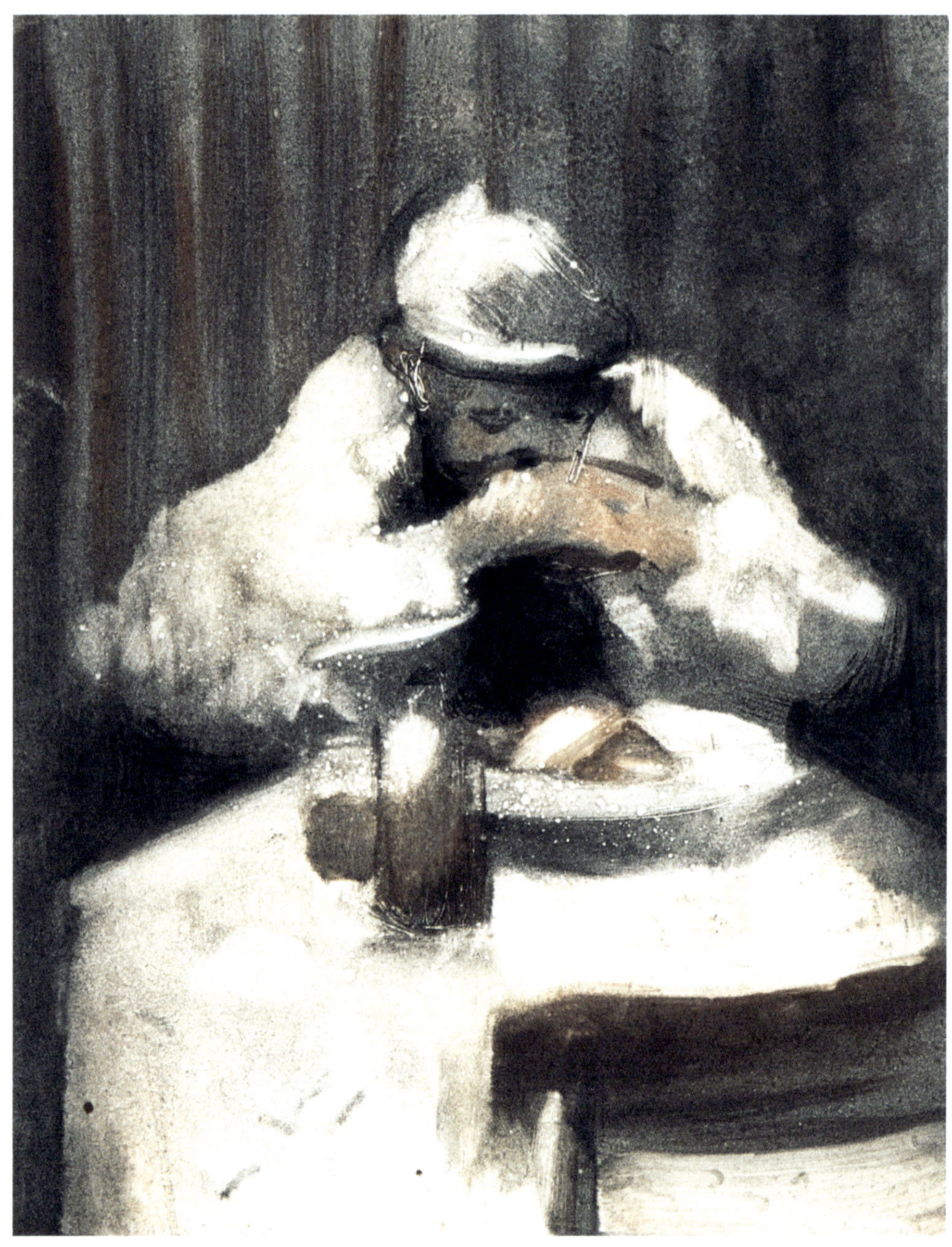

25
Sandwich Eater I, 2007
Monotype, 10 × 8 inches
(25.4 × 20.3 cm)

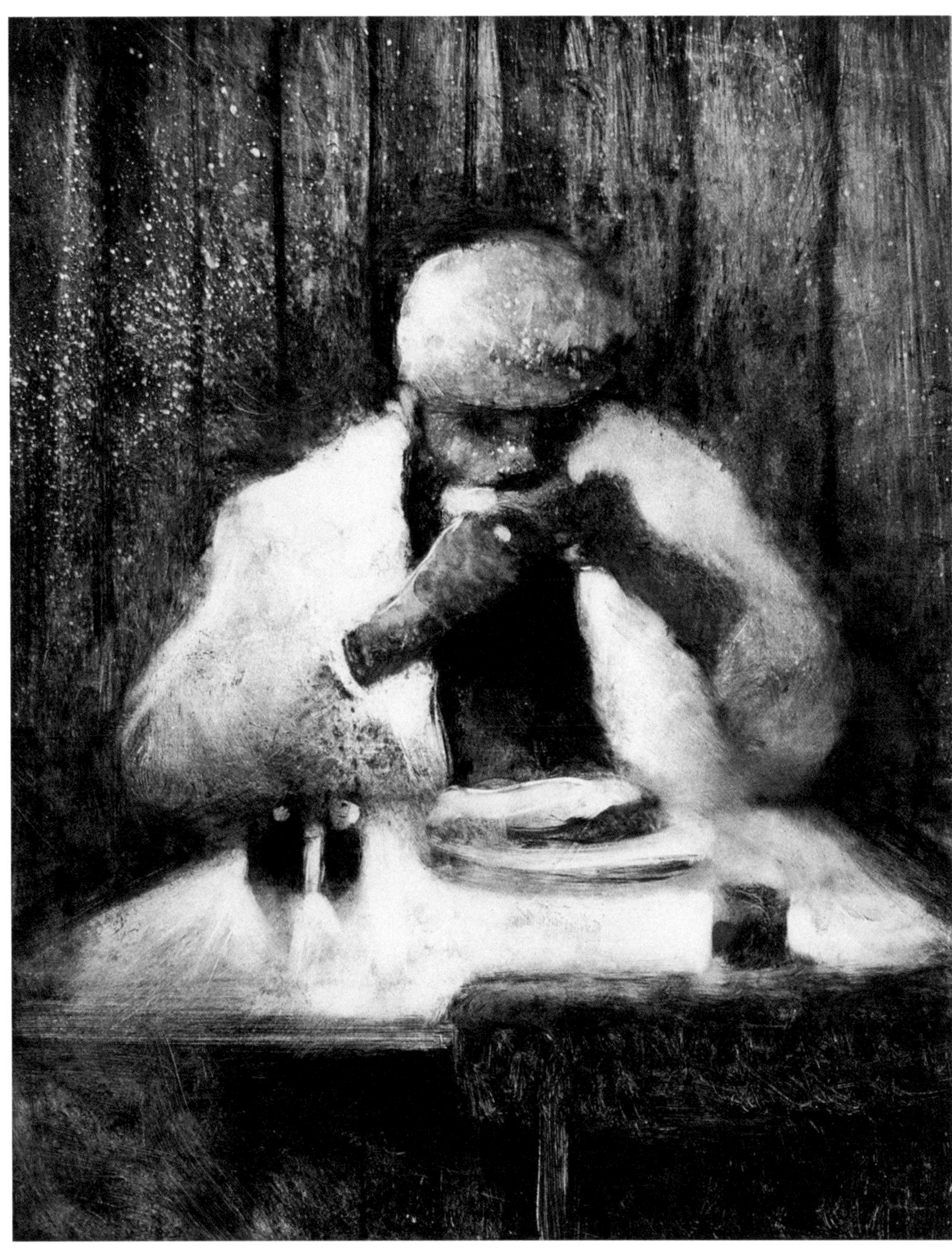

26
Sandwich Eater III, 2007
Monotype, 10 × 8 inches
(25.4 × 20.3 cm)

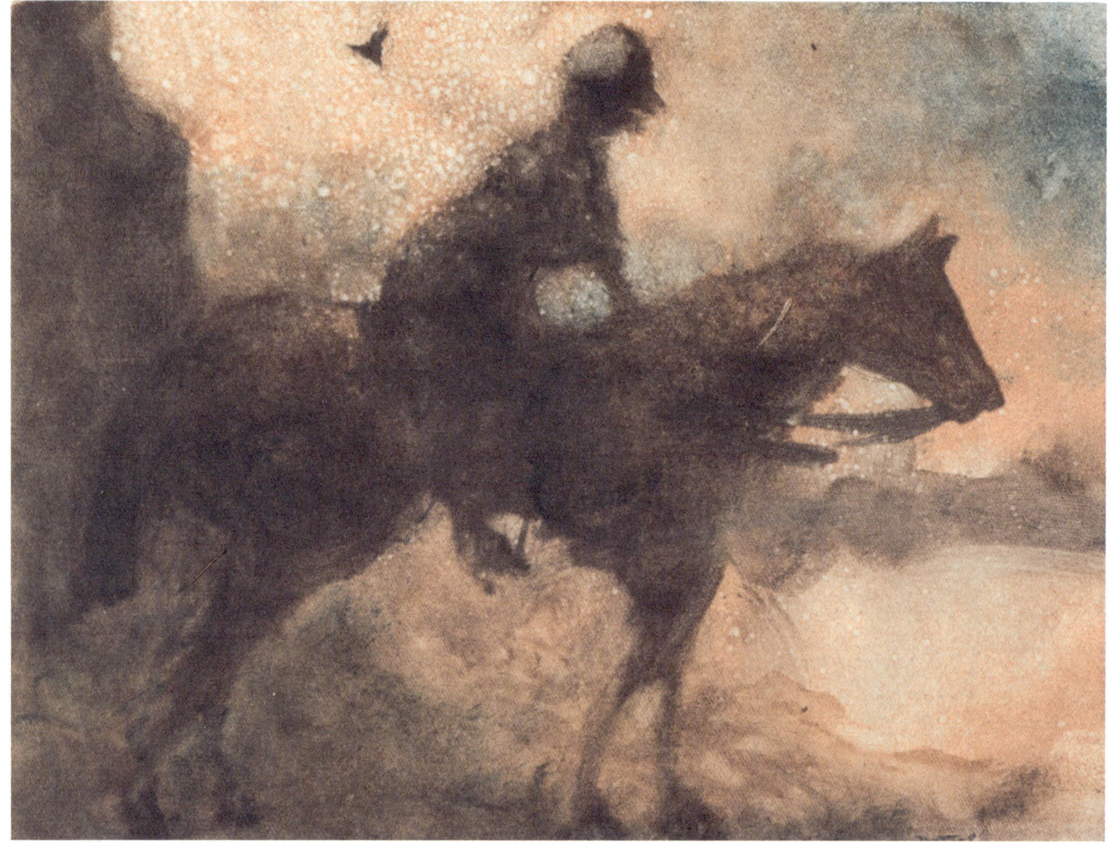

27
Mounted Policeman, NYC, 2001
Monotype, 4½ × 6 inches
(11.4 × 15.2 cm)

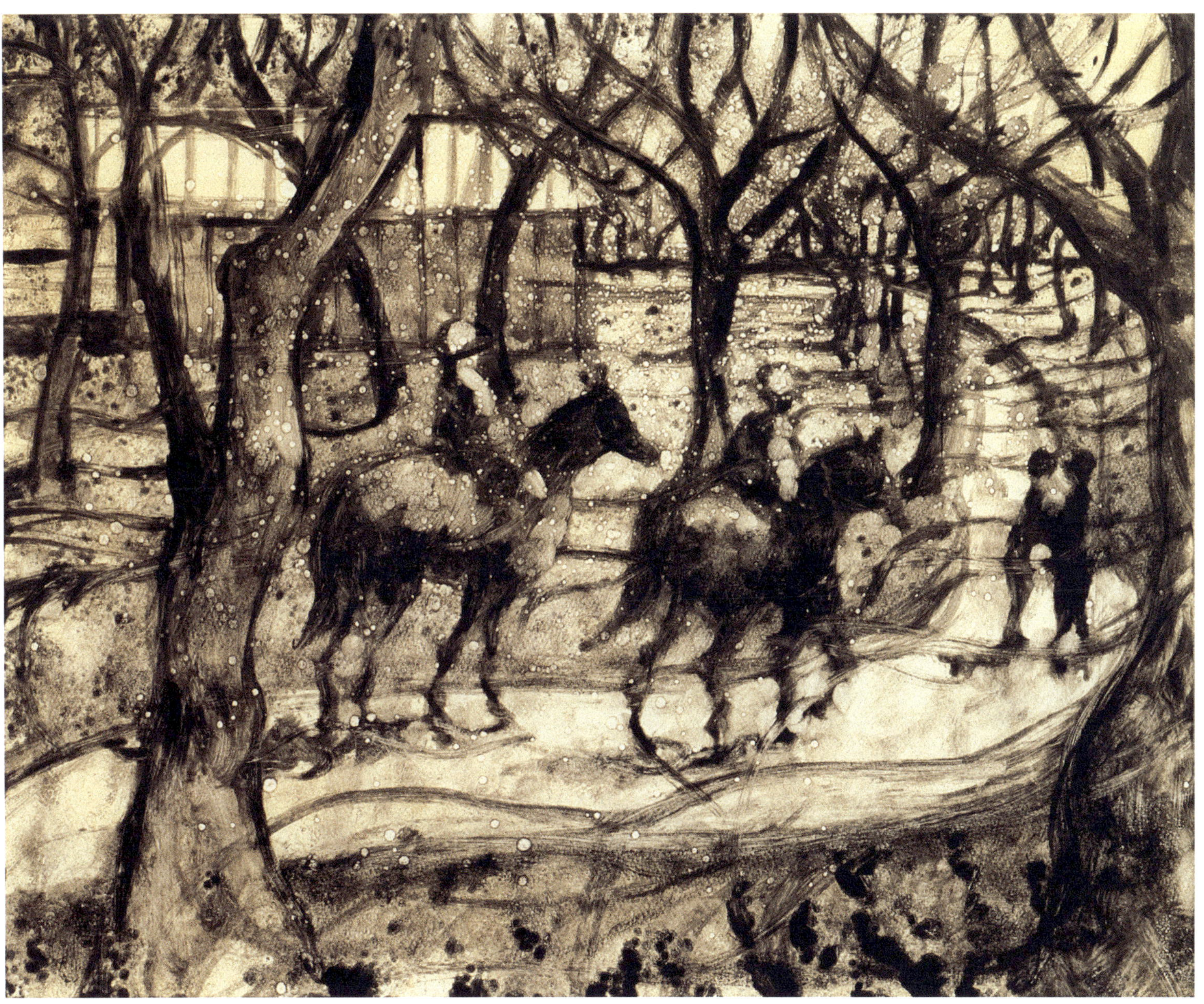

28
Mounted Police C.P. I, 2003
Monotype, 15 × 19¾ inches
(38.4 × 50.2 cm)

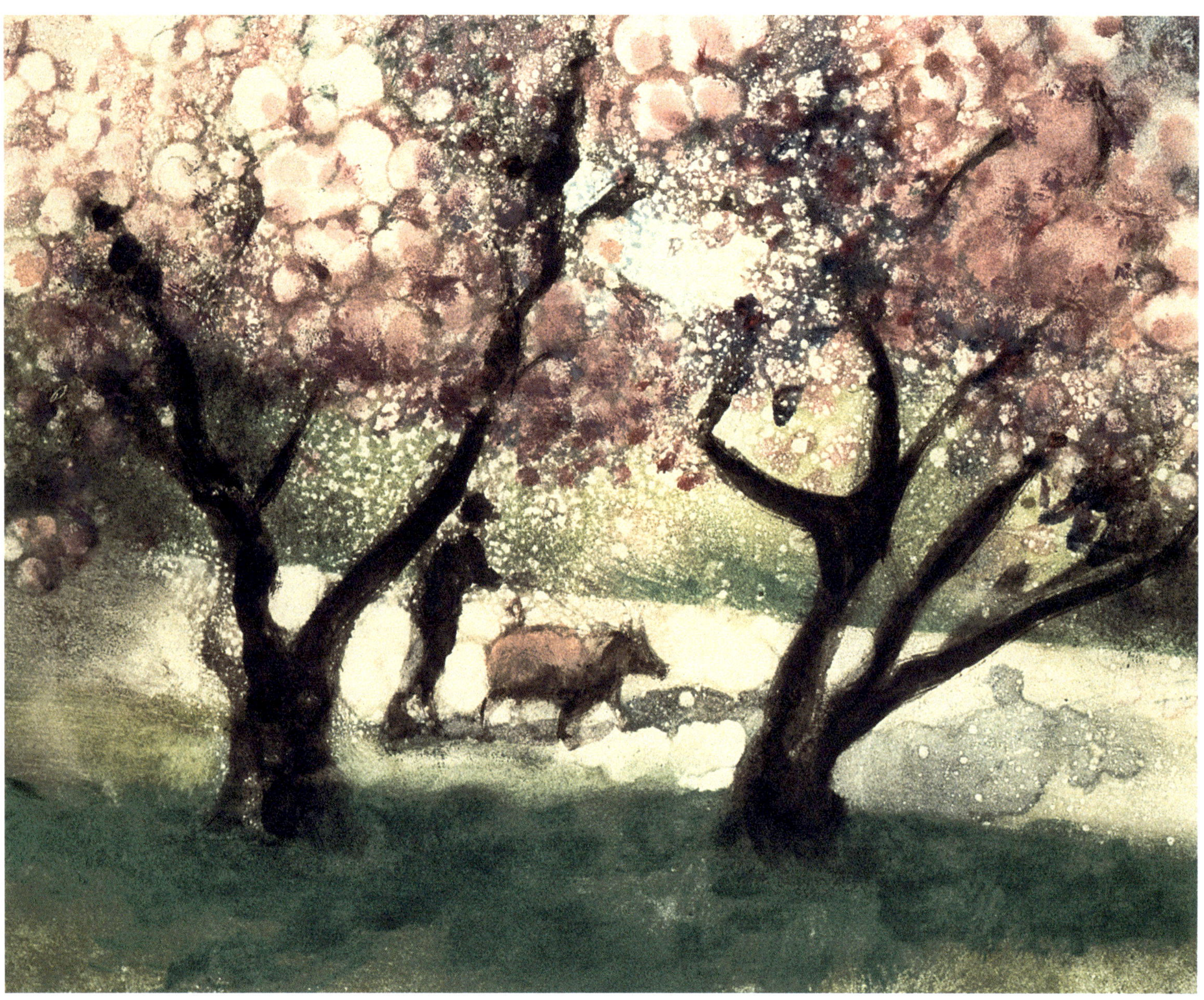

29
Man with Pig and Cherry Tree NYC, 2001
Monotype, 15½ × 18 inches
(39.4 × 45.7 cm)

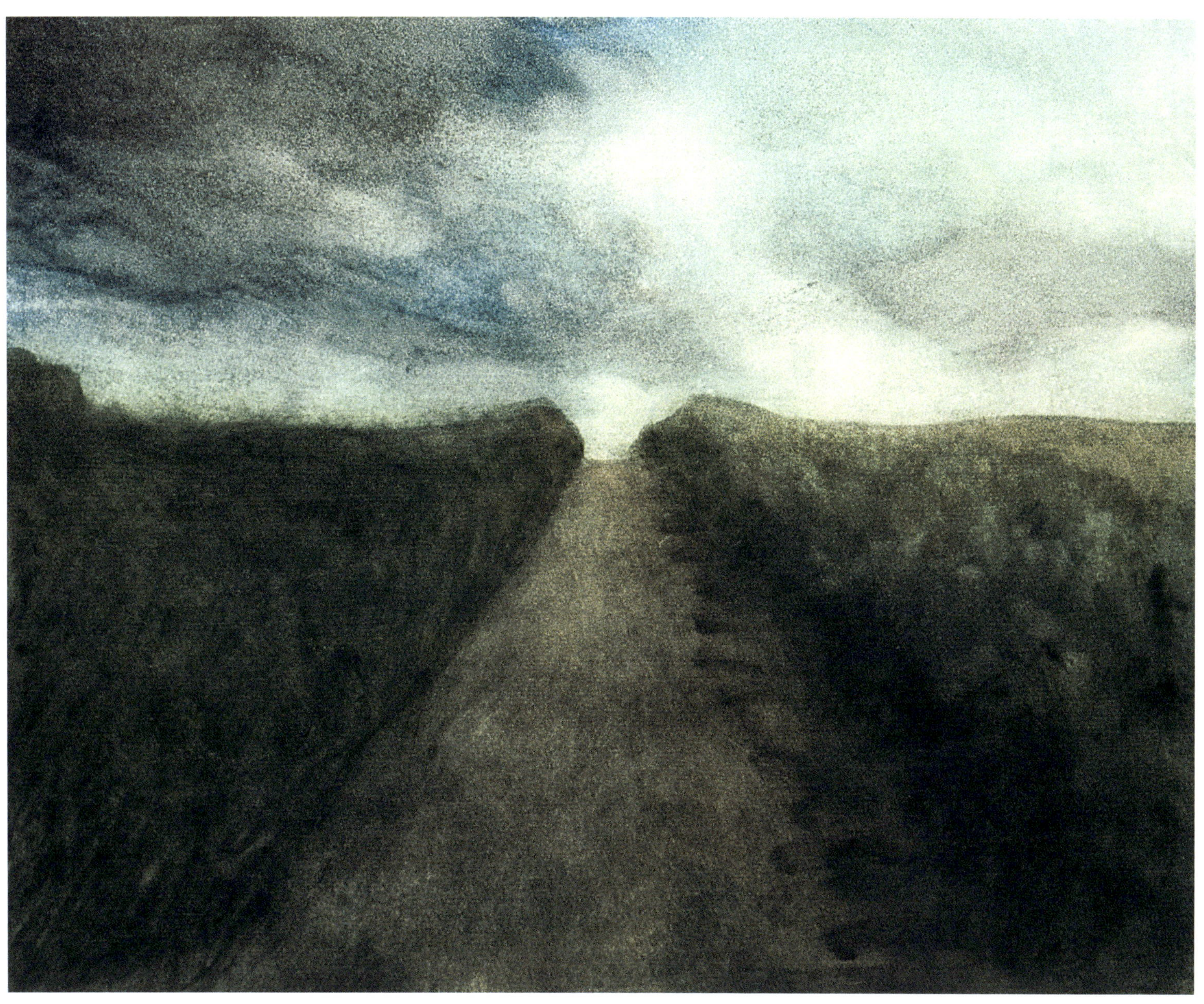

30
Road to the Sky I, 2001
Monotype, 15½ × 19½ inches
(39.4 × 49.5 cm)

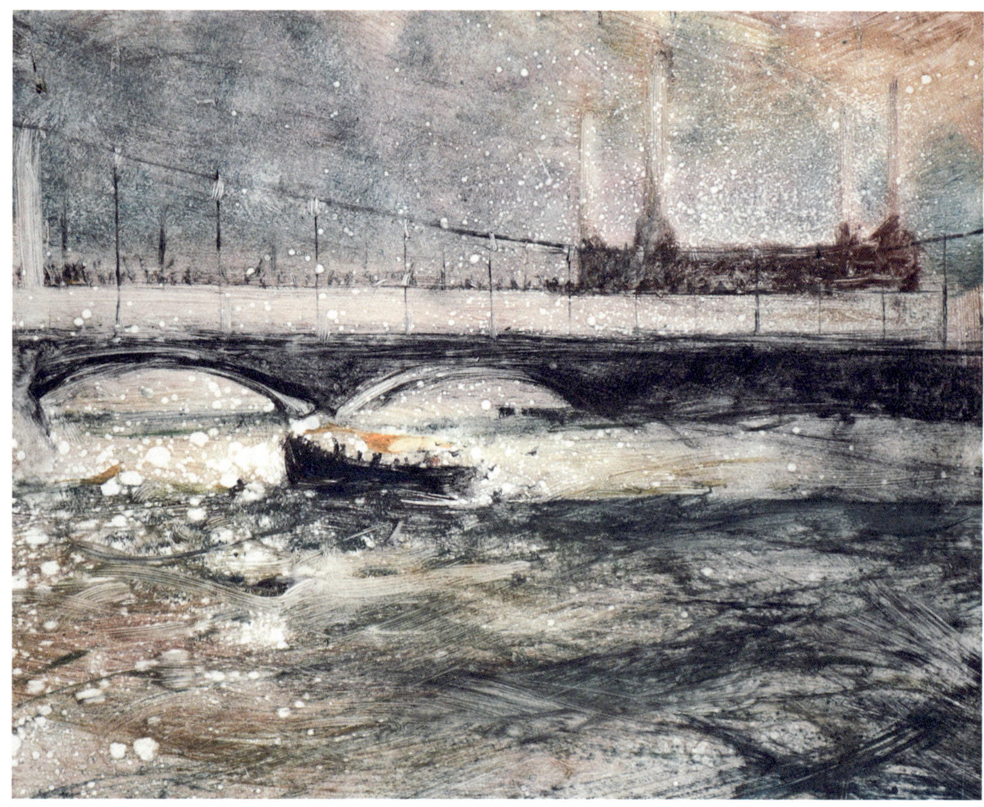

31
Towards Battersea Bridge VII, 2006
Monotype, 16 × 20 inches
(40.6 × 50.8 cm)

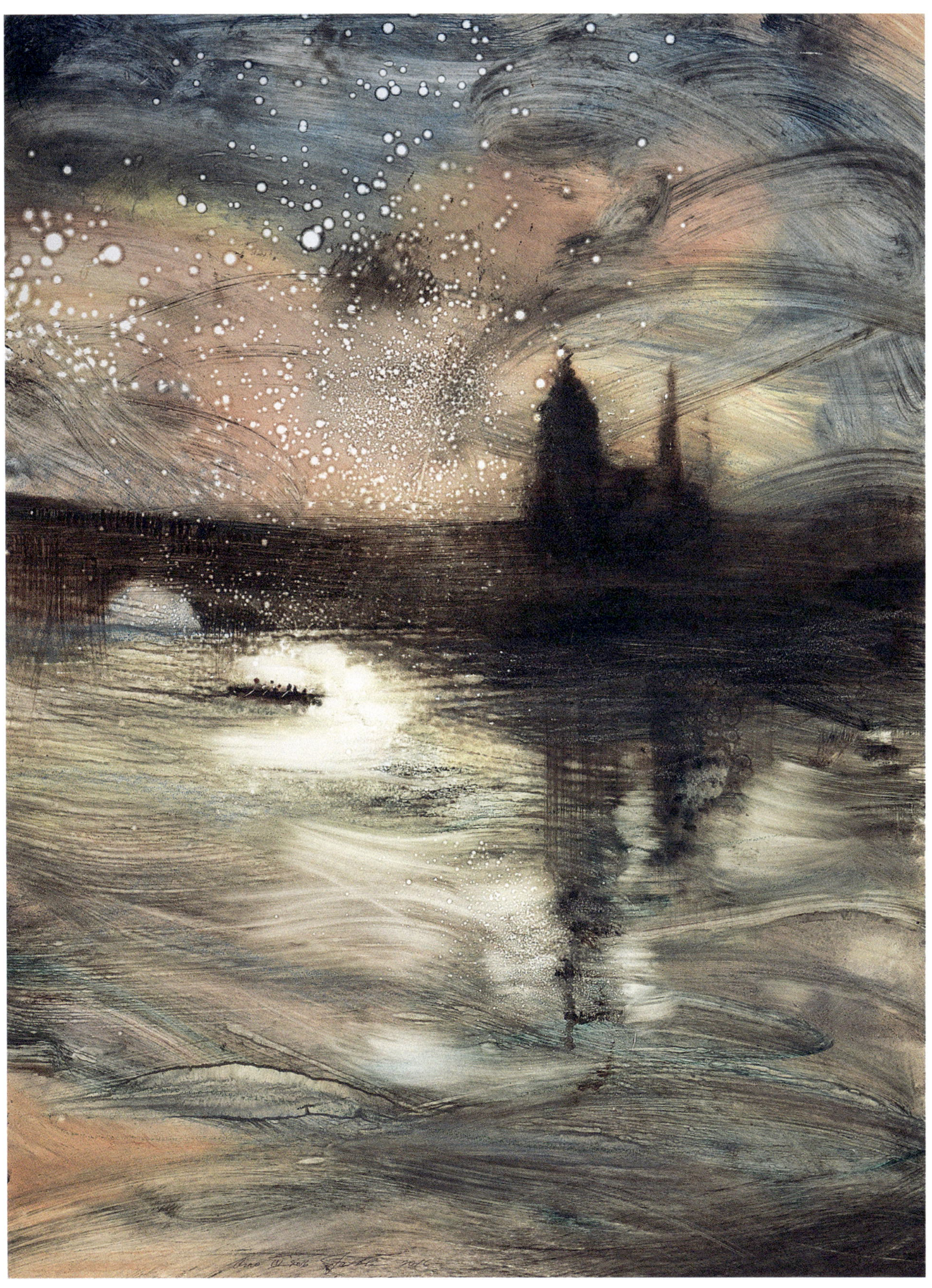

32
Arno IV, 2016
Monotype, 39½ × 29½ inches
(100.3 × 74.9 cm)

33
Prima della tempesta III, 2003
Monotype, 29 × 40 inches
(73.7 × 101.6 cm)

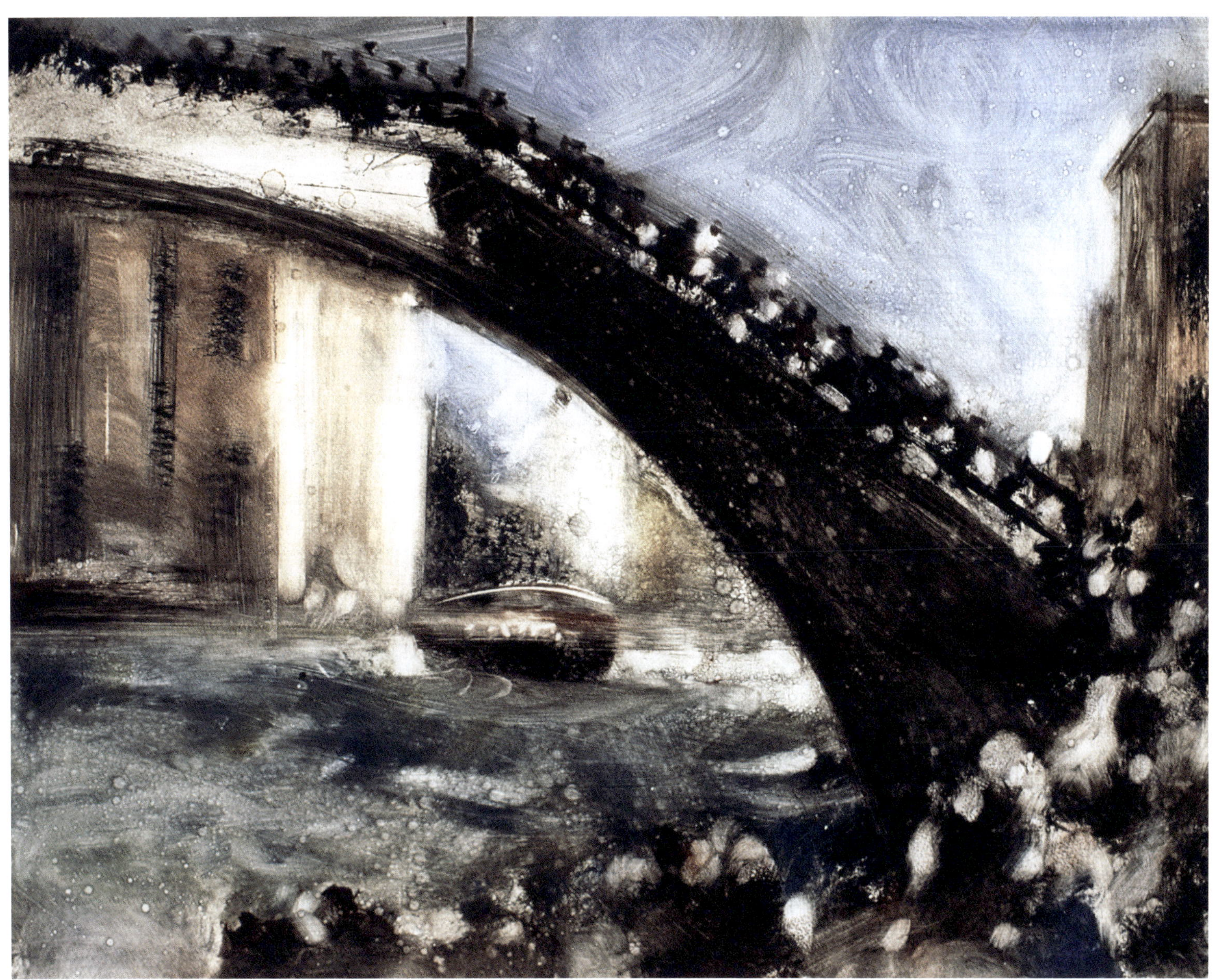

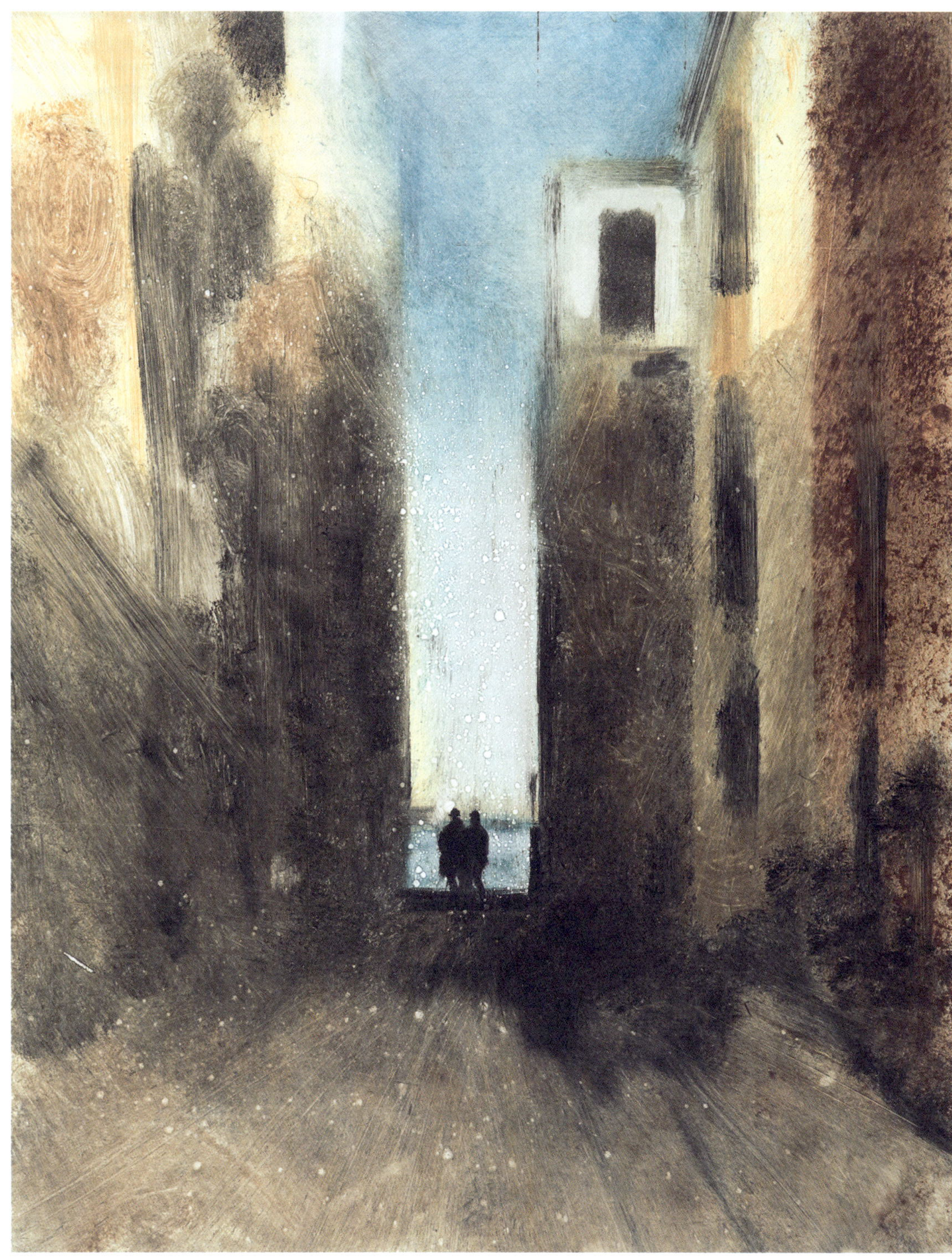

34
Verso il mare II, 2004
Monotype, 19¾ × 15¾ inches
(50.2 × 40 cm)

35
Fire III, 2007
Monotype, 20 × 16 inches
(50.8 × 40.6 cm)

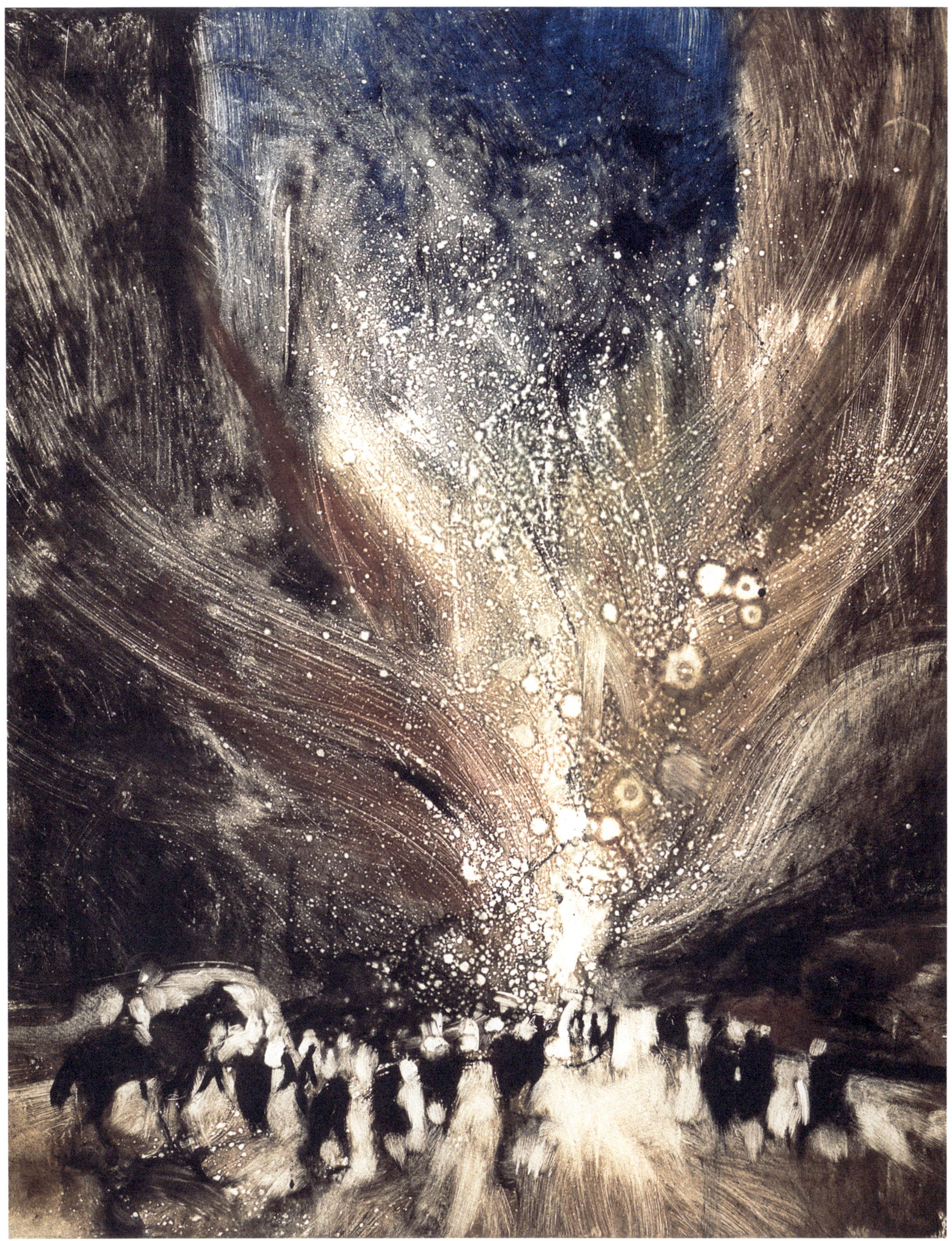

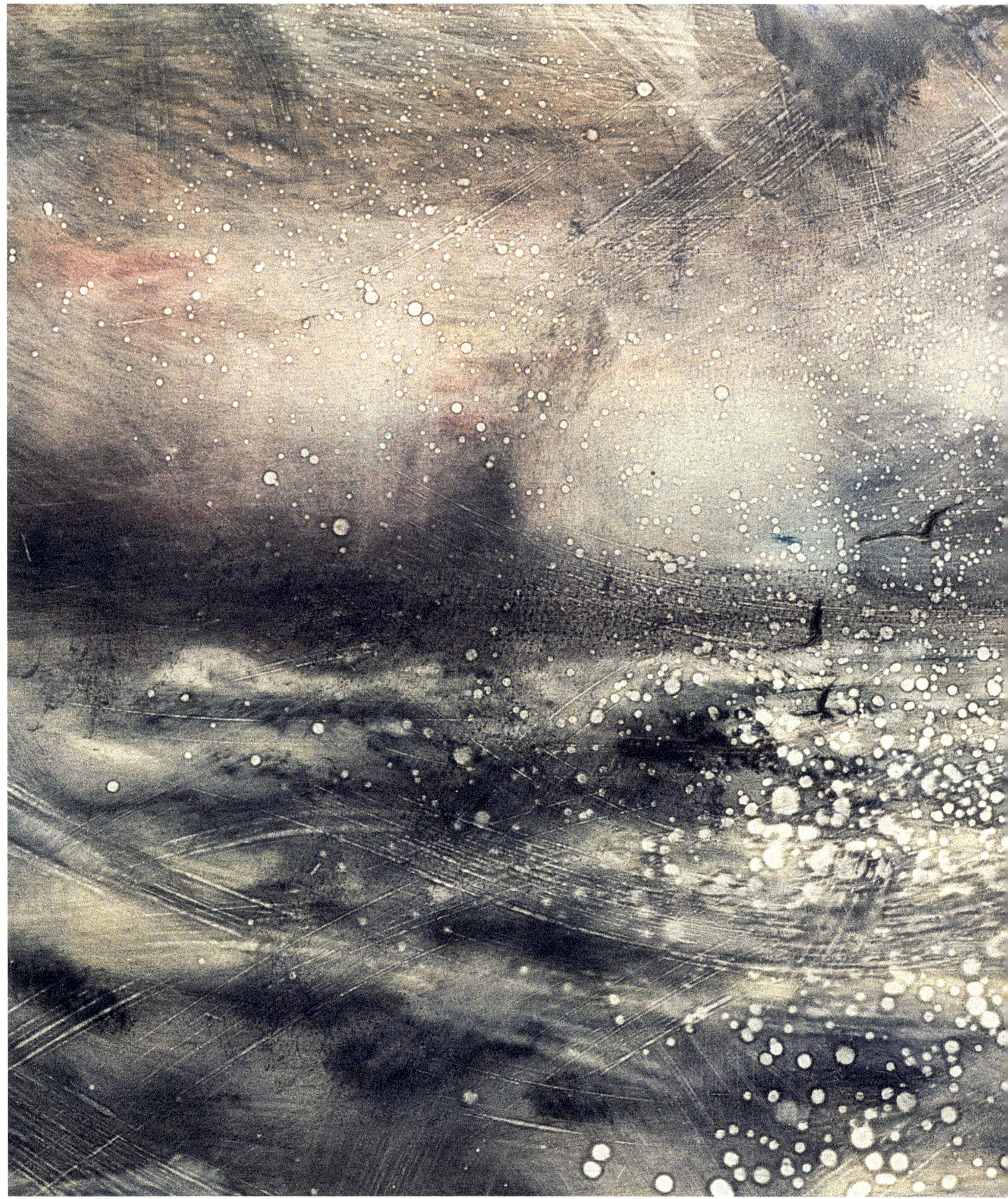

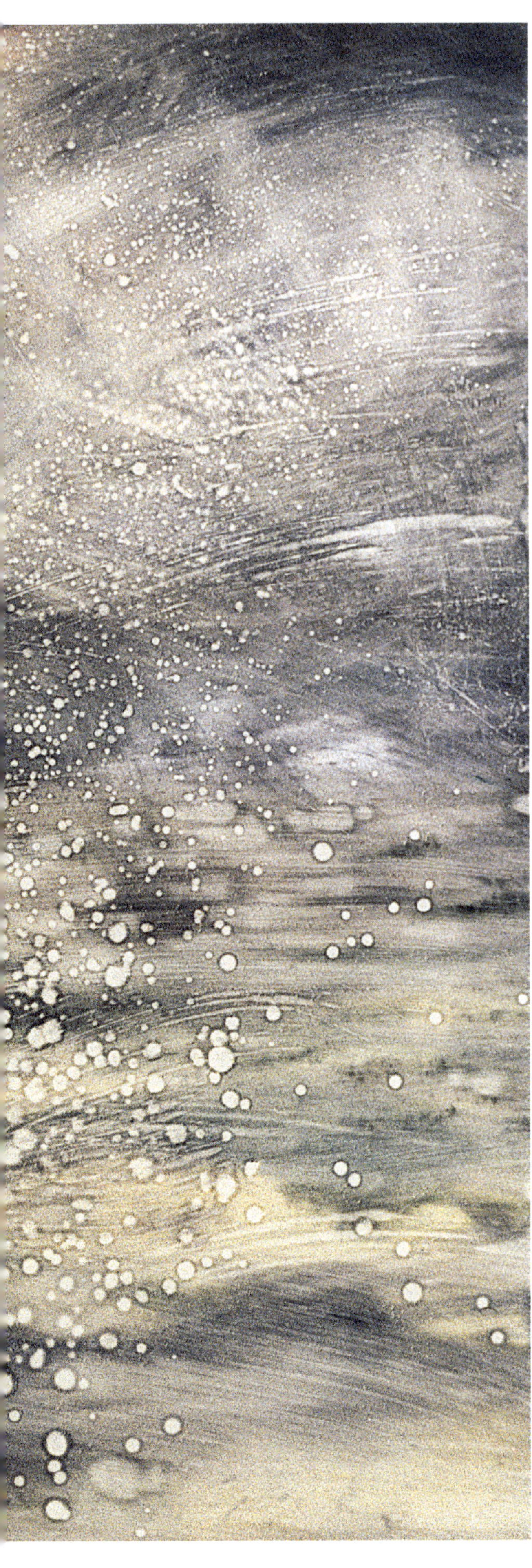

36
New York Harbour, 2003
Monotype, 15¾ × 19¾ inches
(40 × 50.2 cm)

37
The Black Umbrella A, 2007
Monotype, 20 × 16 inches
(50.8 × 40.6 cm)

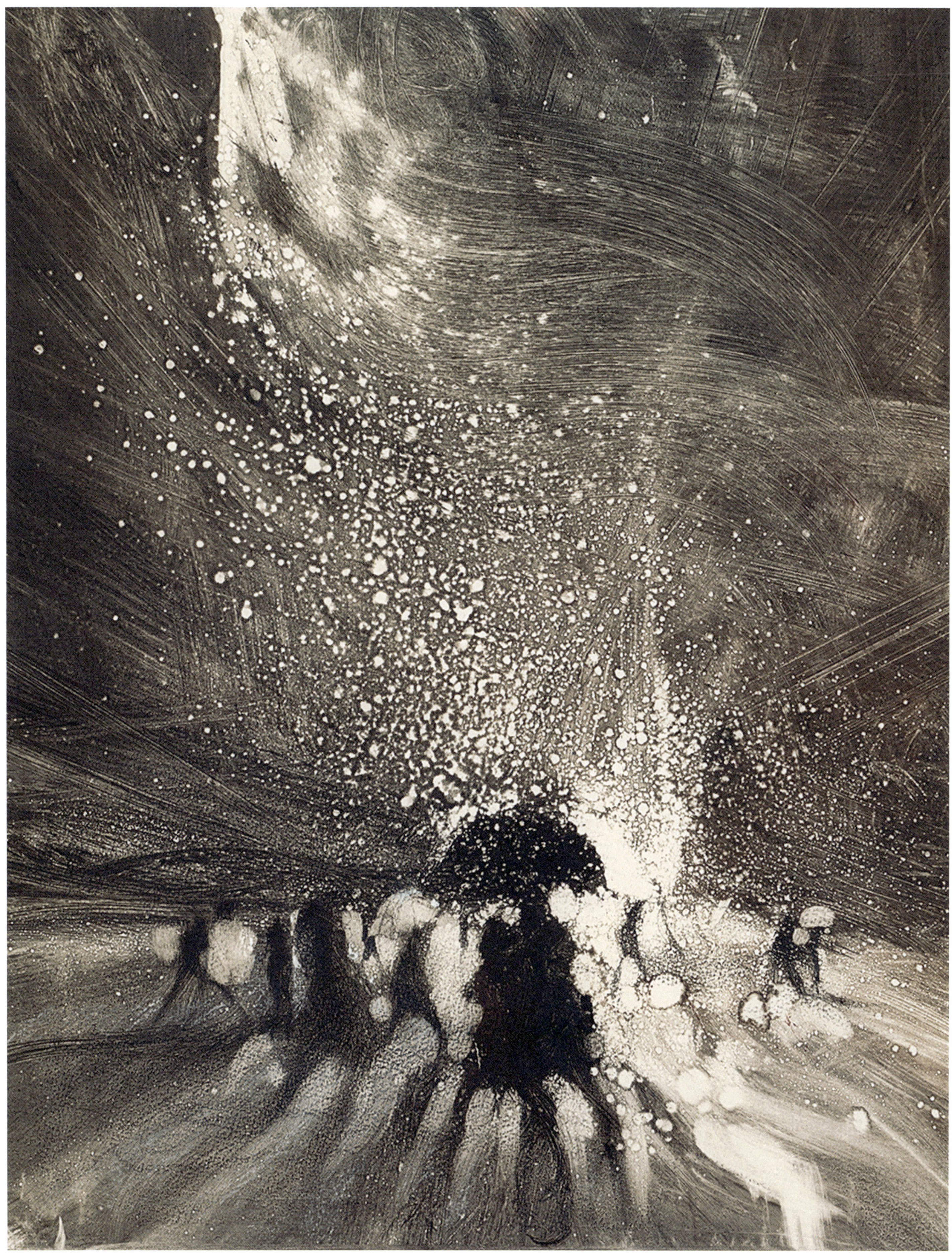

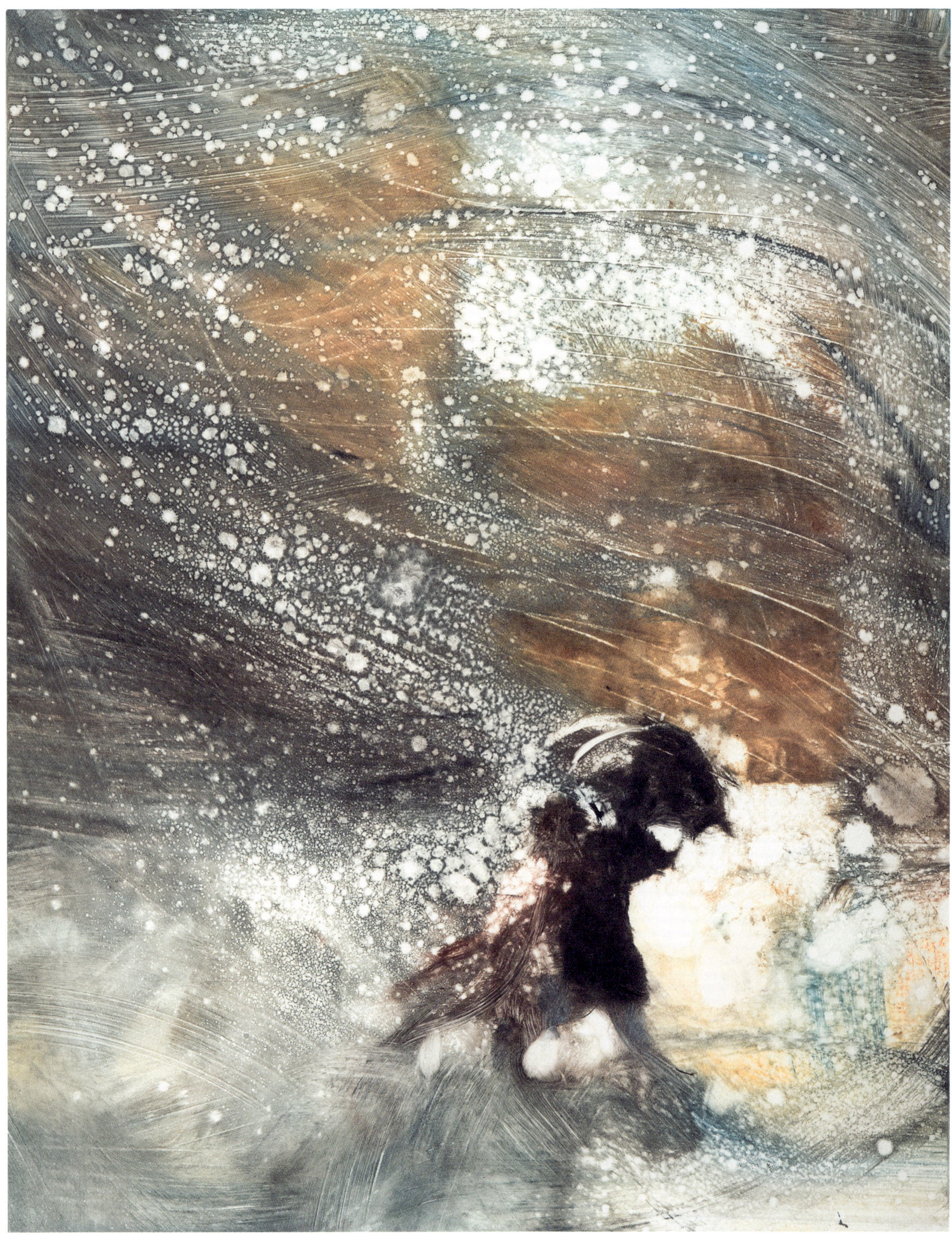

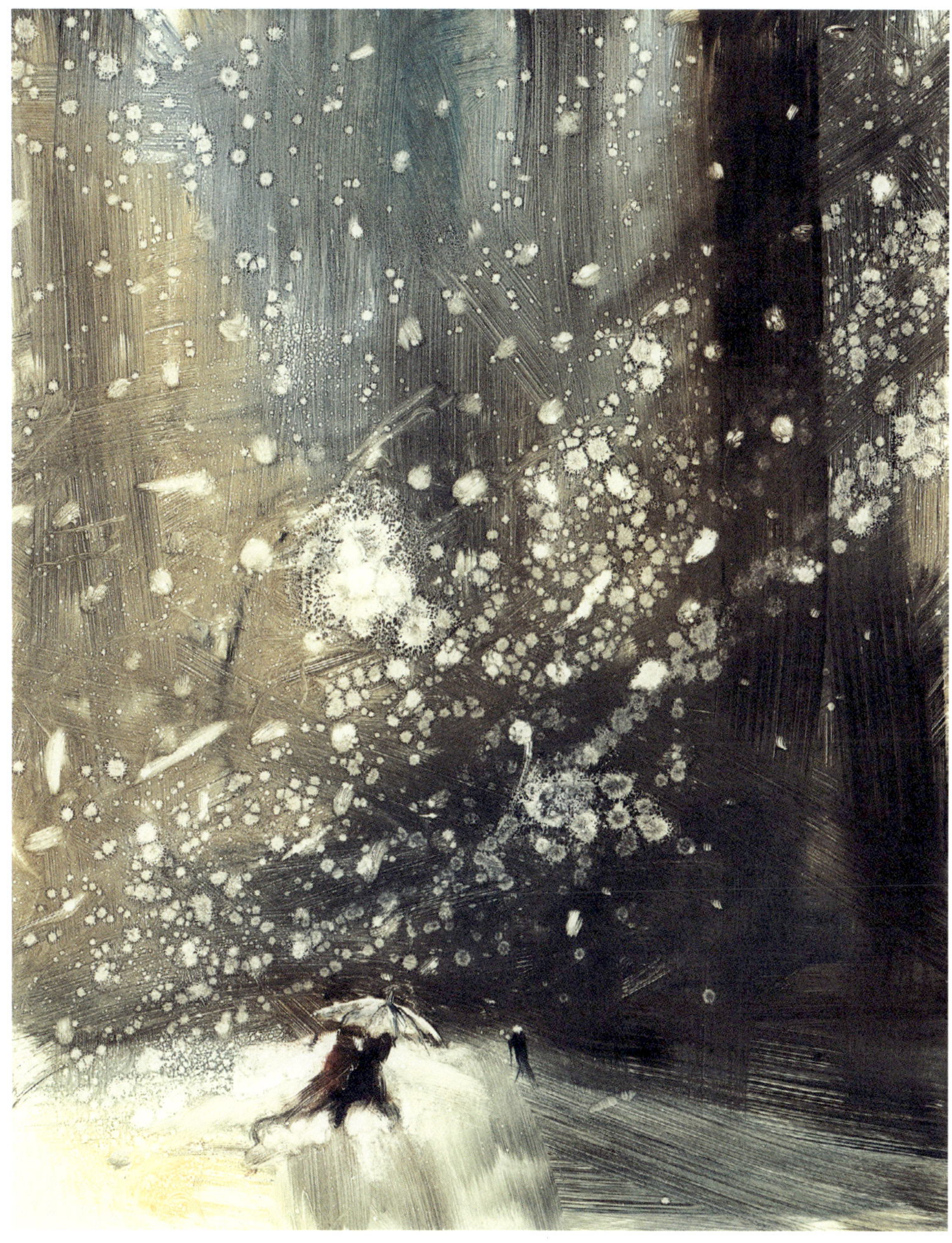

38
Crossing the Square in the Snow VI, 2009
Monotype, 20 × 16 inches
(50.8 × 40.6 cm)

39
Crossing the Square in the Snow V, 2009
Monotype, 19½ × 15½ inches
(49.5 × 39.4 cm)

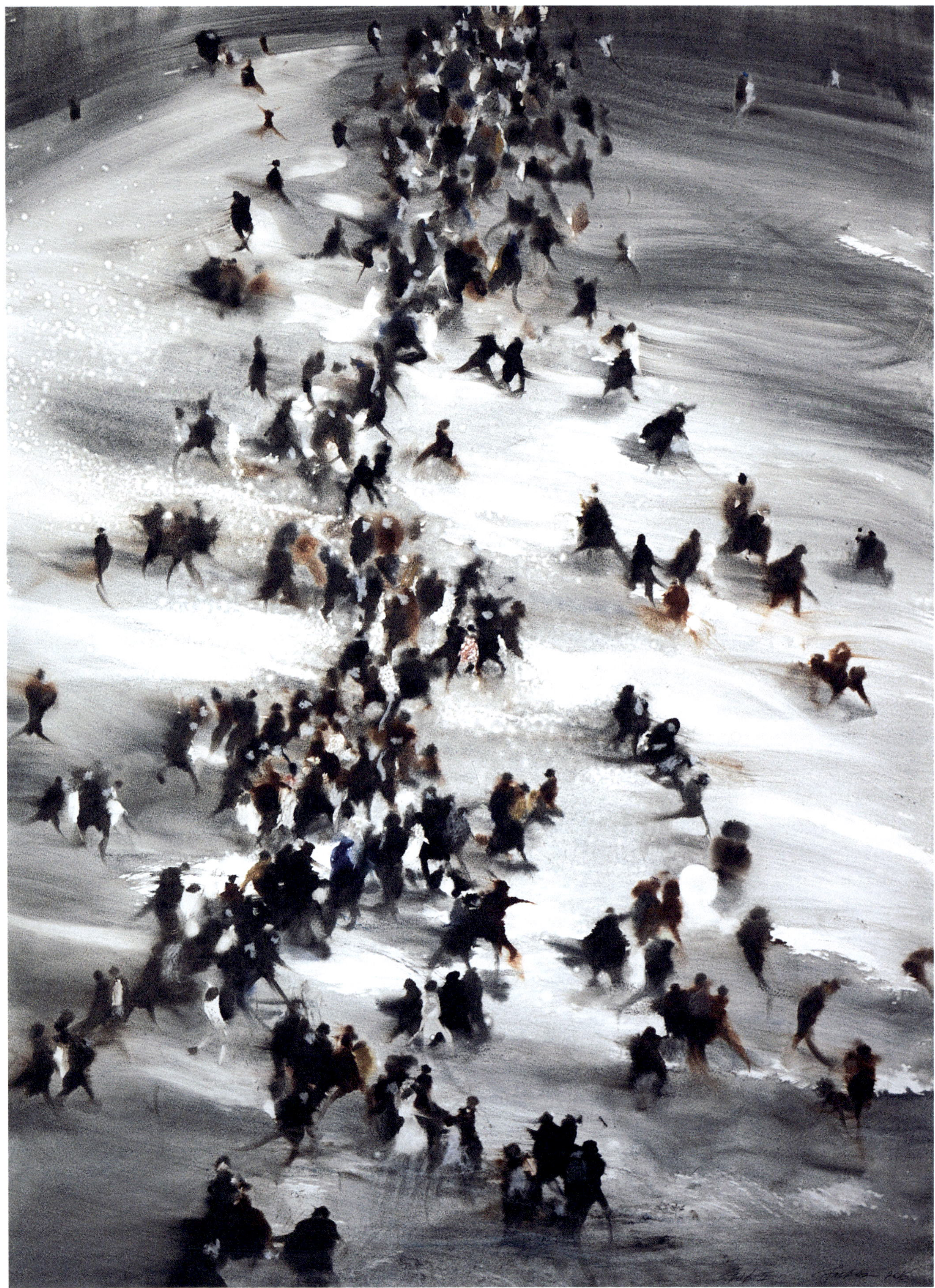

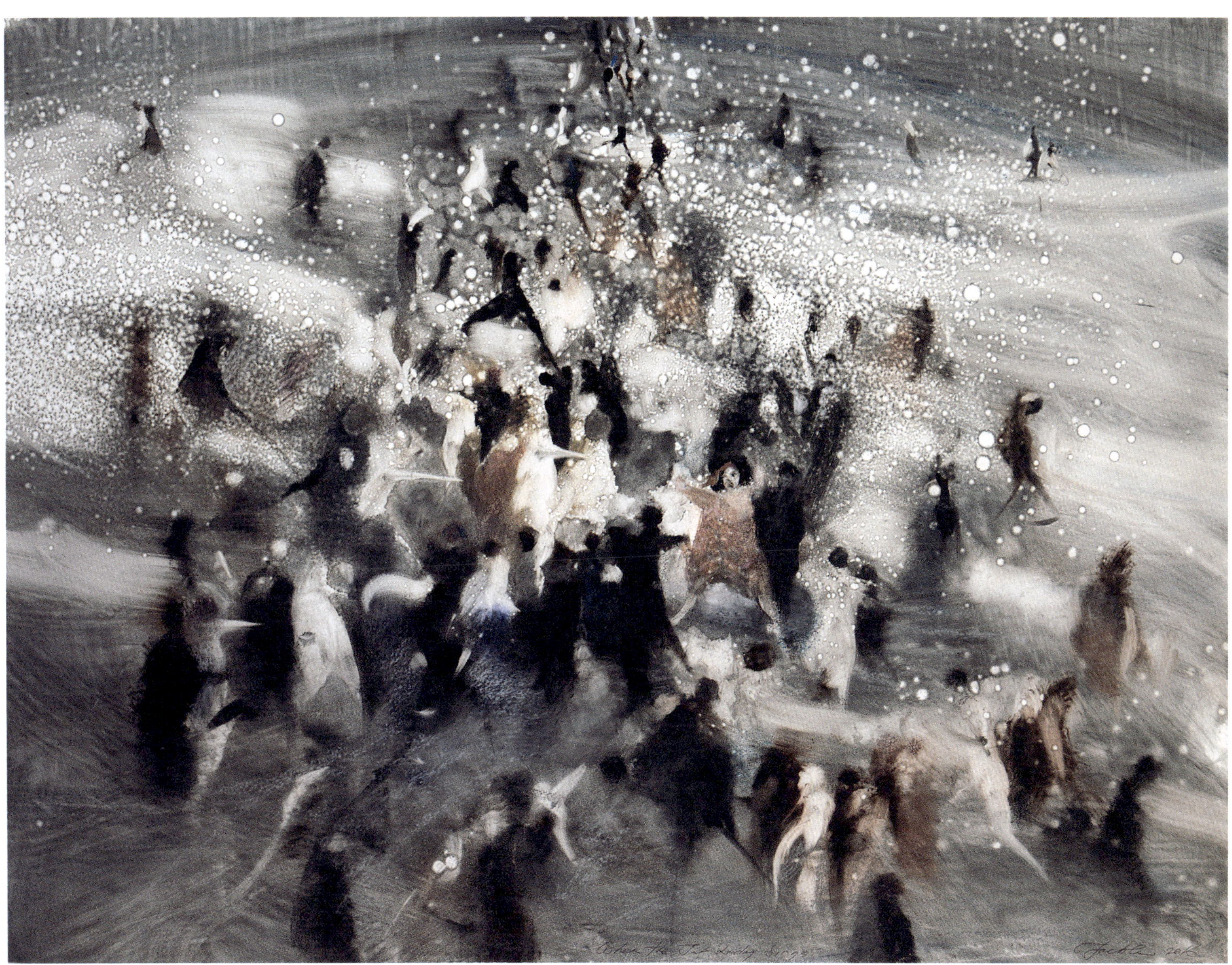

40
Hub I, NYC, 2016
Monotype, 39½ × 29½ inches
(100.3 × 74.9 cm)

41
When the Fat Lady Sings, 2016
Monotype, 29½ × 39½ inches
(74.9 × 100.3 cm)

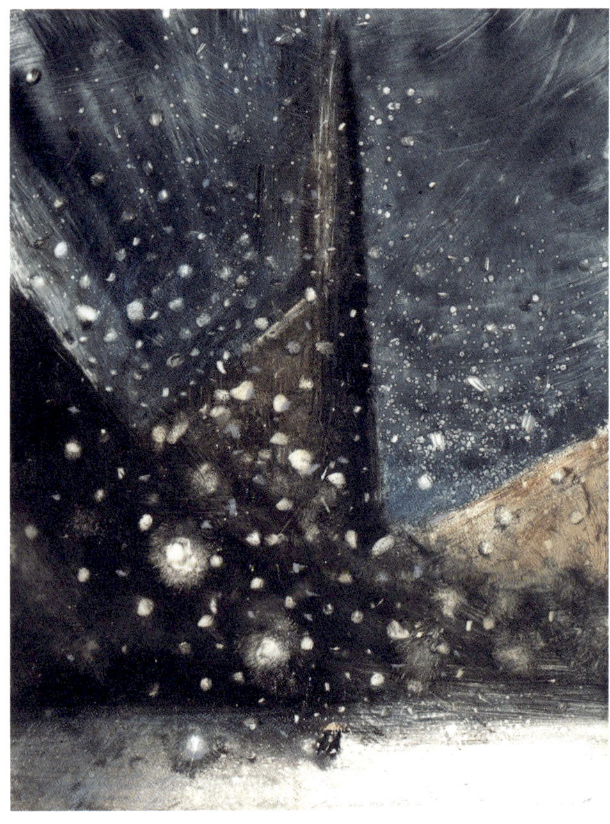

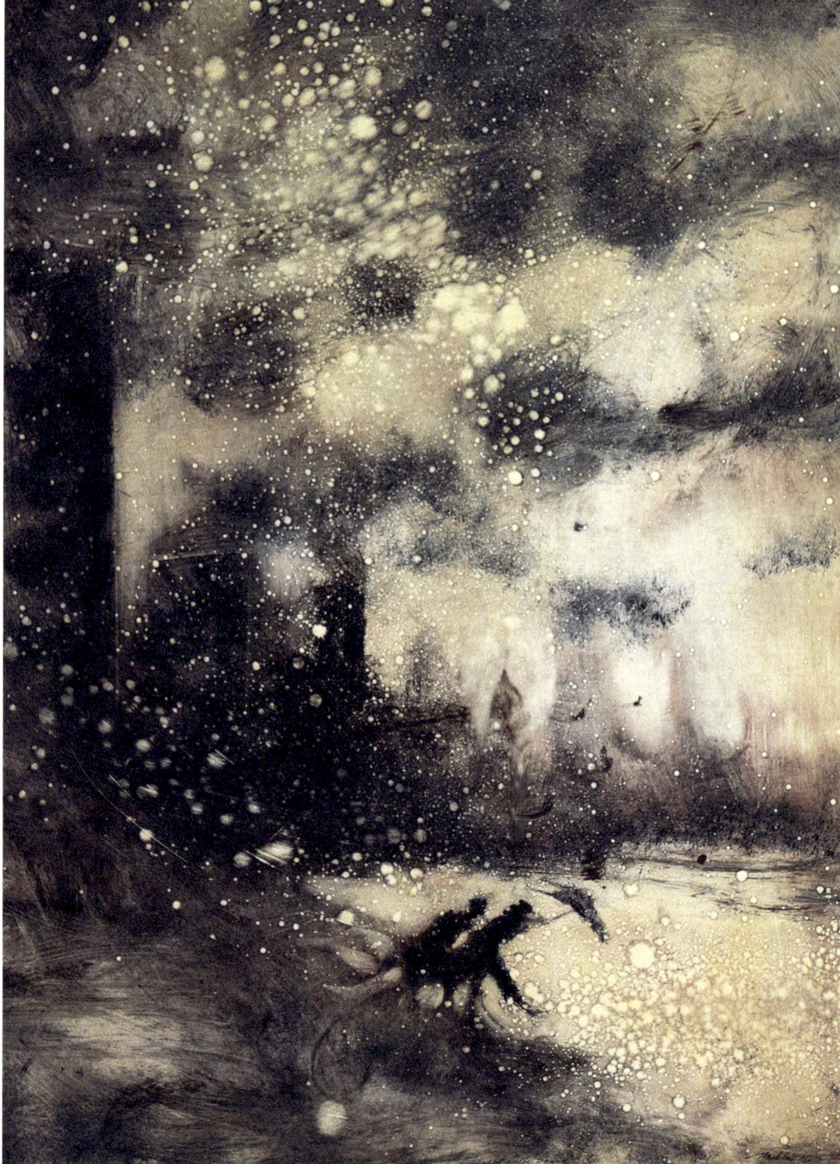

42
Snow in the City II, 2015
Monotype, 27 × 21 inches
(68.6 × 53.3 cm)

43
Tempest in the Square IX, 2016
Monotype, 39½ × 29½ inches
(100.3 × 74.9 cm)

44
Tempest in the Square VI, 2016
Monotype, 39½ × 29½ inches
(100.3 × 74.9 cm)

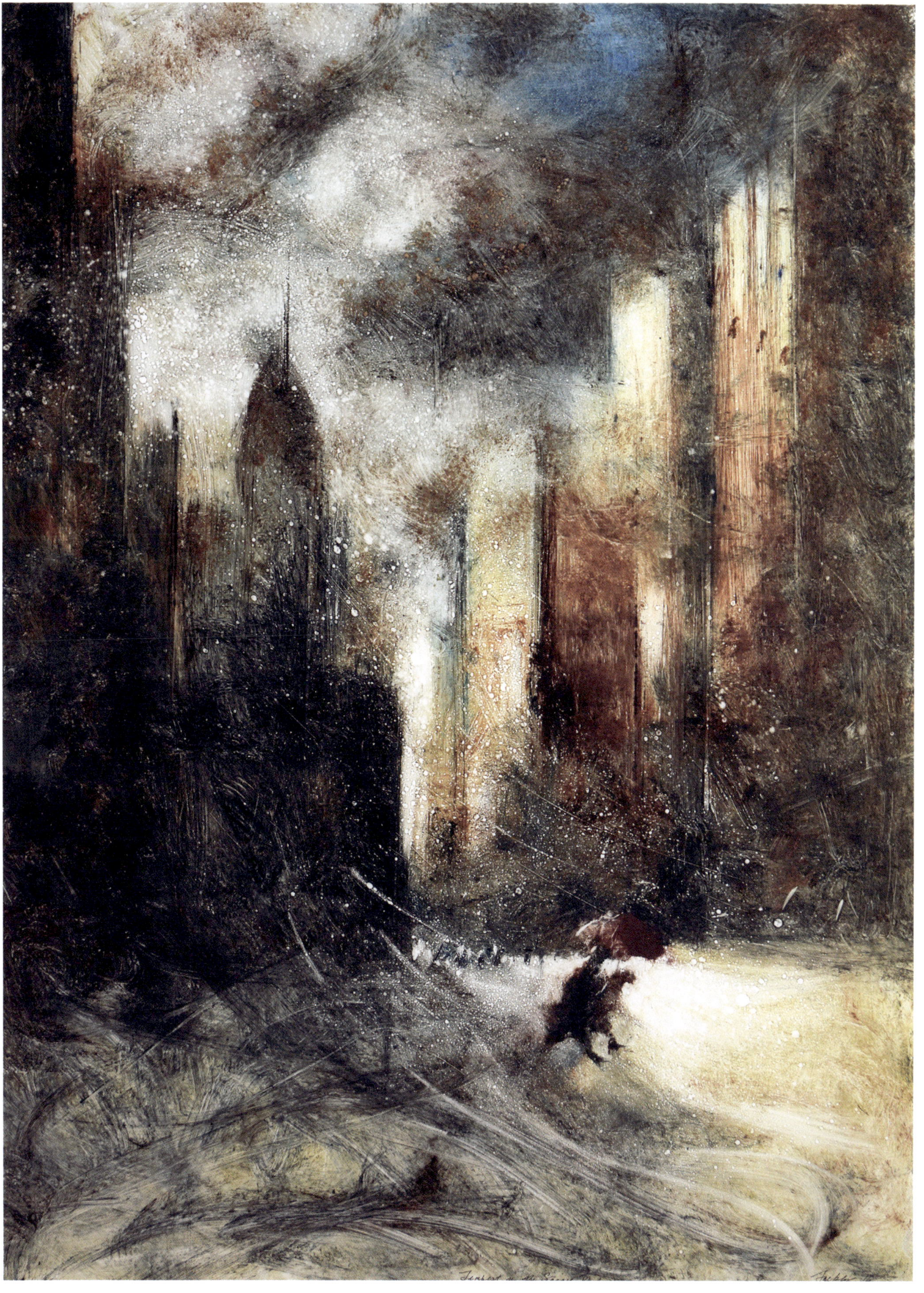

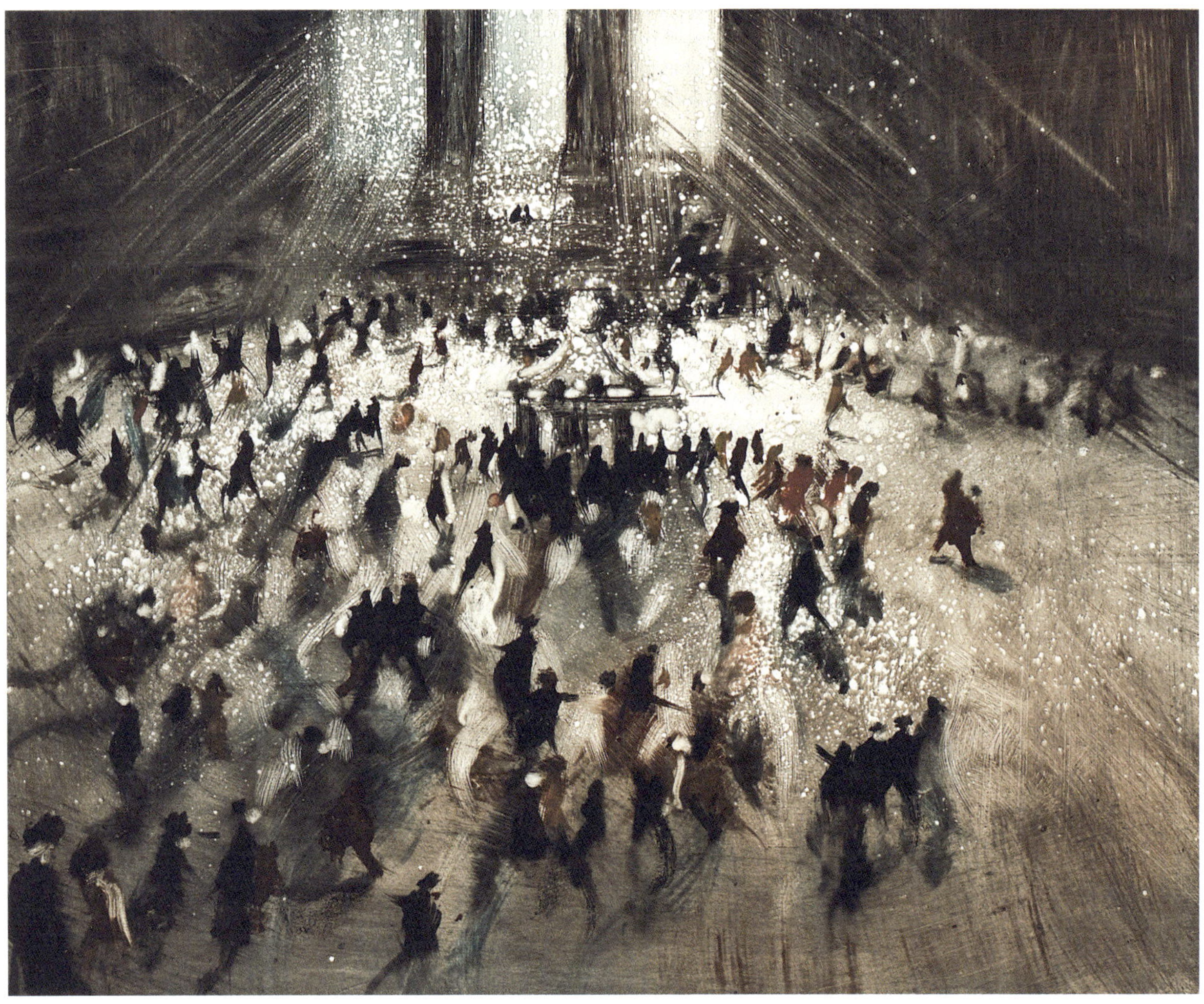

45
Chance Encounter, Grand Central I, 2006
Monotype, 16 × 20 inches
(40.6 × 50.8 cm)

46
Lucky Strike, Grand Central I, 2007
Monotype, 20 × 16 inches
(50.8 × 40.6 cm)

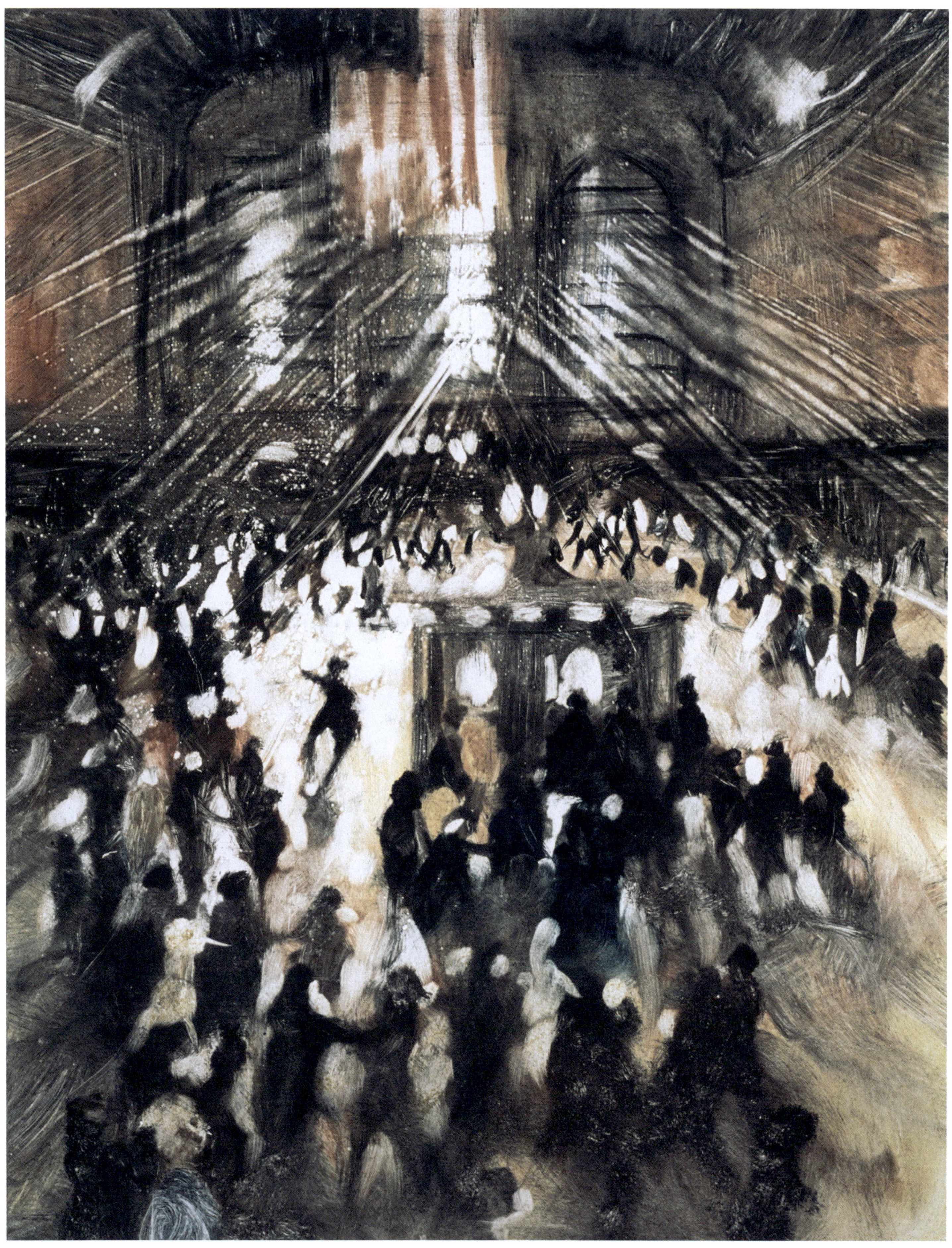

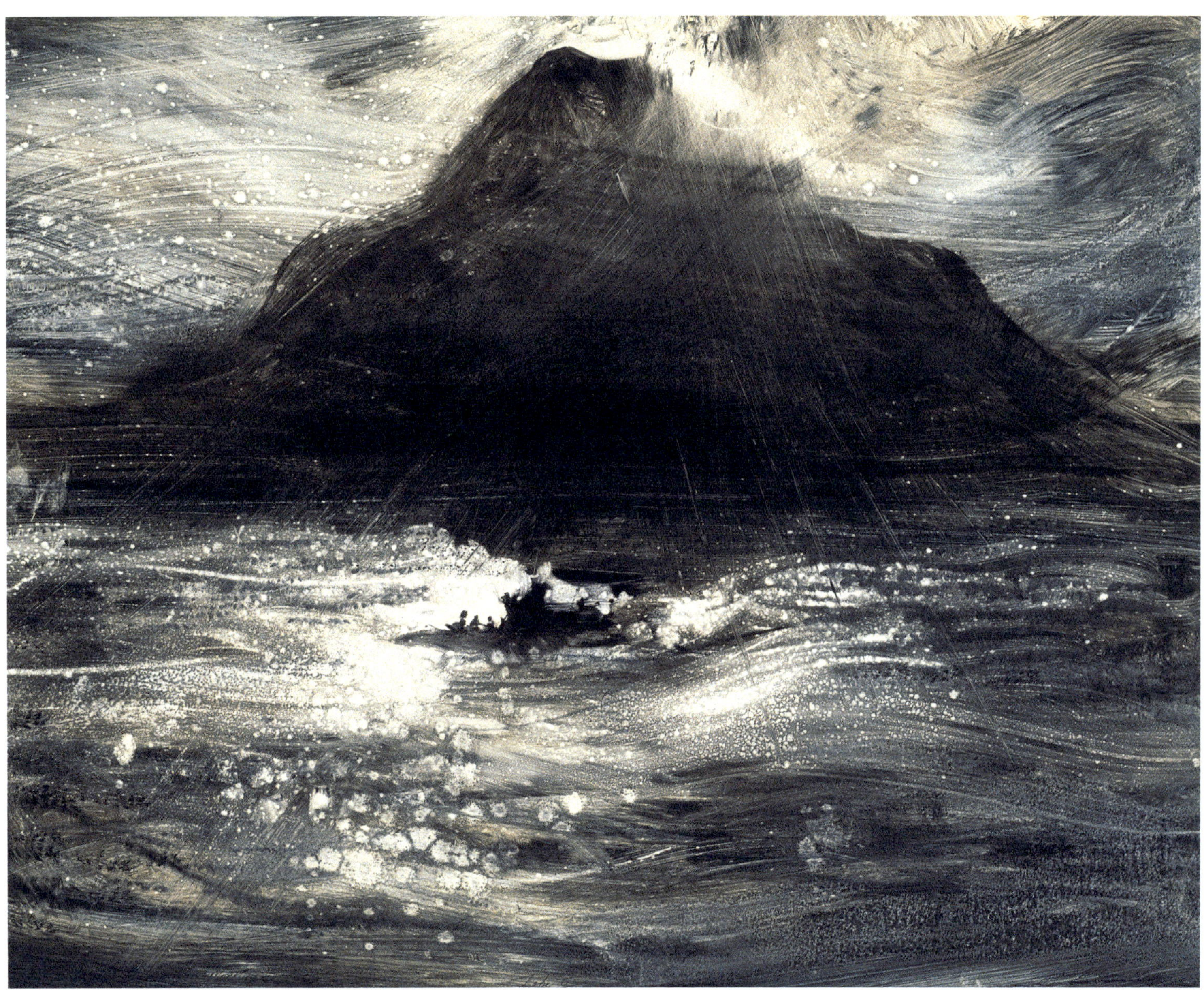

47
Lake VI, 2009
Monotype, 16 × 20 inches
(40.6 × 50.8 cm)

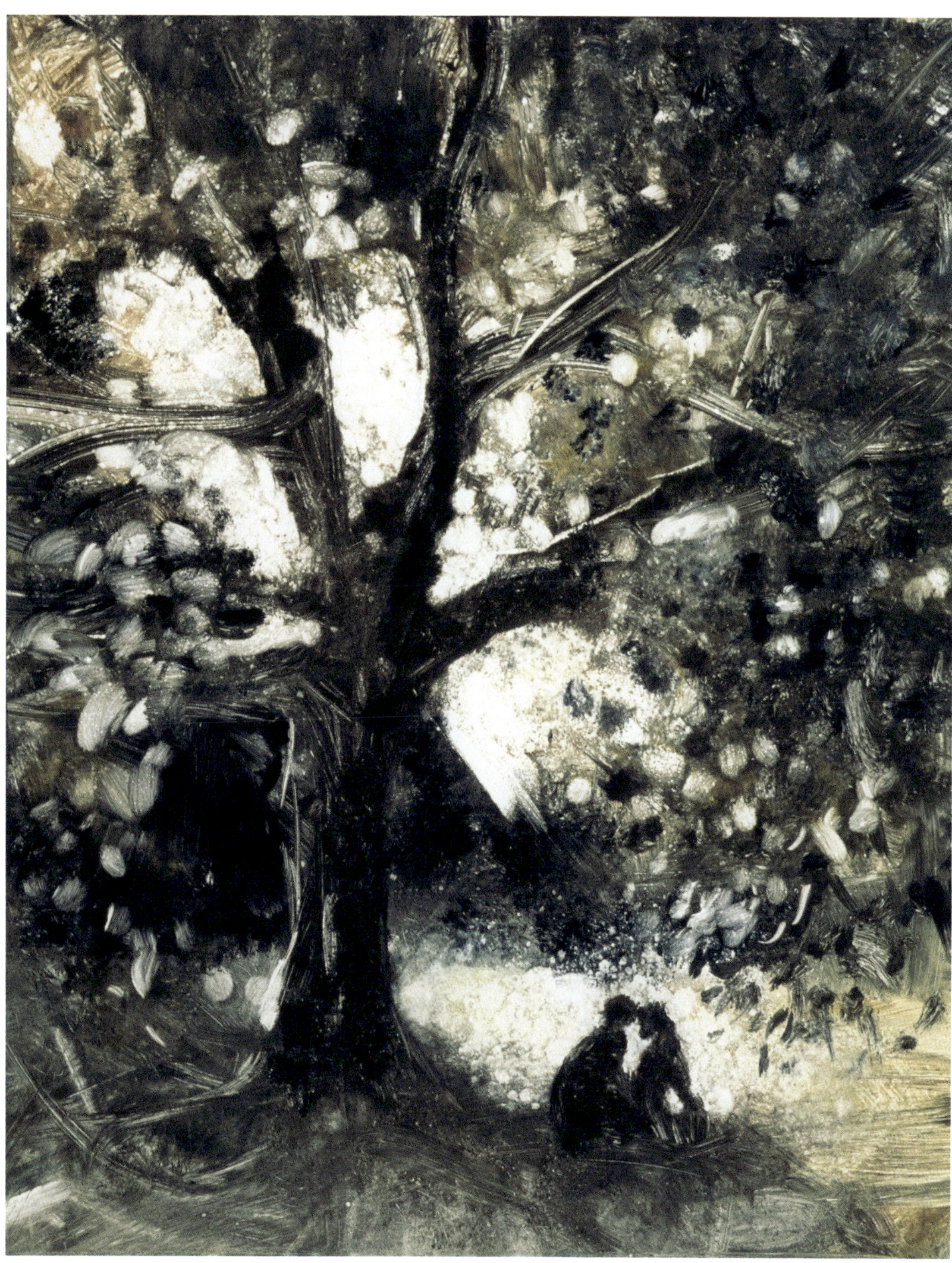

48
Under the Tree II, 2008
Monotype, 20 × 16 inches
(50.8 × 40.6 cm)

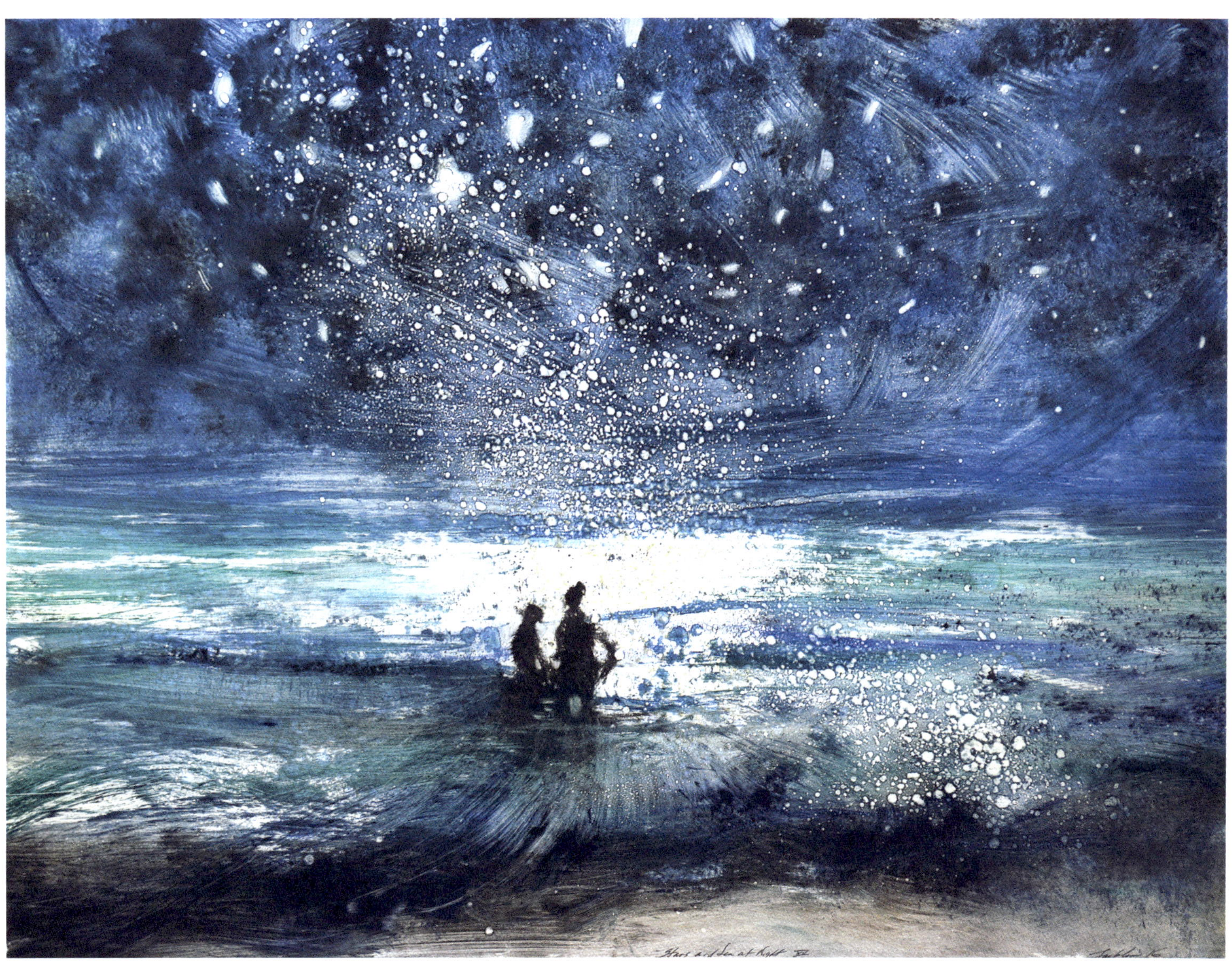

49
Stars and Sea at Night XV, 2016
Monotype, 29½ × 39½ inches
(74.9 × 100.3 cm)

50
Into the Sea at Night I, 2011
Monotype, 32 × 25¾ inches
(81.5 × 65.5 cm)

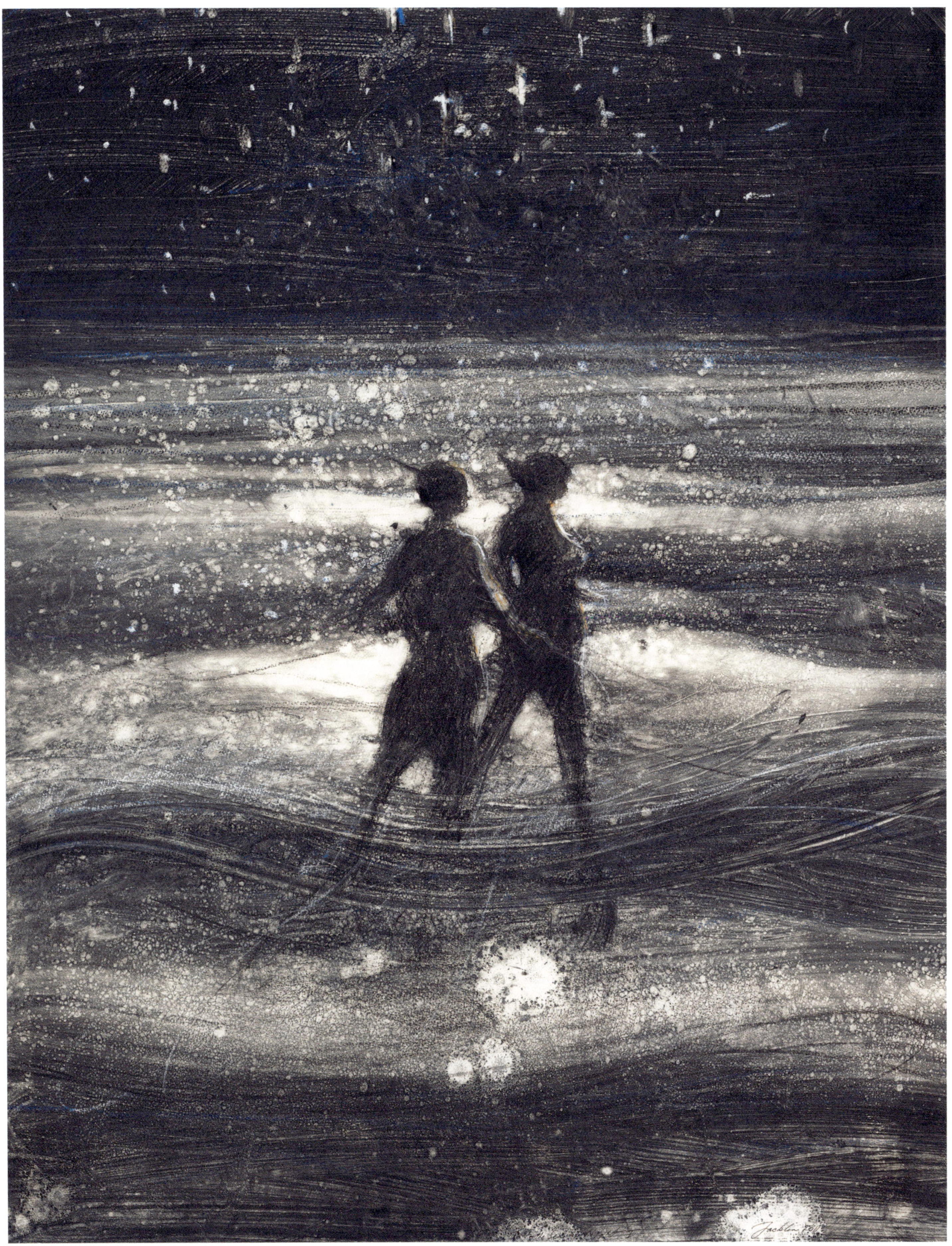

51
Stars and Sea at Night III, 2015
Monotype, 27 × 22 inches
(68.6 × 55.9 cm)

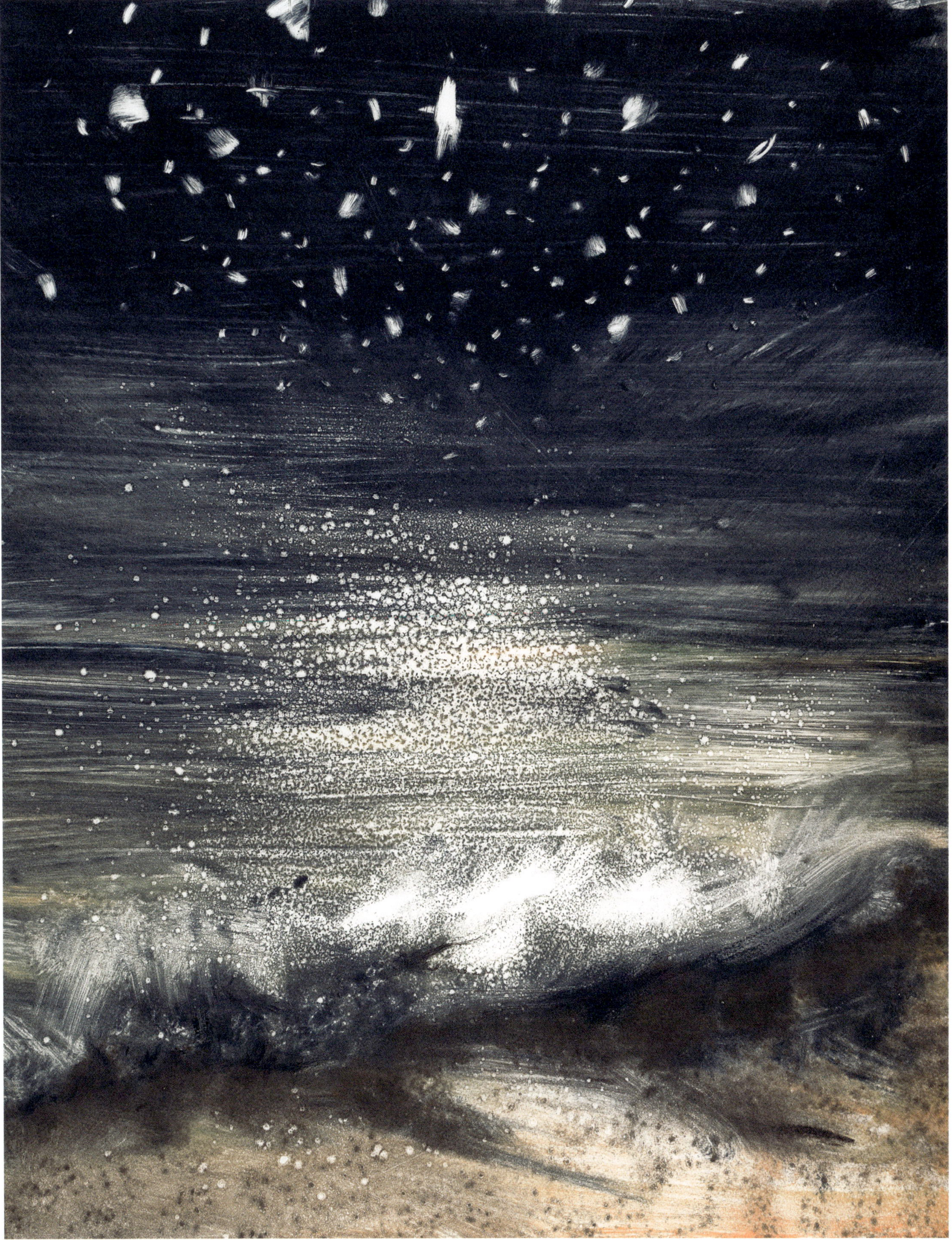

52
Stars and Sea at Night VII, 2015
Monotype, 27½ × 21½ inches
(69.9 × 54.6 cm)

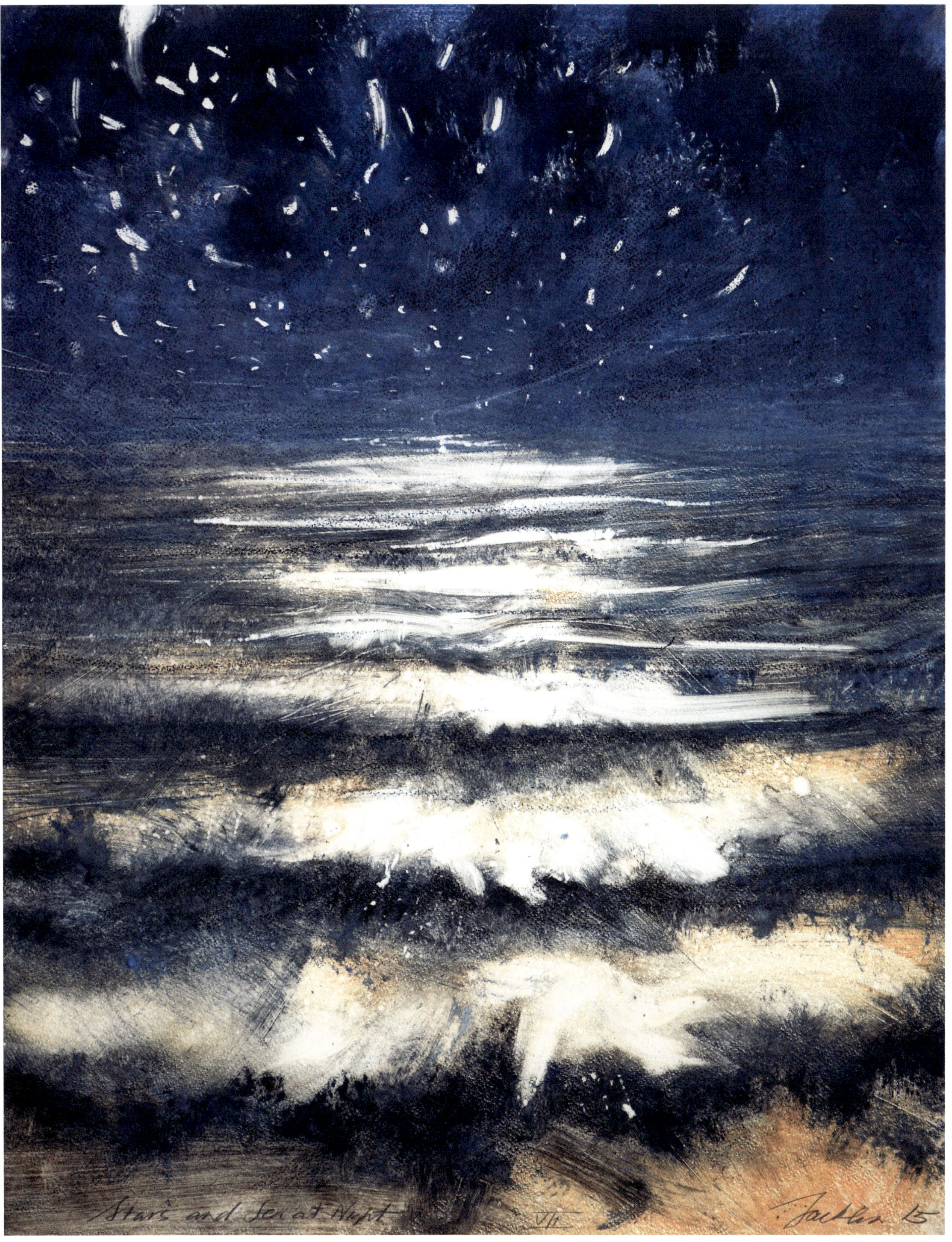
Stars and Sea at Night
VII
Jacklin 15

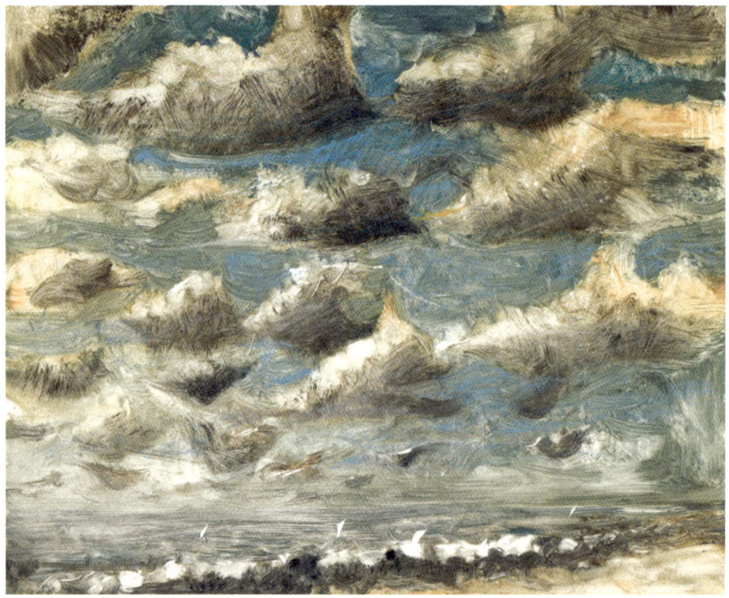

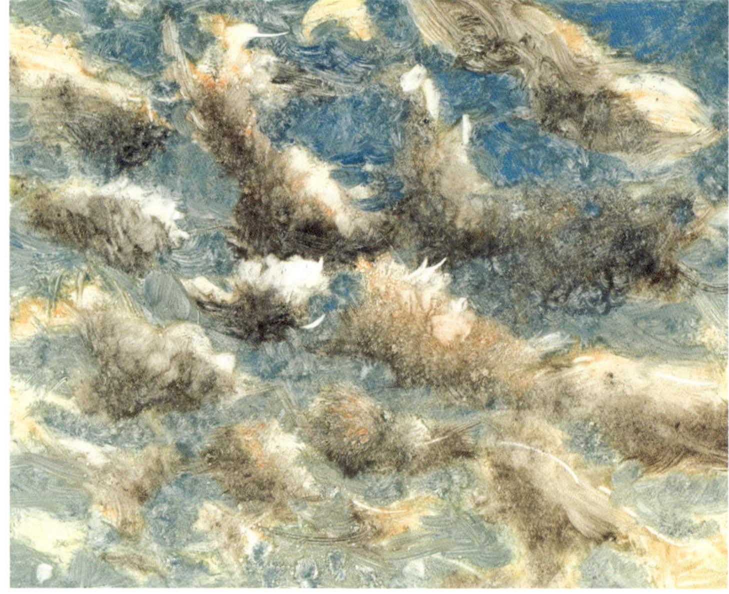

53
Clouds and Sea I, 2015
Monotype, 16 × 20 inches
(40.6 × 50.8 cm)

54
Clouds and Sky I, 2015
Monotype, 16 × 20 inches
(40.6 × 50.8 cm)

55
Stars and Sea at Night with Clouds, 2015
Monotype, 27 × 21 inches
(68.6 × 53.3 cm)

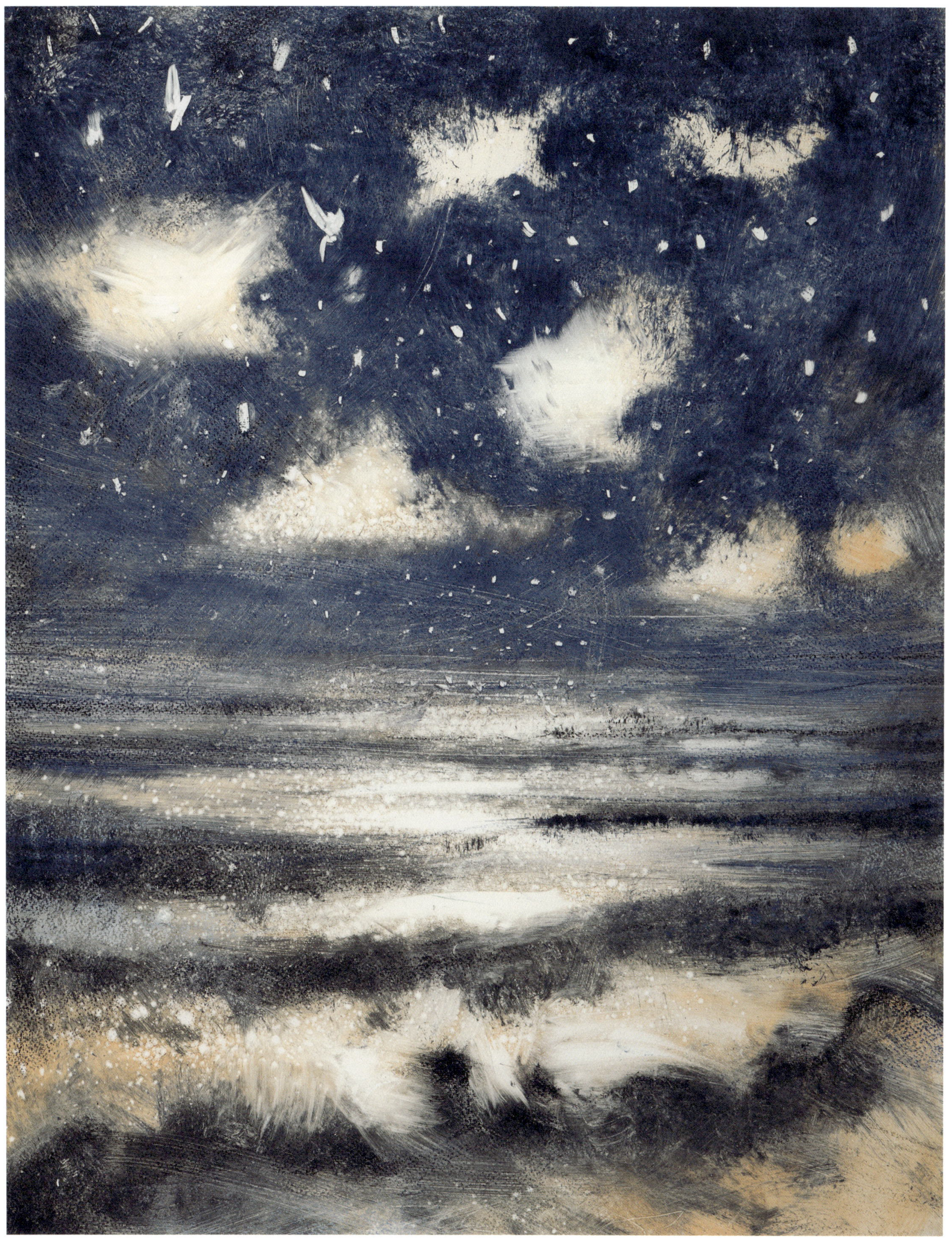

56
Stars and Sea at Night XIII, 2016
Monotype, 39½ × 29½ inches
(100.3 × 74.9 cm)

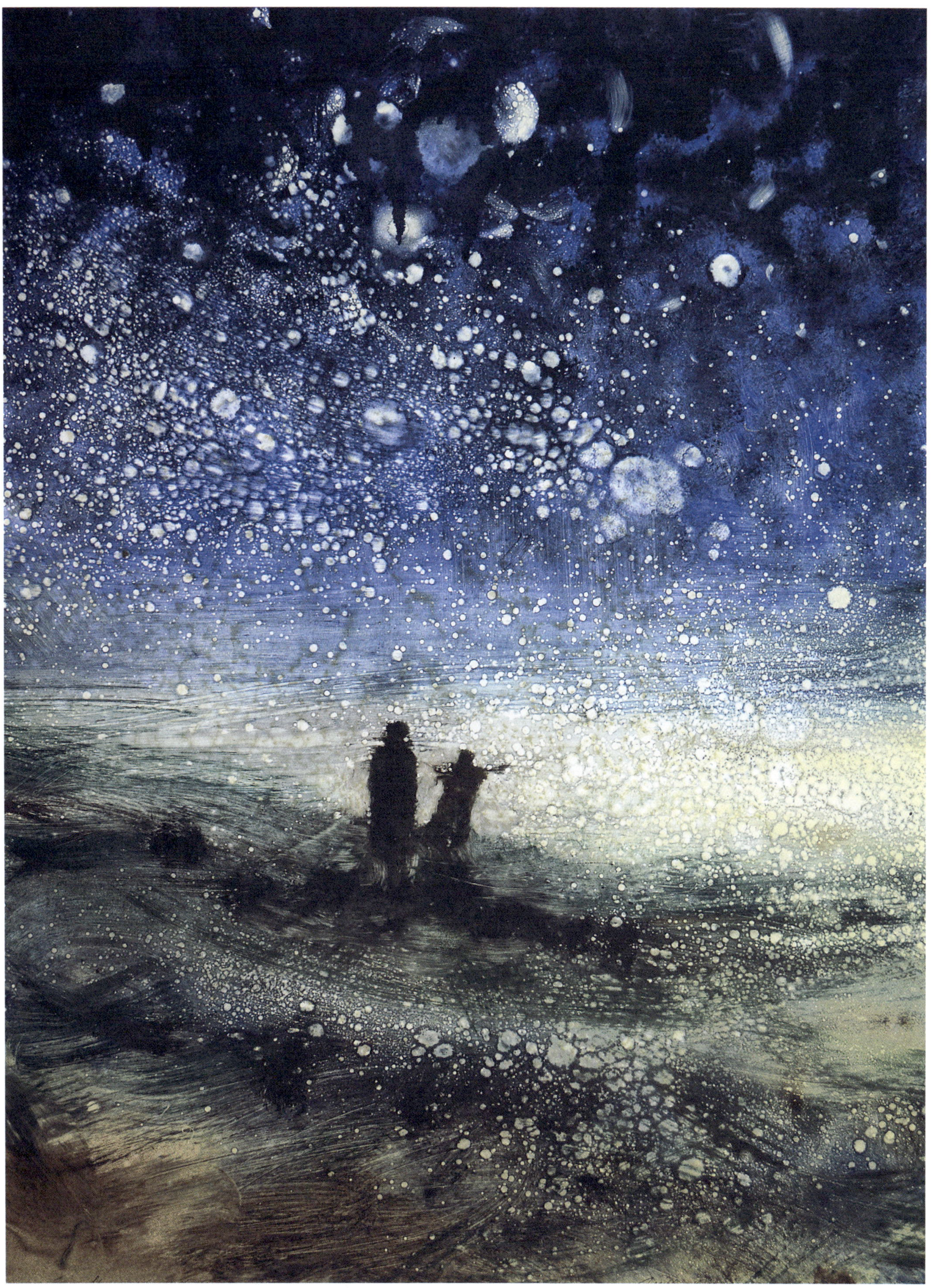

57
Stars and Sea at Night II, 2015
Monotype, 27 × 21 inches
(68.6 × 53.3 cm)

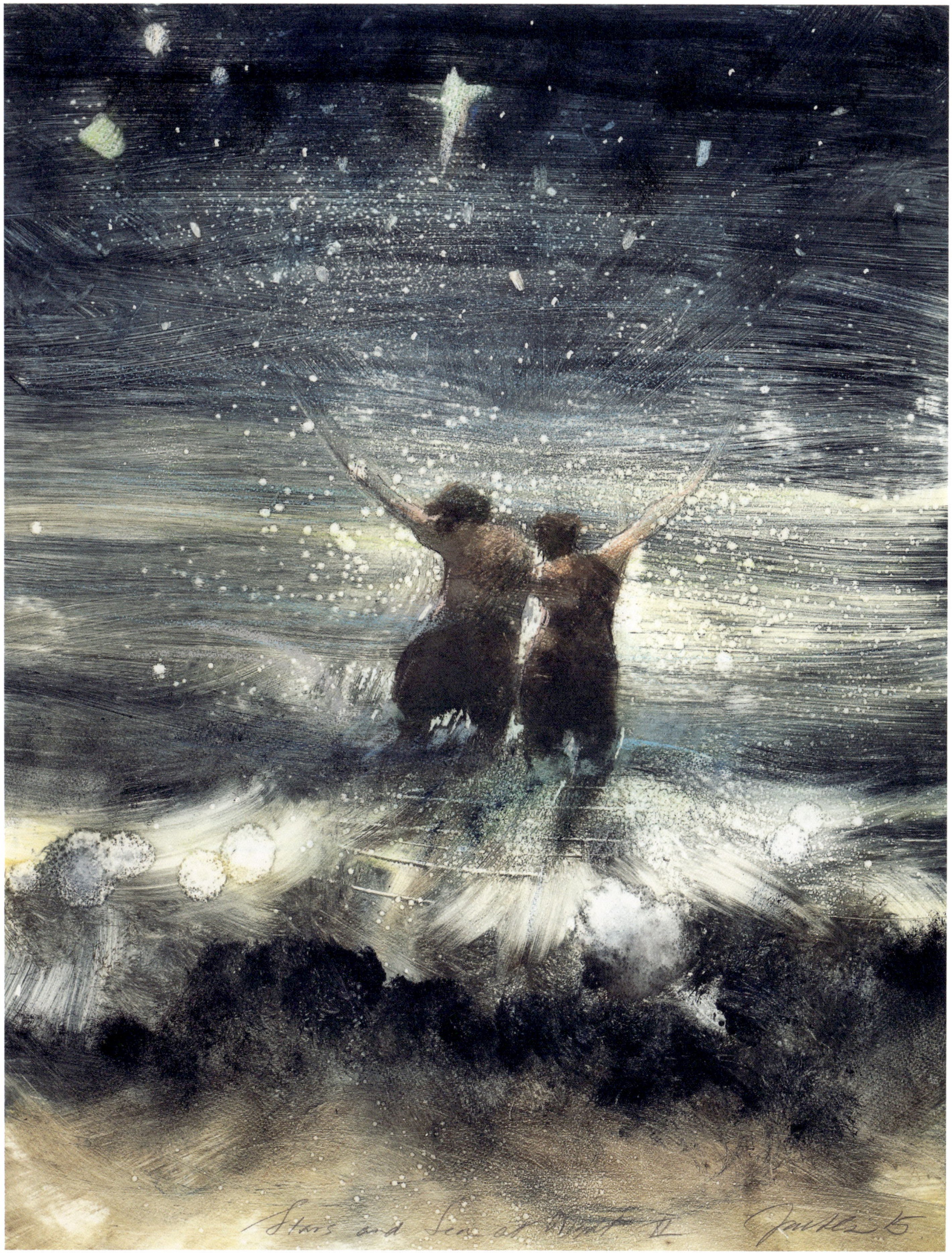
Stars and Sea at Night V

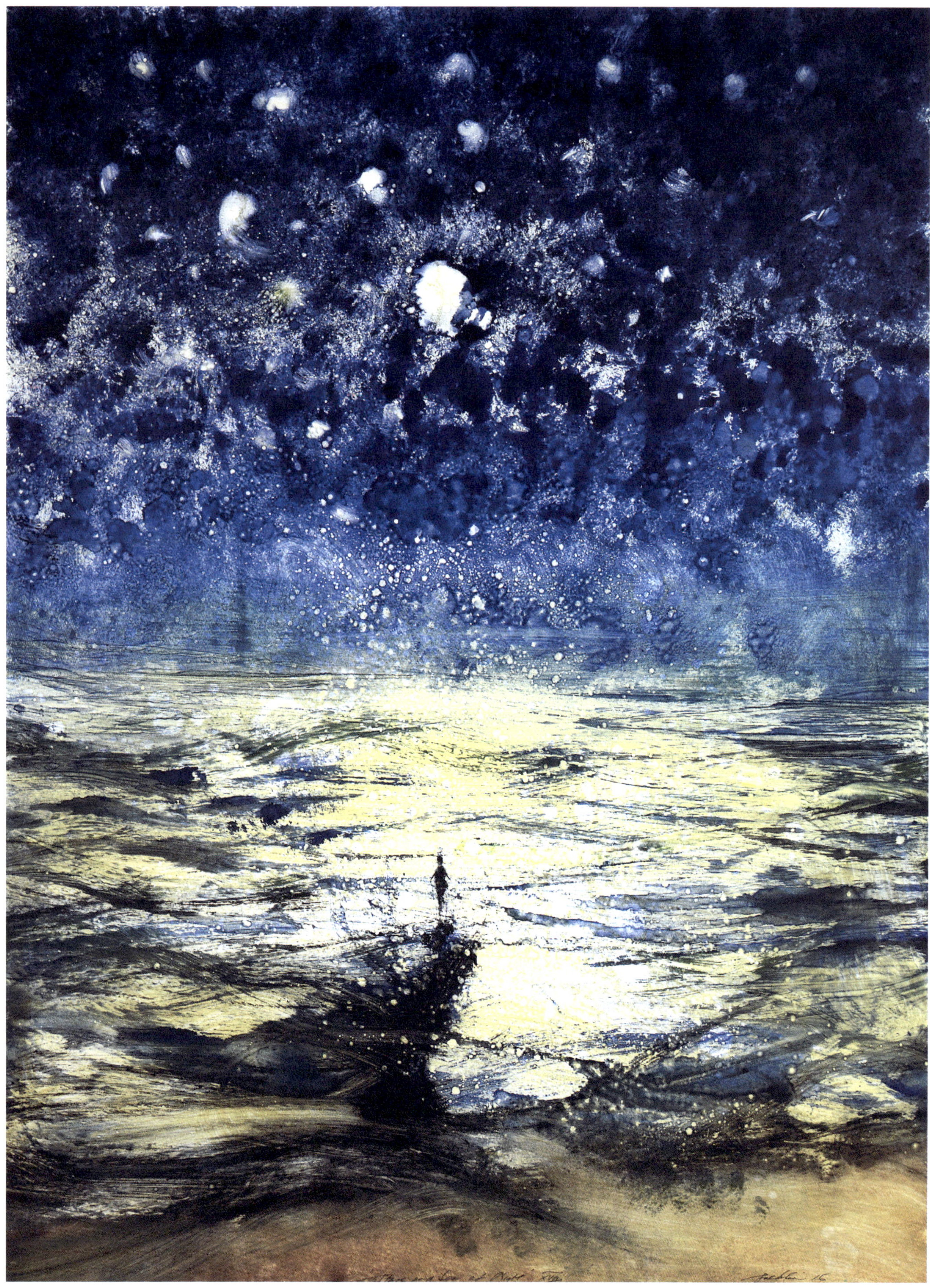

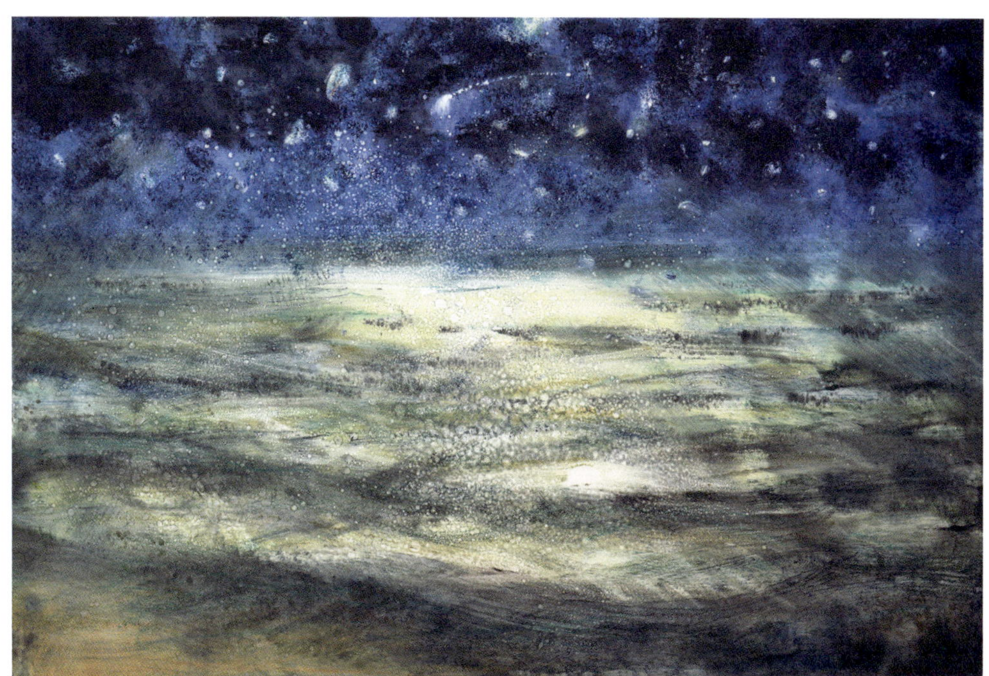

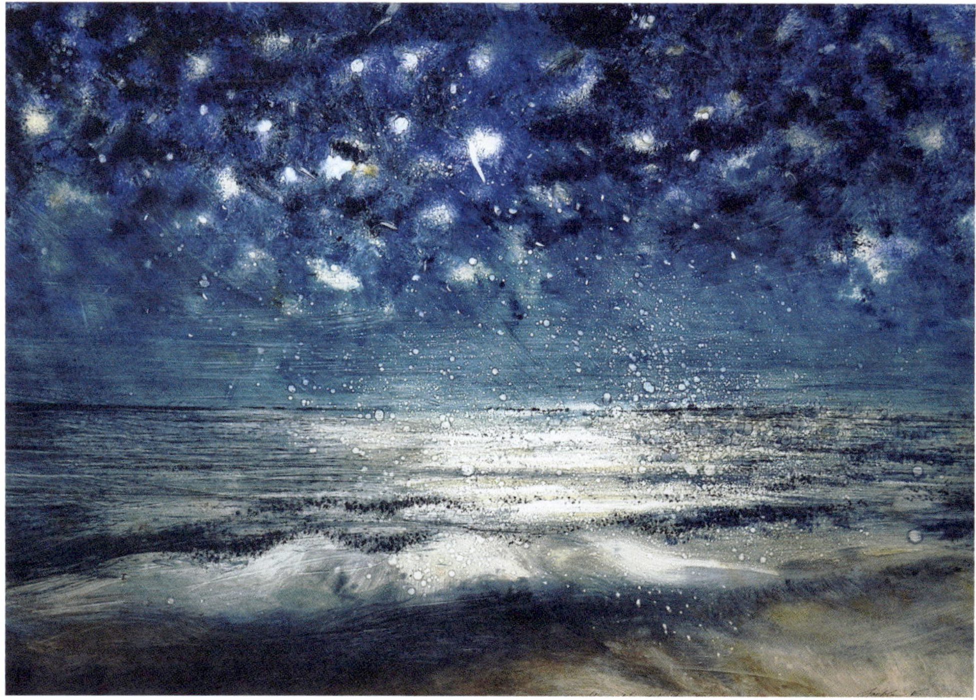

59
Shooting Star IX, 2016
Monotype, 32 × 48 inches
(81.3 × 121.9 cm)

58
Stars and Sea at Night XVII, 2016
Monotype, 39½ × 29½ inches
(100.3 × 74.9 cm)

60
Stars and Sea at Night XIX, 2016
Monotype, 31½ × 45½ inches
(80 × 115.7 cm)

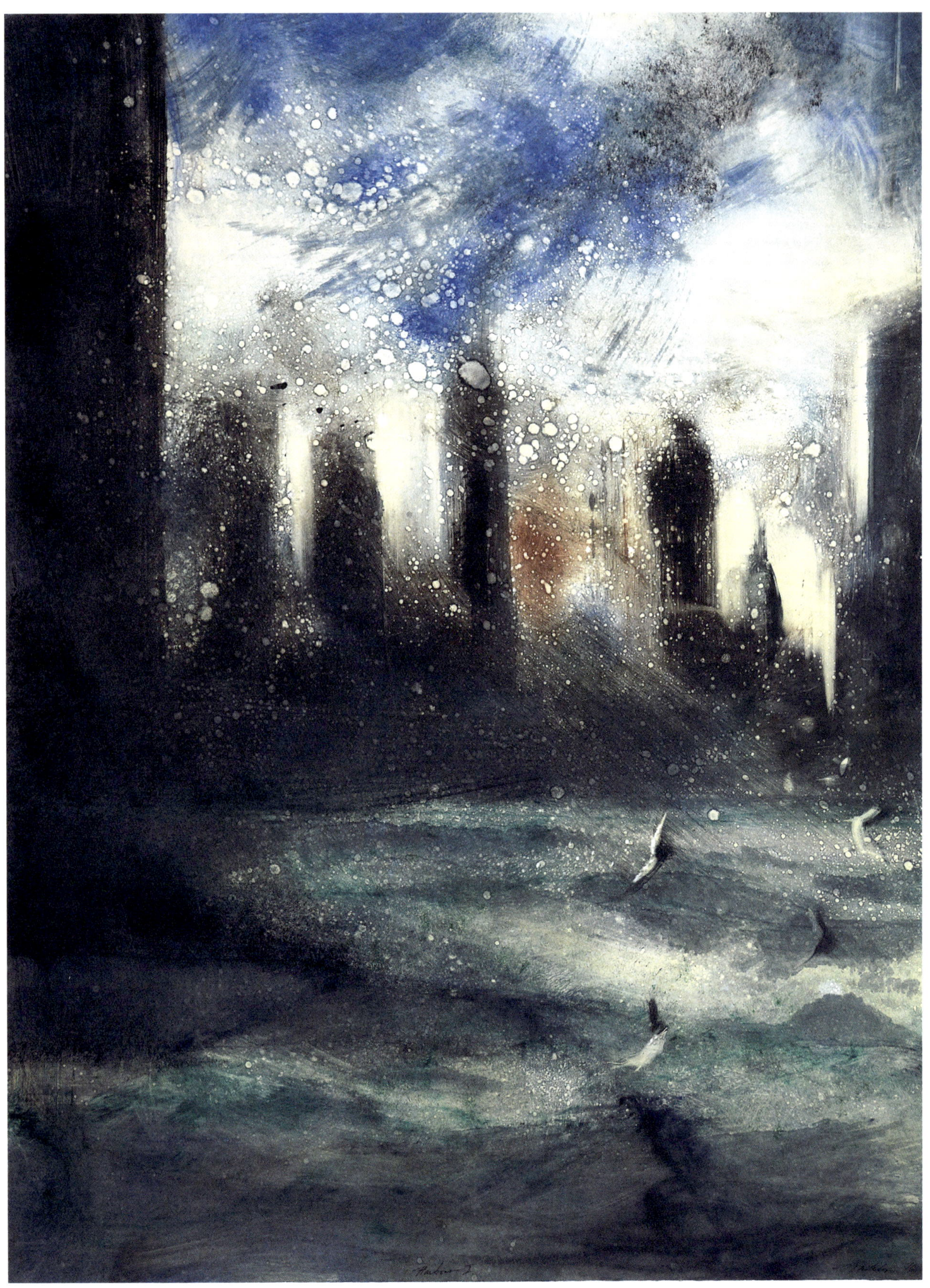

61
Harbour I, 2016
Monotype, 39½ × 29½ inches
(100.3 × 74.9 cm)

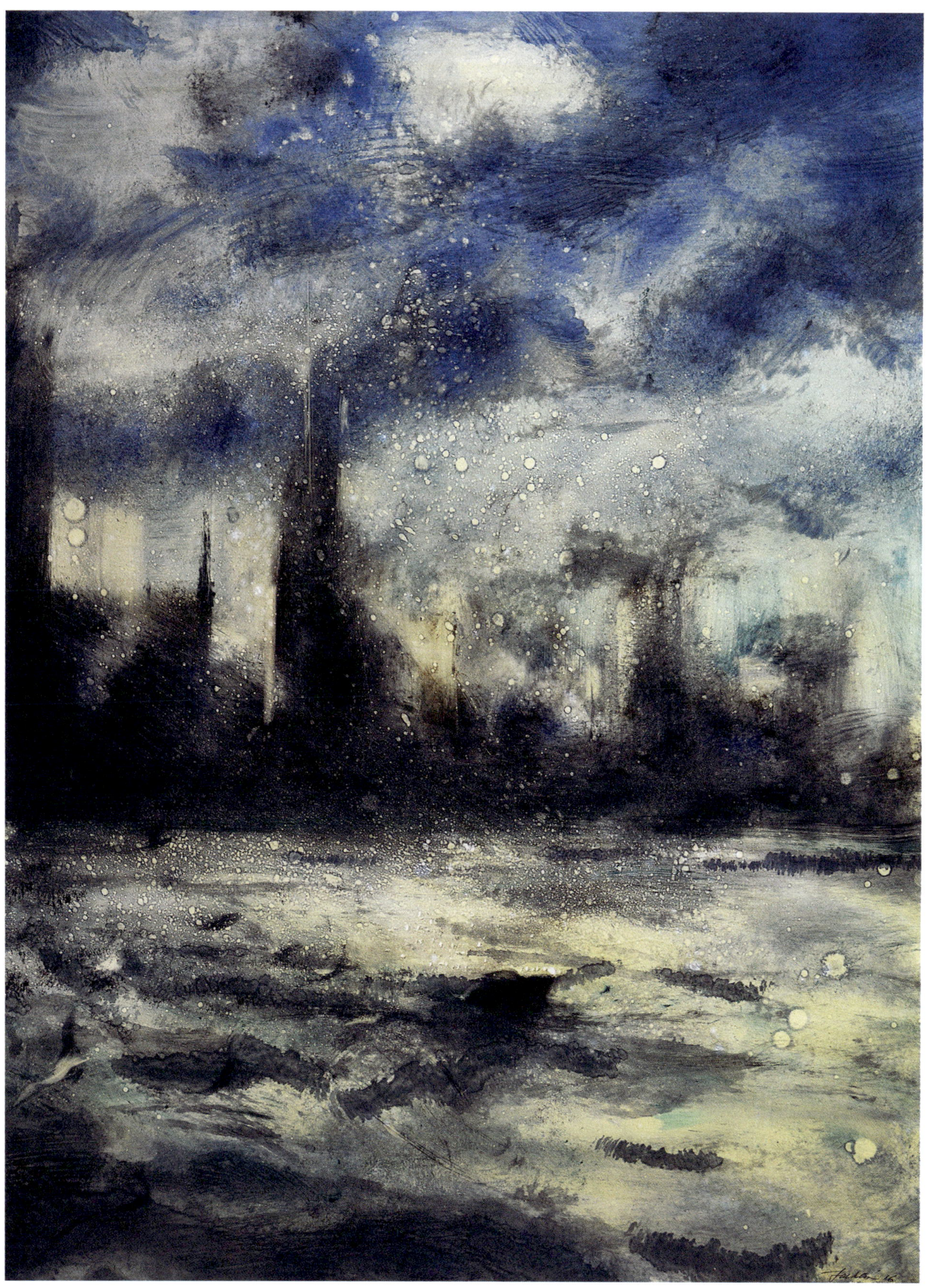

62
Harbour II, 2016
Monotype, 39½ × 29½ inches
(100.3 × 74.9 cm)

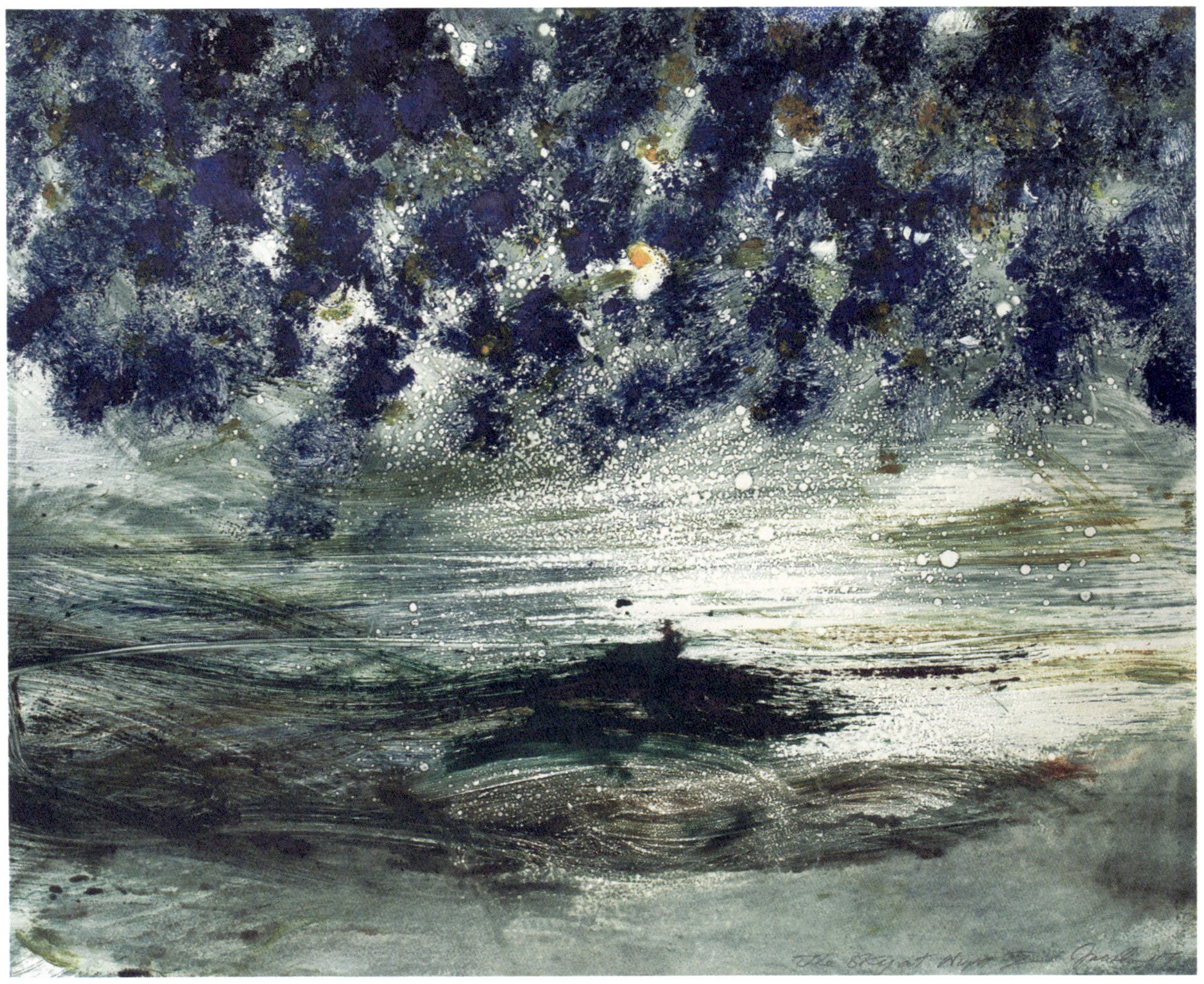

63
Stars and Sea at Night X, 2017
Monotype, 21 × 27½ inches
(53.3 × 69.9 cm)

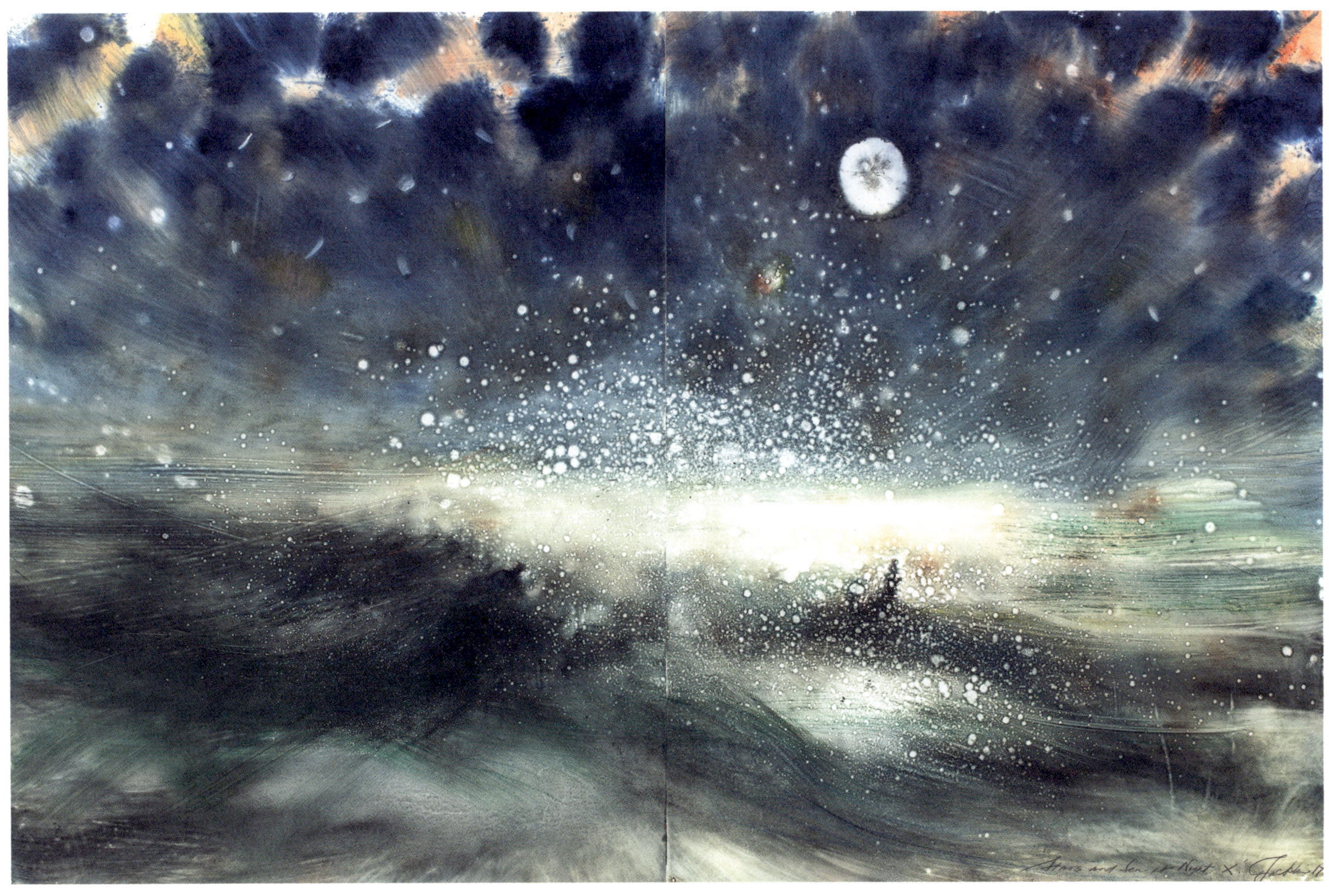

64
Stars and Sea at Night X, 2017
Monotype, diptych, each 27½ × 21 inches
(69.9 × 53.3 cm)

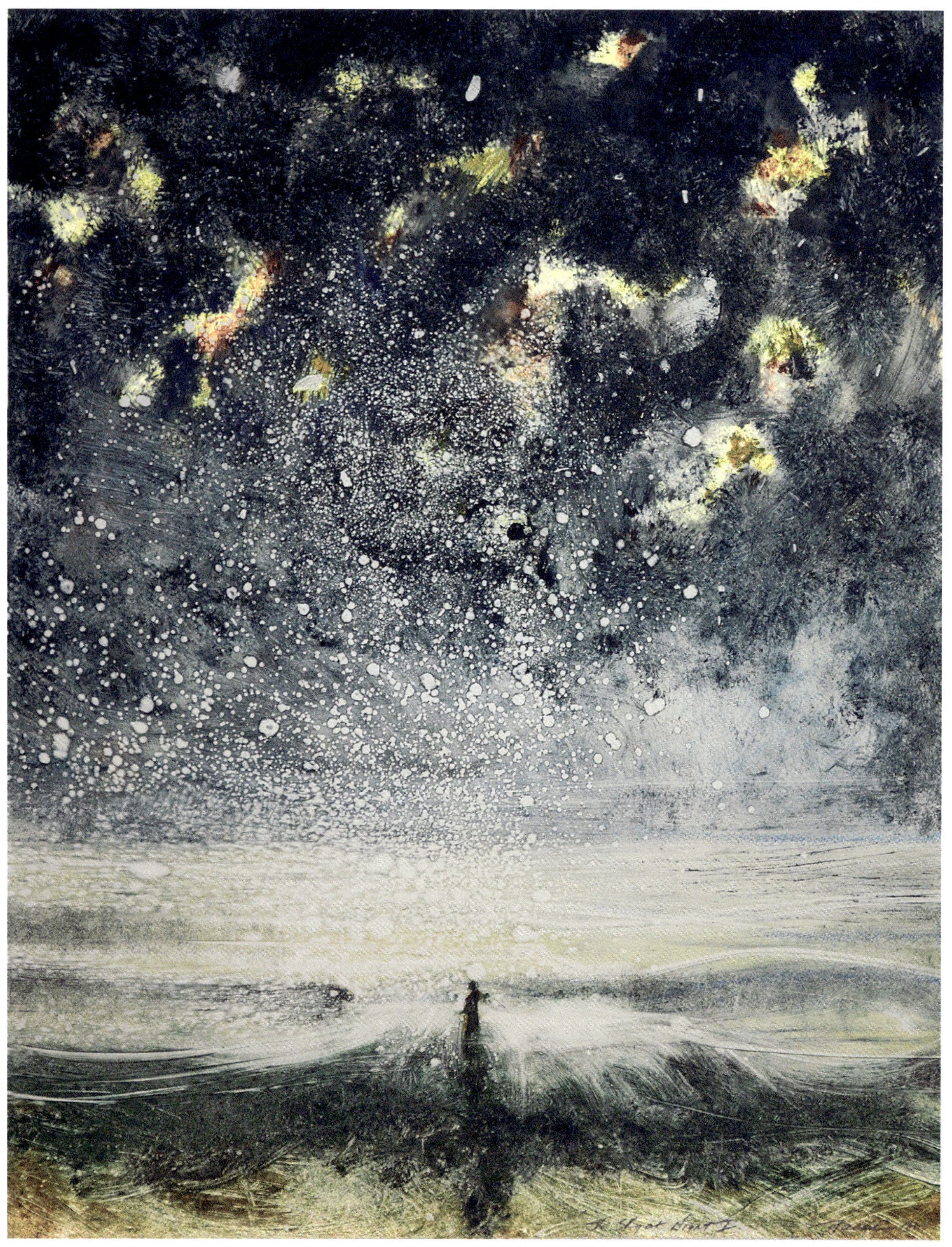

65
The Sky at Night I, 2017
Monotype, 27½ × 21 inches
(69.9 × 53.3 cm)

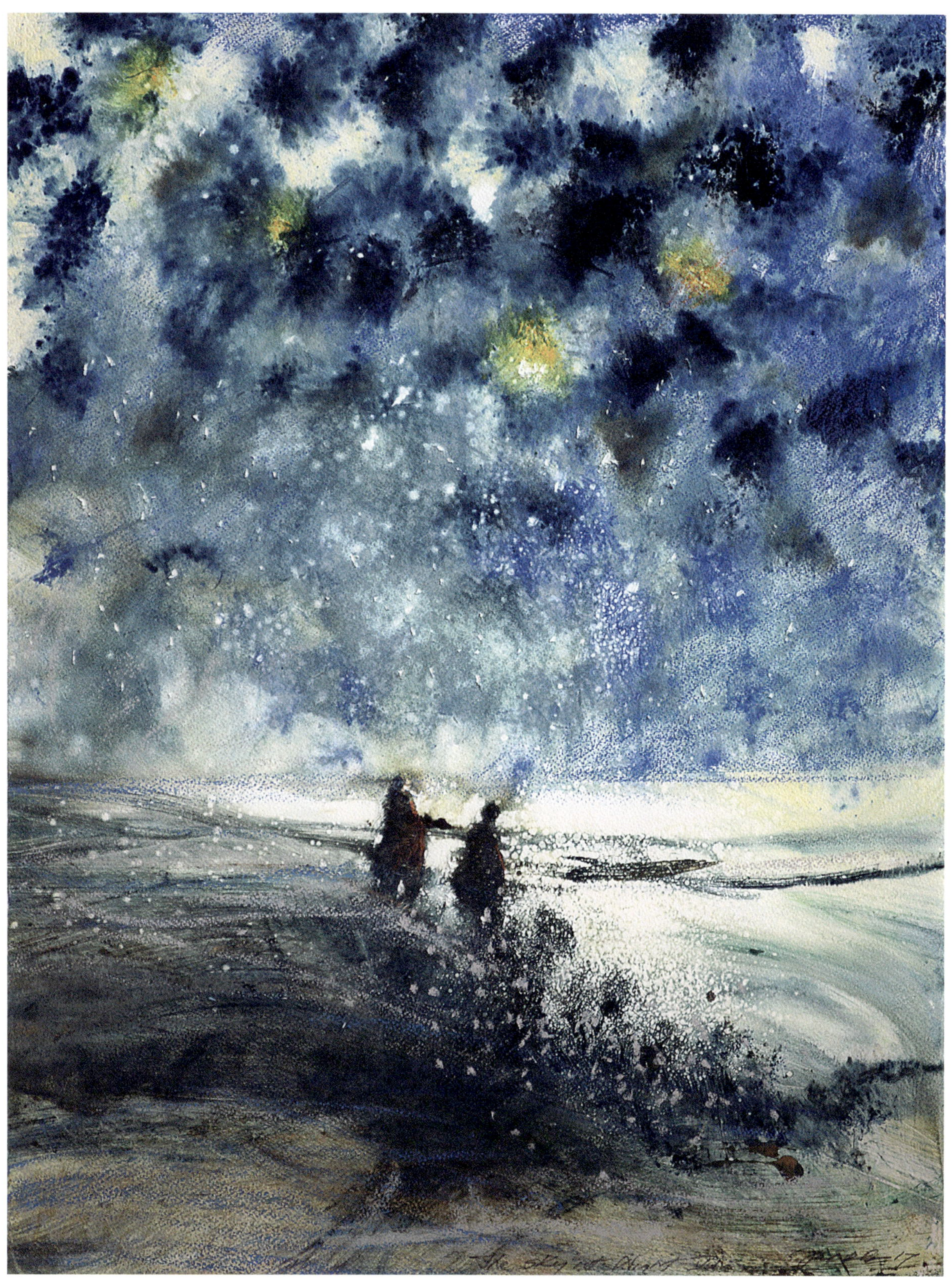

66
The Sky at Night VI, 2017
Monotype, 27½ × 21 inches
(69.9 × 53.3 cm)

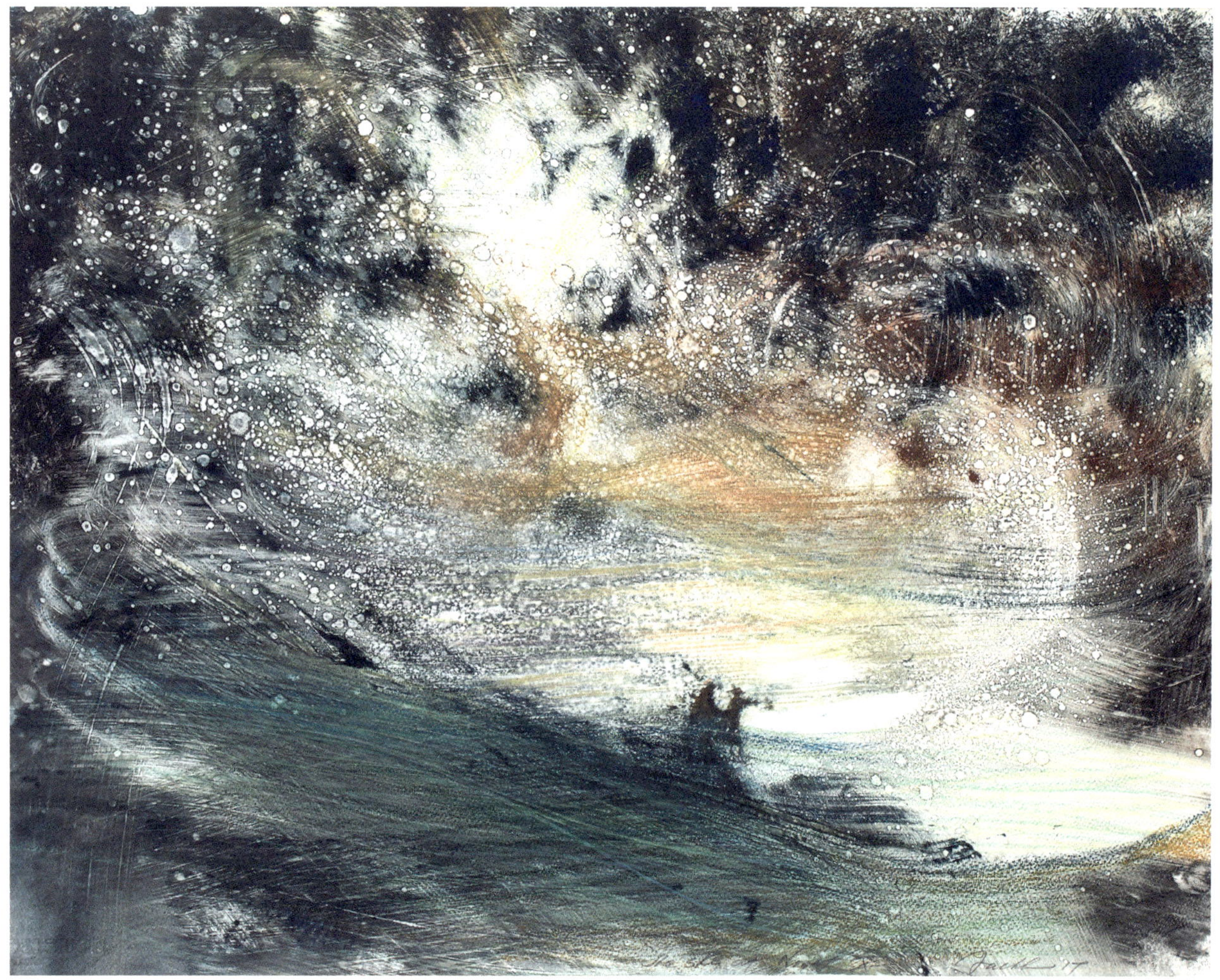

67
The Sky at Night XI, 2017
Monotype, 21½ × 27½ inches
(54.6 × 69.9 cm)

68
The Sky at Night XII, 2017
Monotype, 27½ × 21½ inches
(69.9 × 54.6 cm)

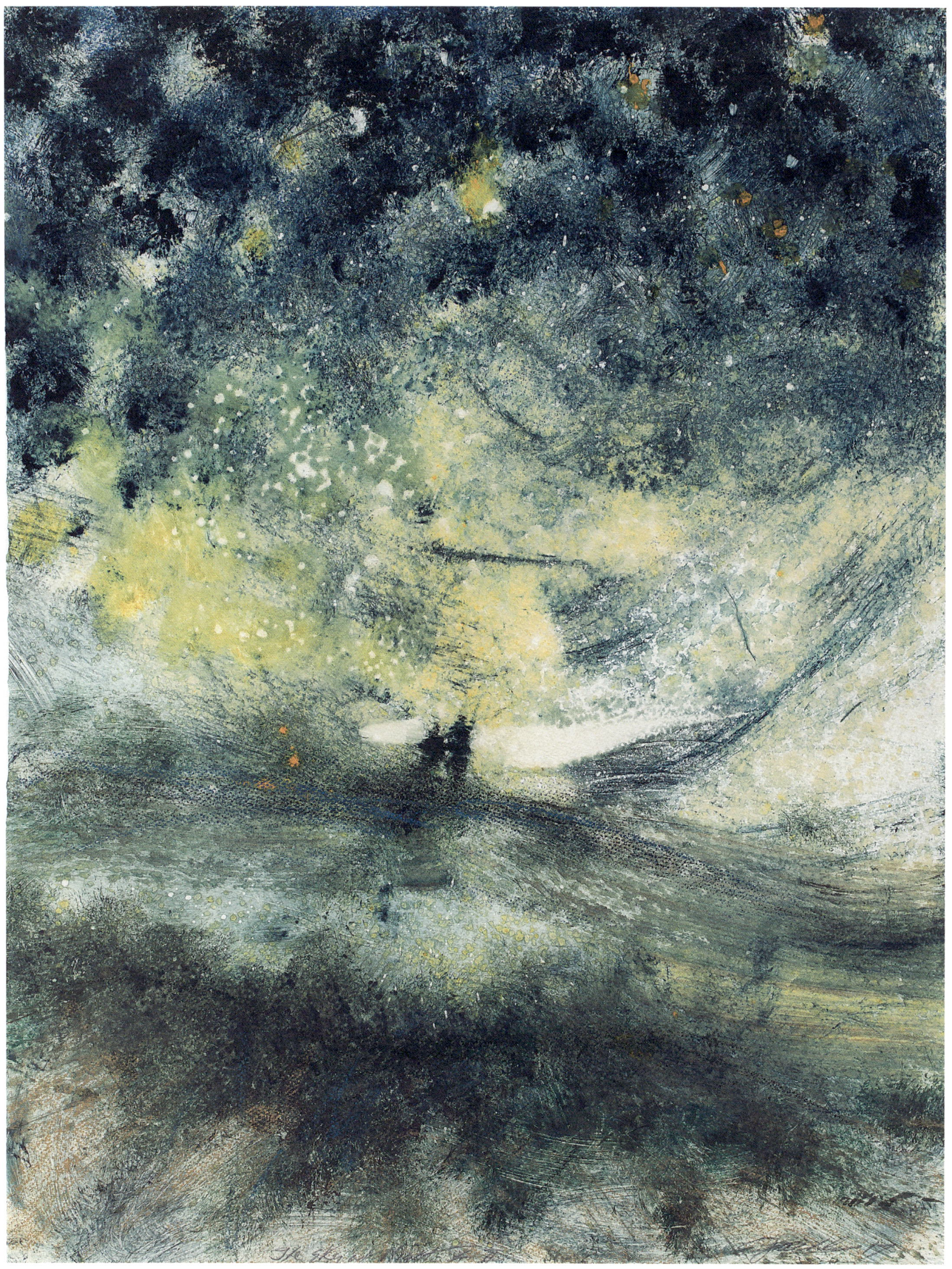

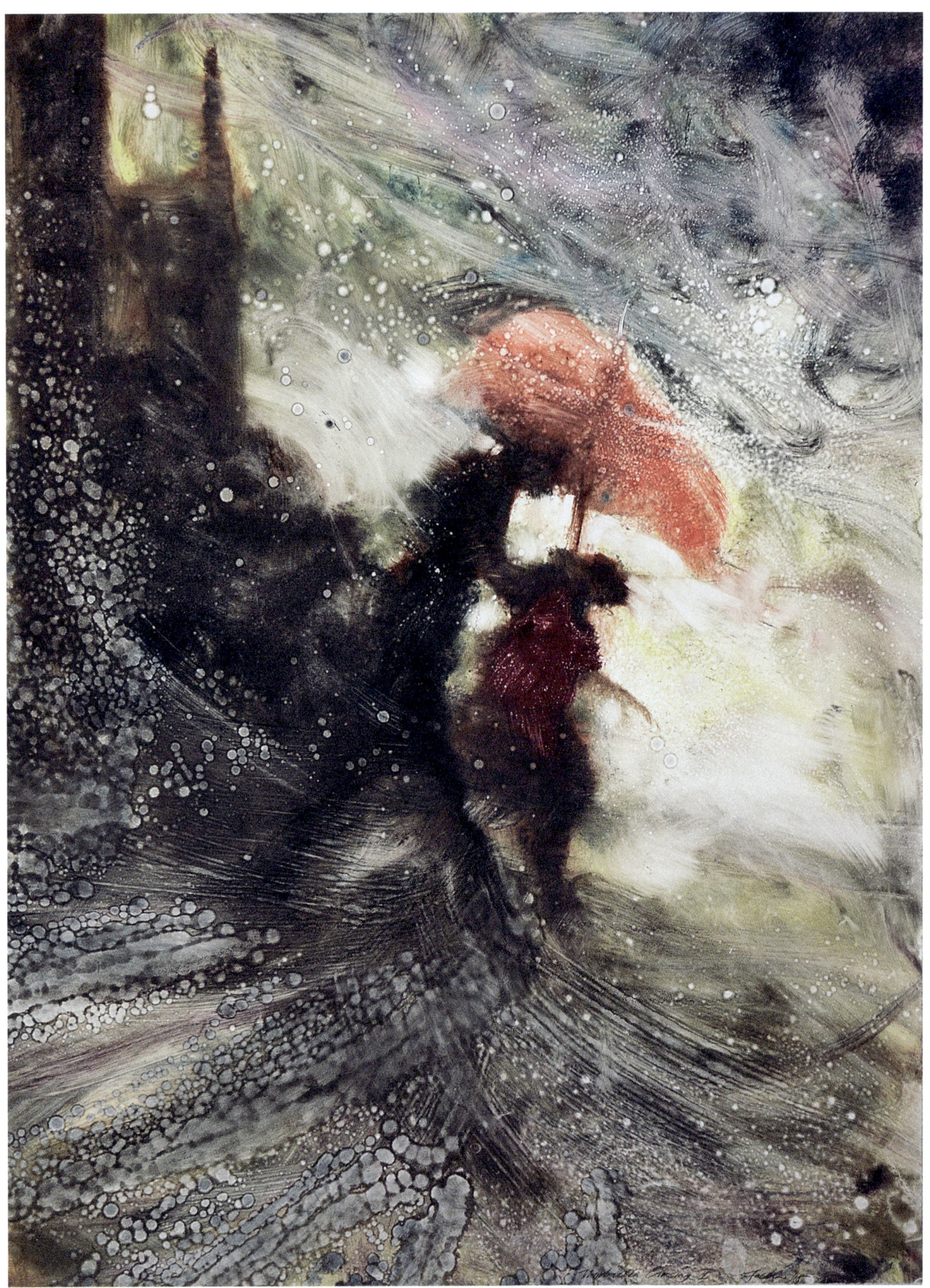

69
Umbrella Crossing I, 2018
Monotype, 39½ × 29½ inches
(100.3 × 74.9 cm)

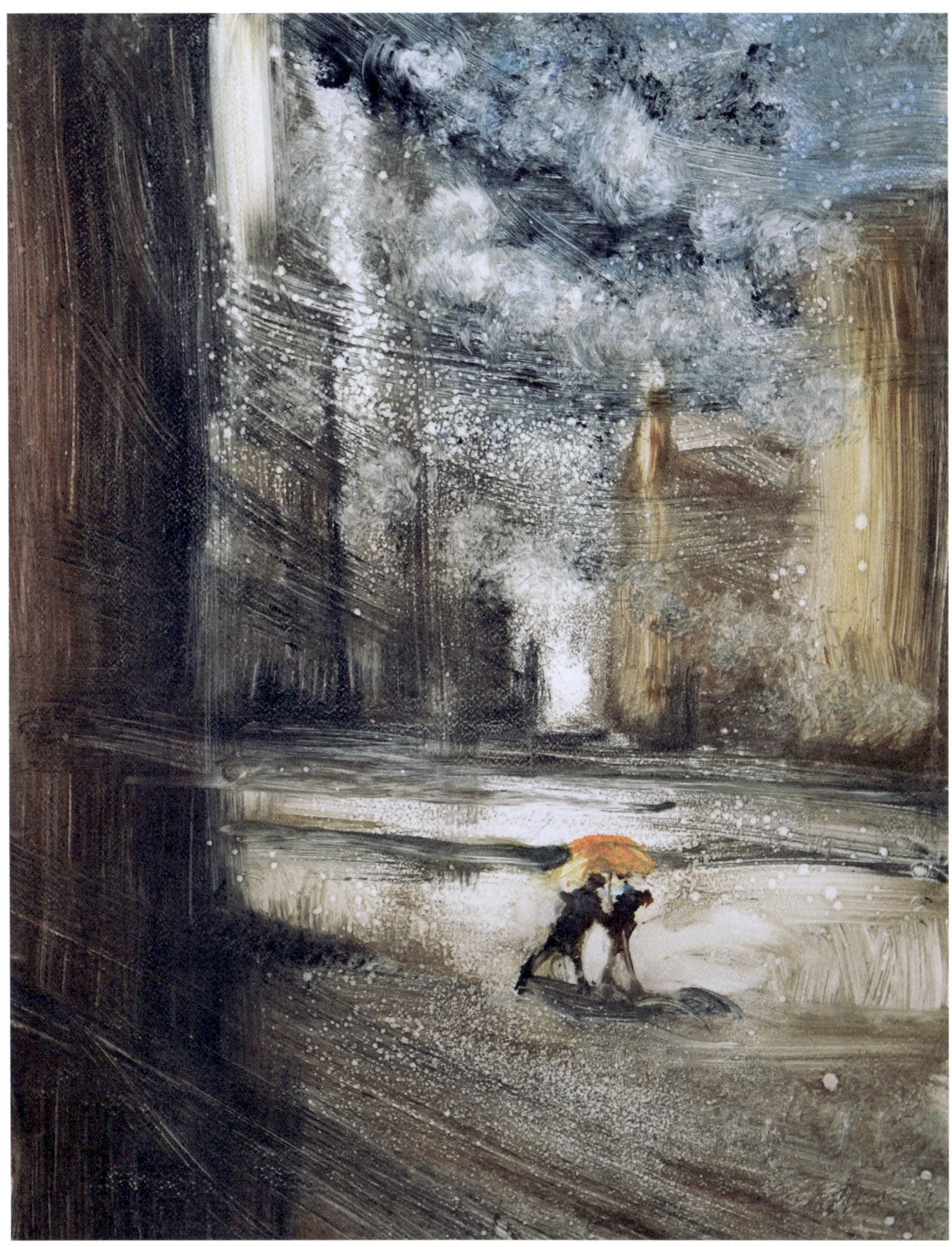

70
Yellow Umbrella II, 2023
Monotype, 27 × 21¼ inches
(68.6 × 54 cm)

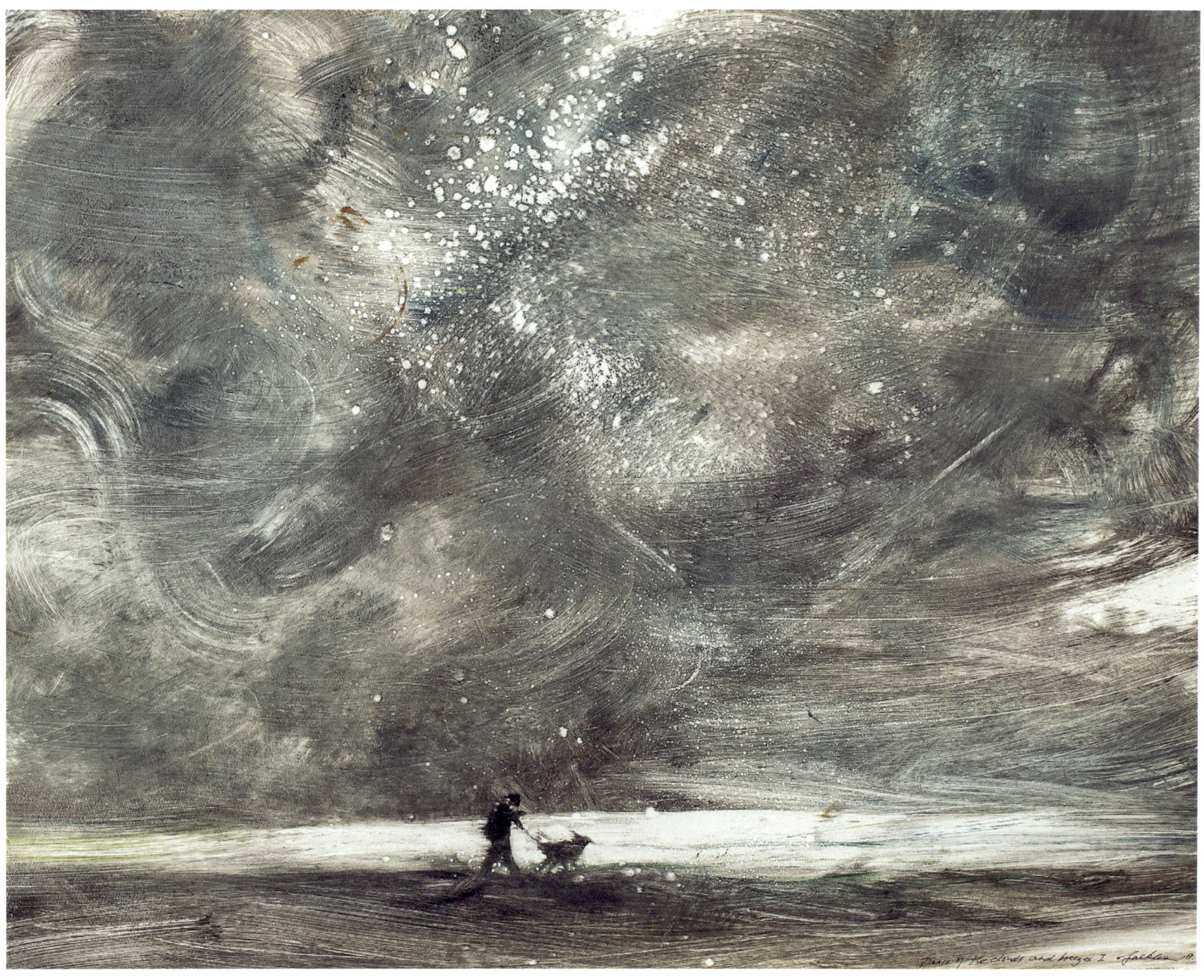

71
Dance of the Cloud and Breezes I, 2019
Monotype, 21½ × 27½ inches
(54.6 × 69.9 cm)

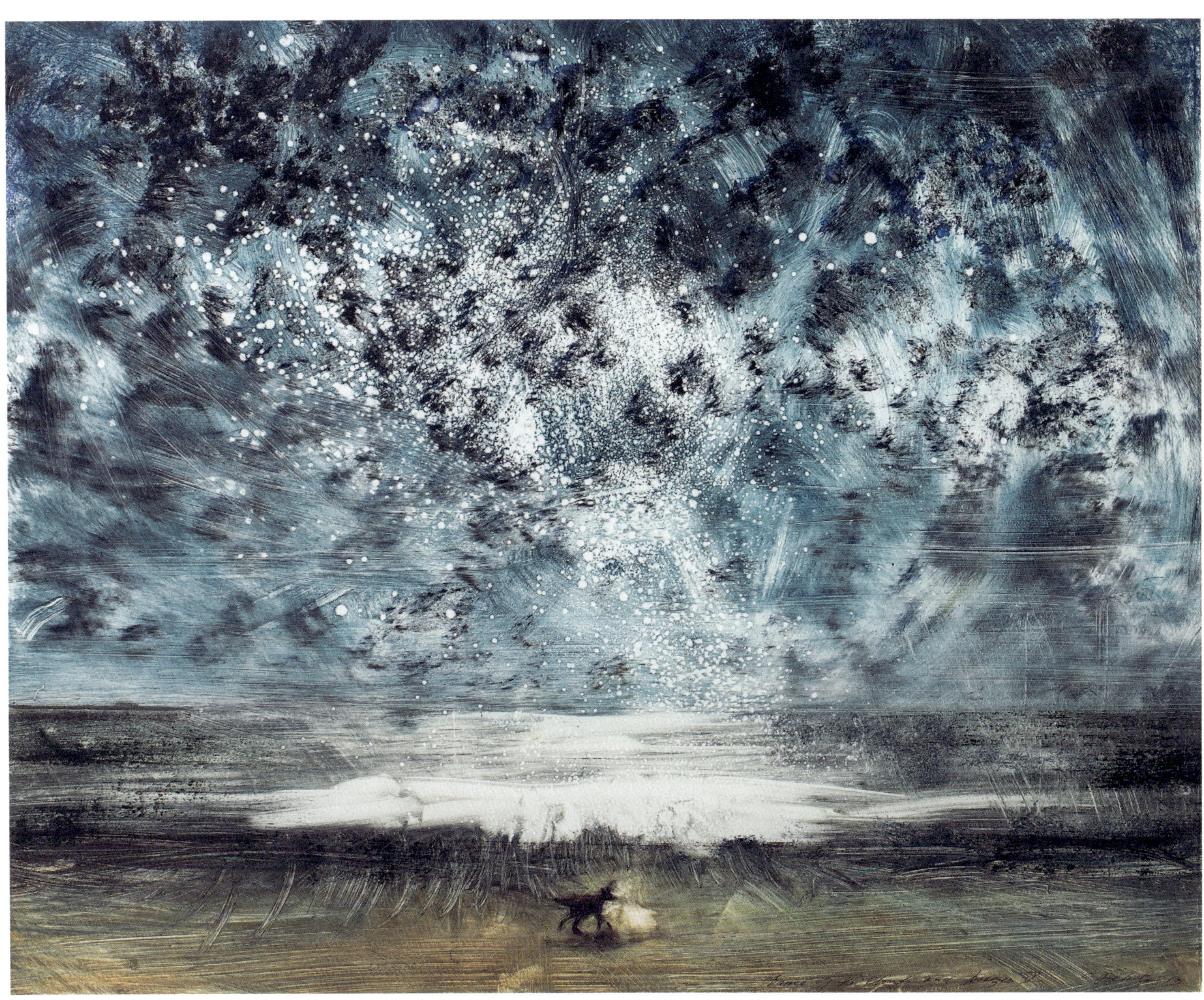

72
Dance of the Cloud and Breezes V, 2019
Monotype, 21½ × 27½ inches
(54.6 × 69.9 cm)

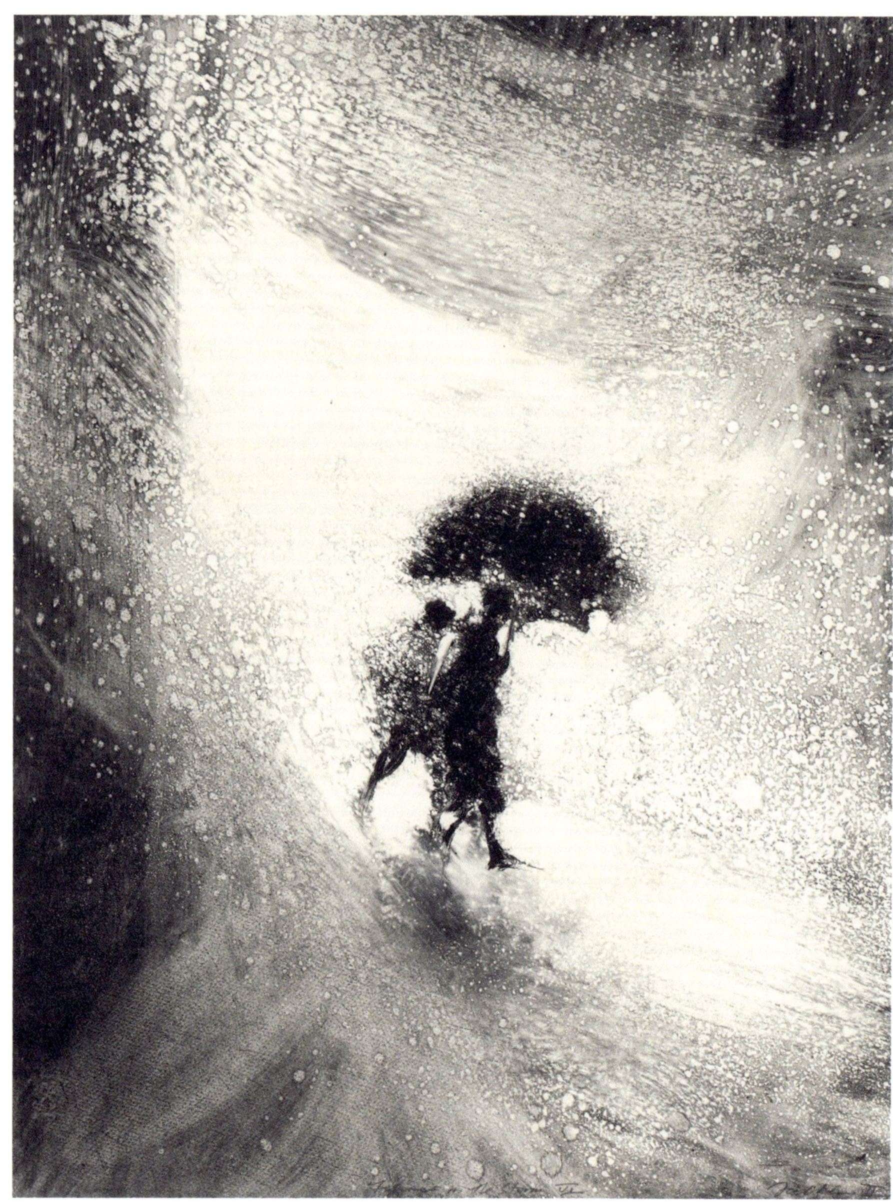

73
Figures in the Storm II, 2018
Monotype, 27 × 21 inches
(68.6 × 53.3 cm)

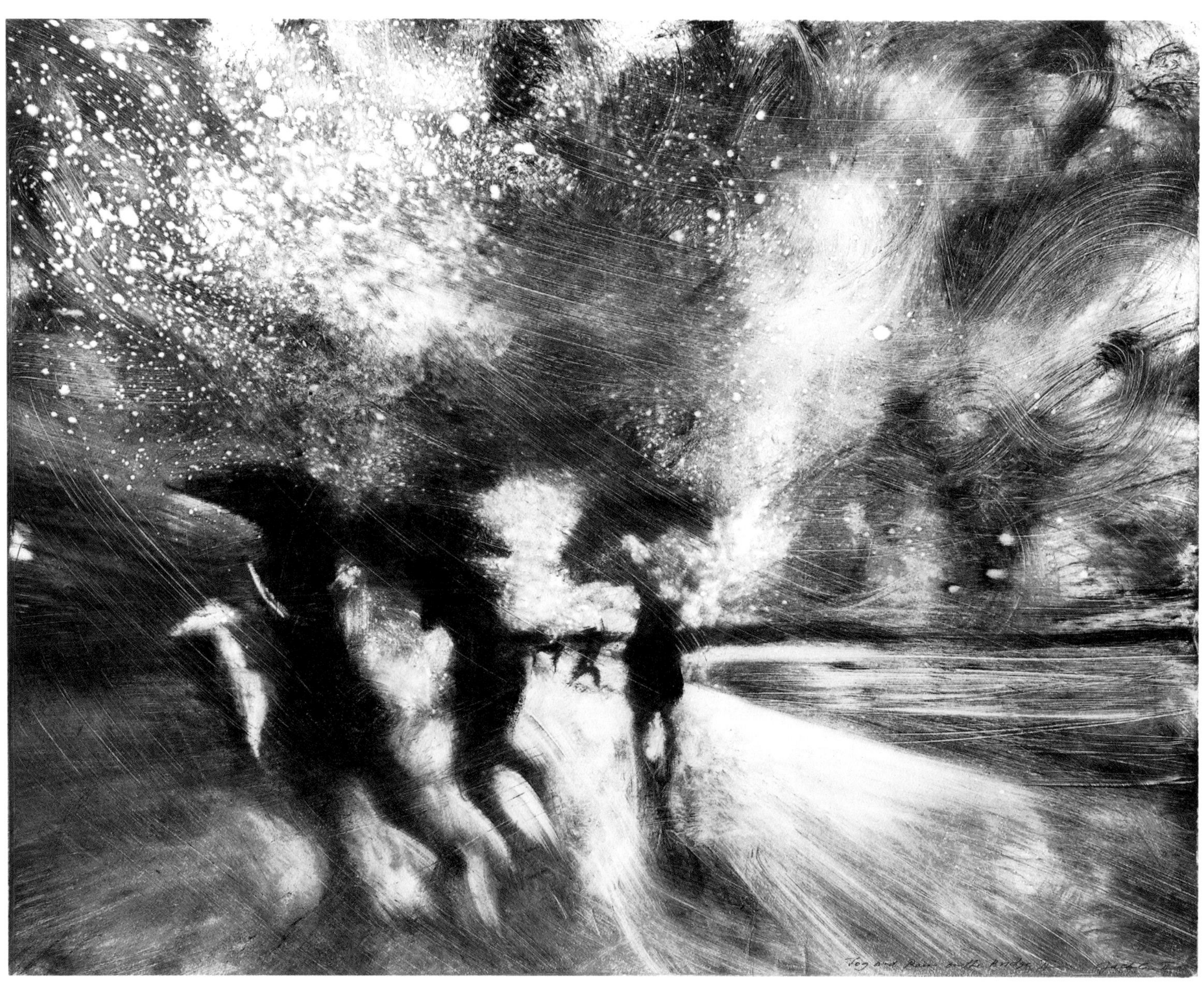

74
Fog and Rain on the Bridge II, 2019
Monotype, 21½ × 27½ inches
(54.6 × 69.9 cm)

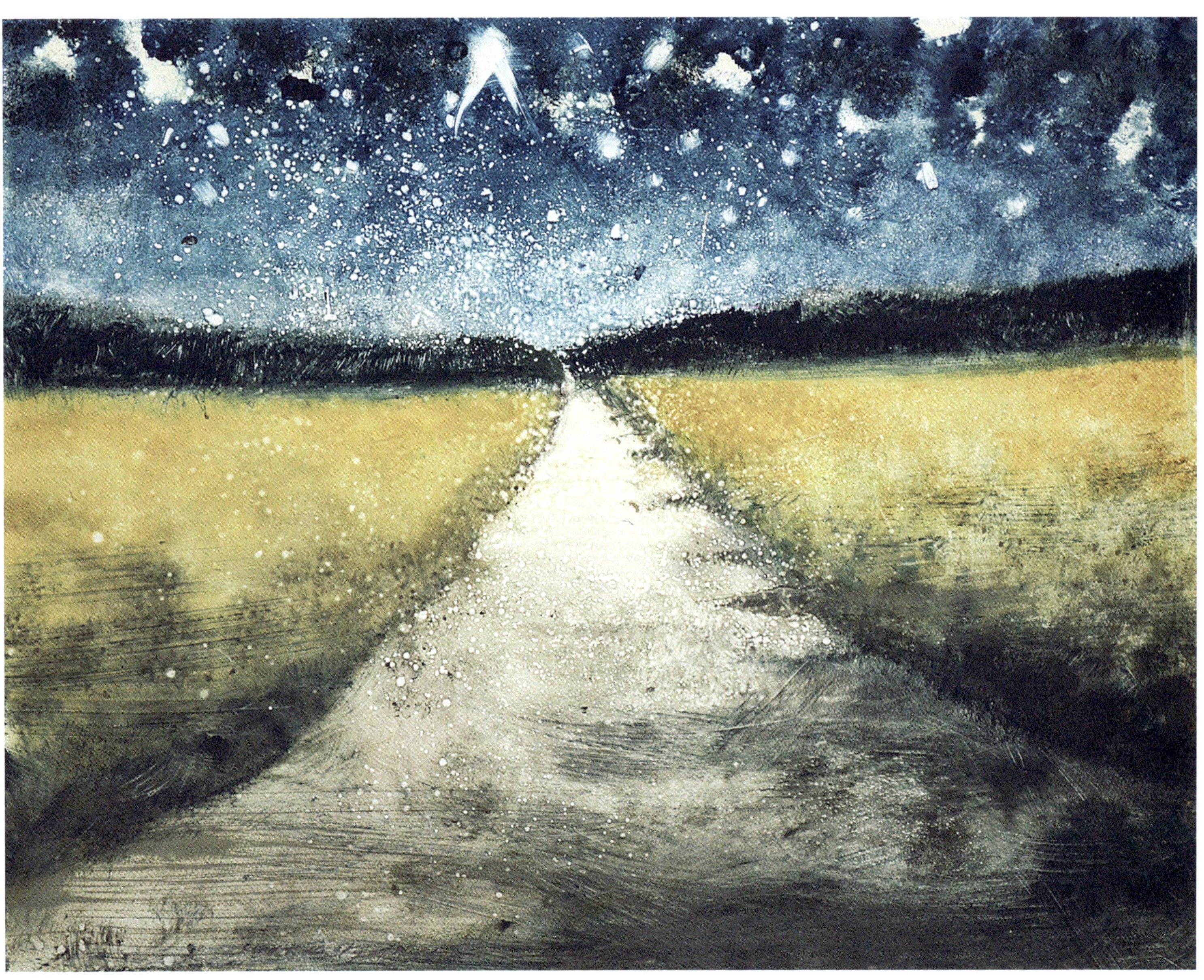

75
Road to the Sky at Night II, 2018
Monotype, 21 × 27½ inches
(53.3 × 69.9 cm)

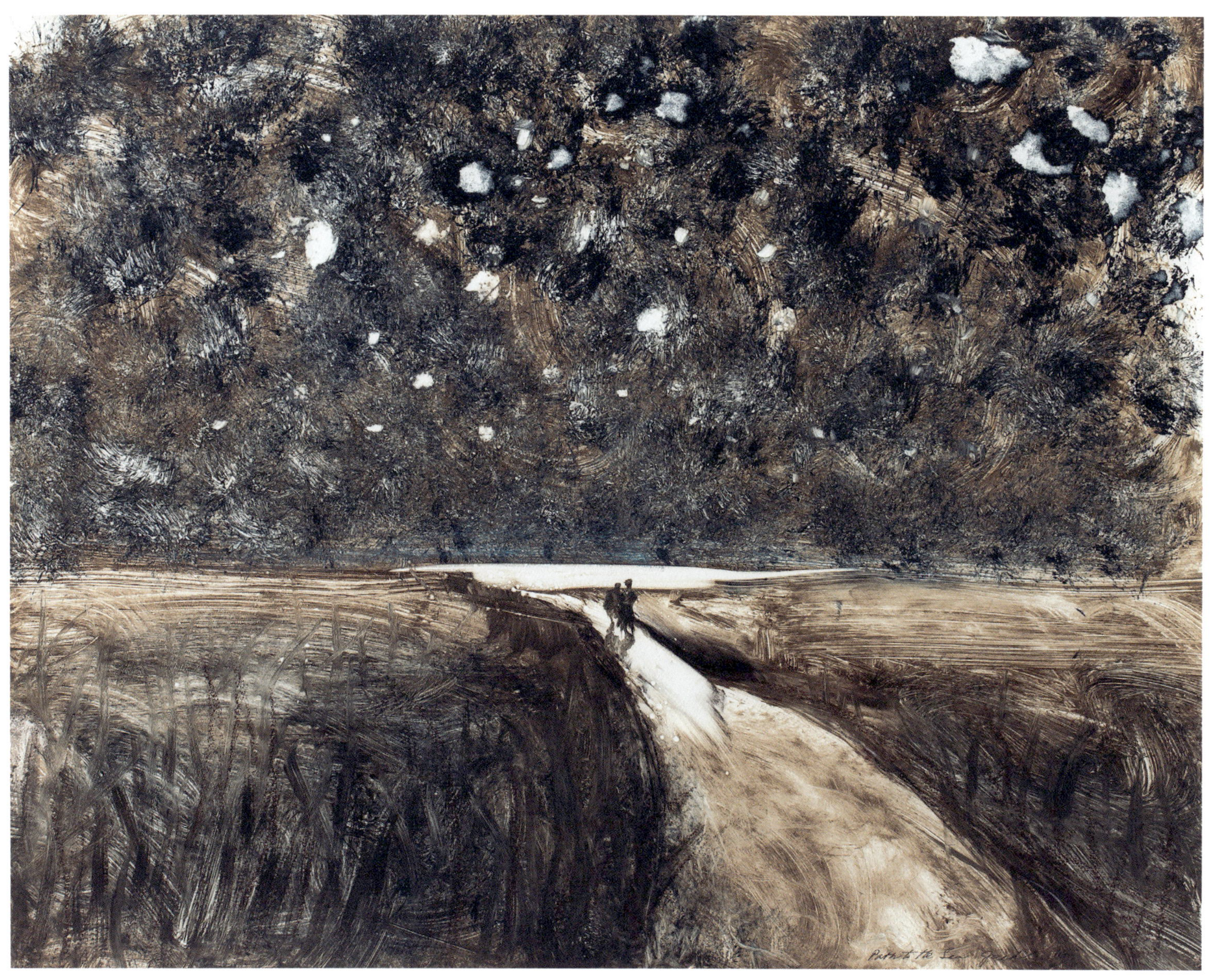

76
Path to the Sea, 2019
Monotype, 21½ × 27½ inches
(54.6 × 69.9 cm)

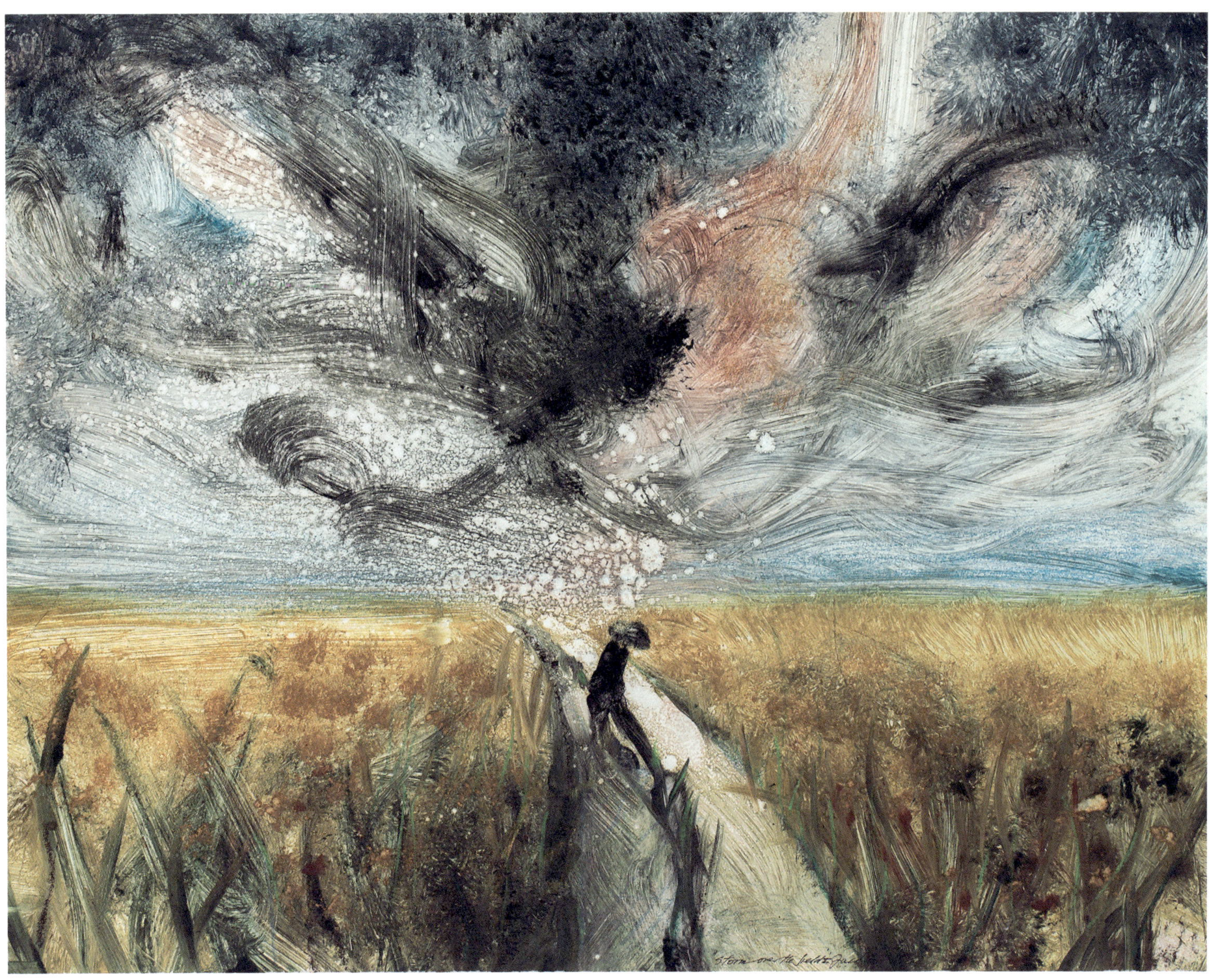

77
Storm over the Field I, 2019
Monotype, 21½ × 27½ inches
(54.6 × 69.9 cm)

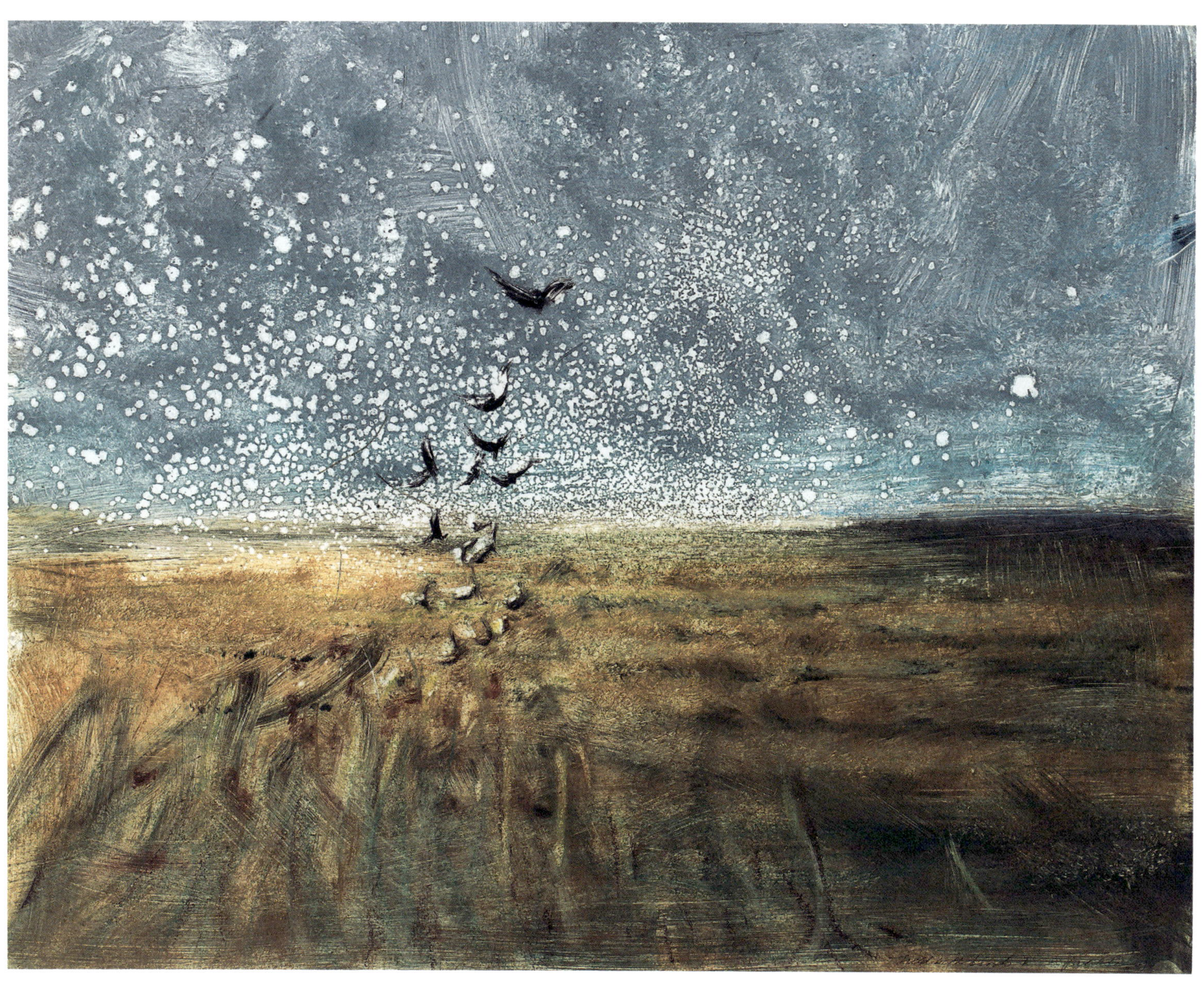

78
Field with Birds I, 2019
Monotype, 21½ × 27½ inches
(54.6 × 69.9 cm)

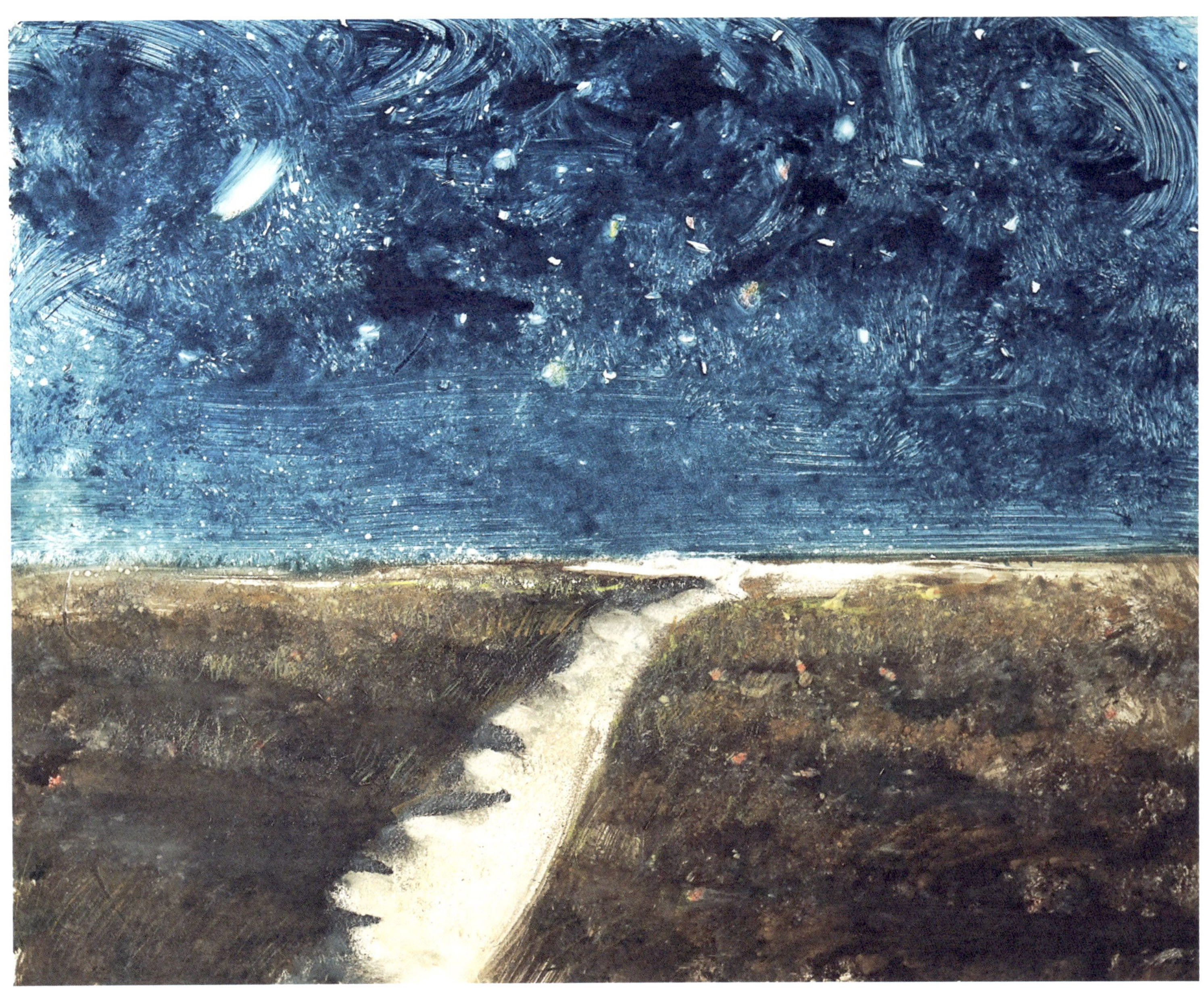

79
Path to the Sea I, 2023
Oil pastel on monotype, 21½ × 27 inches
(54.6 × 68.6 cm)

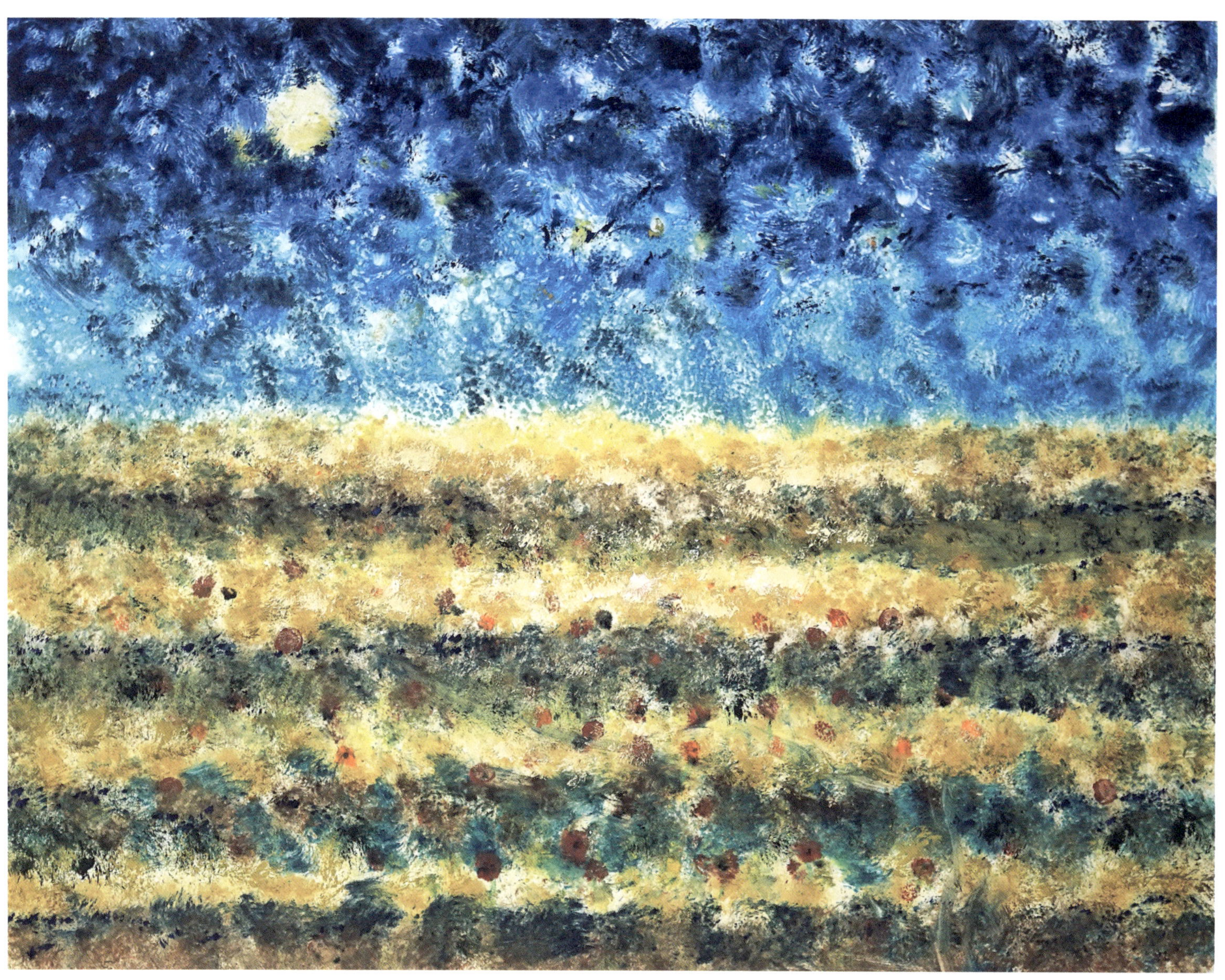

80
Golden Field I, 2023
Oil pastel on monotype, 21¼ × 27¾ inches
(54 × 70.5 cm)

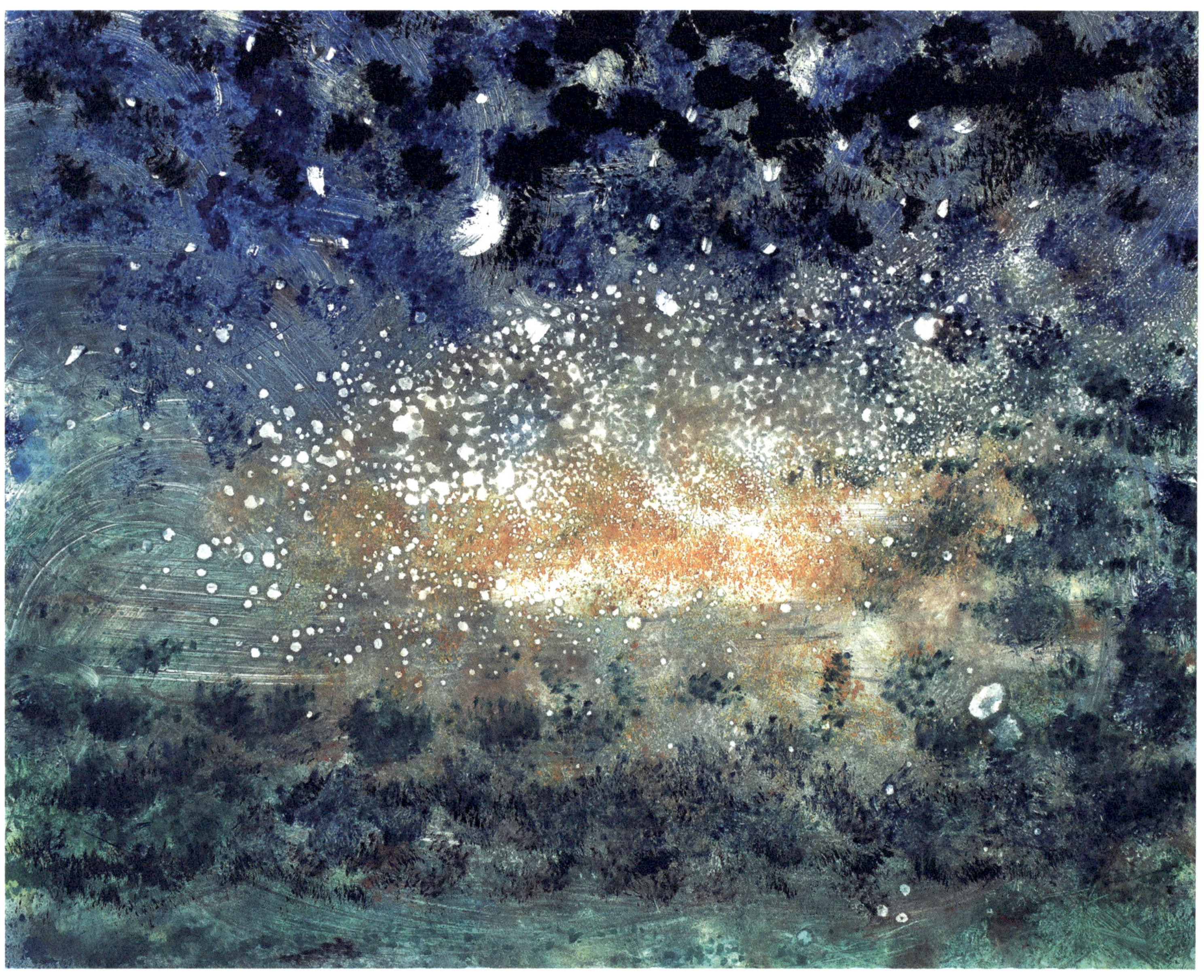

81
Into the Night, 2020
Monotype, 21½ × 27½ inches
(54.6 × 69.9 cm)

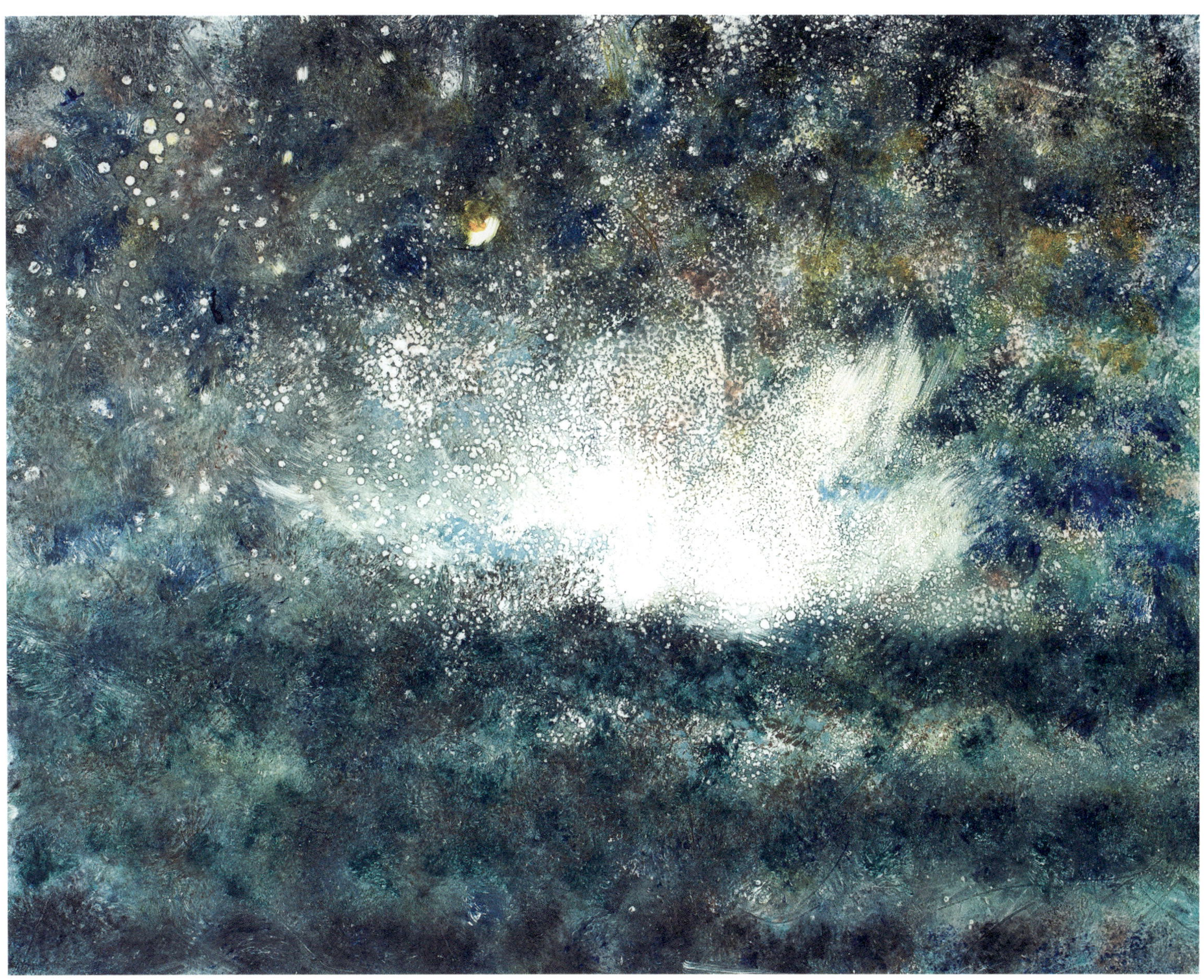

82
Into the Night II, 2020
Monotype, 21½ × 27¼ inches
(54.6 × 69.2 cm)

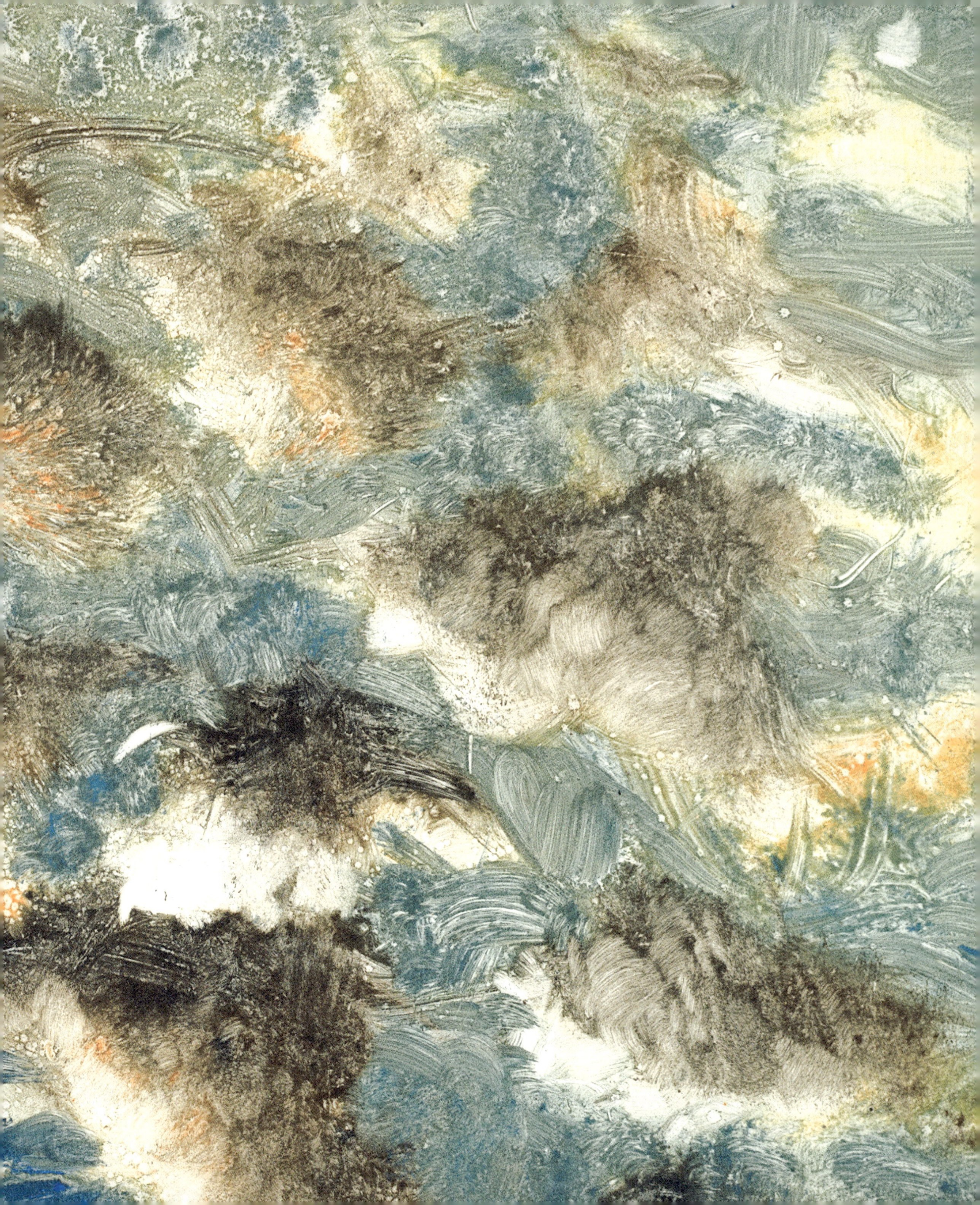

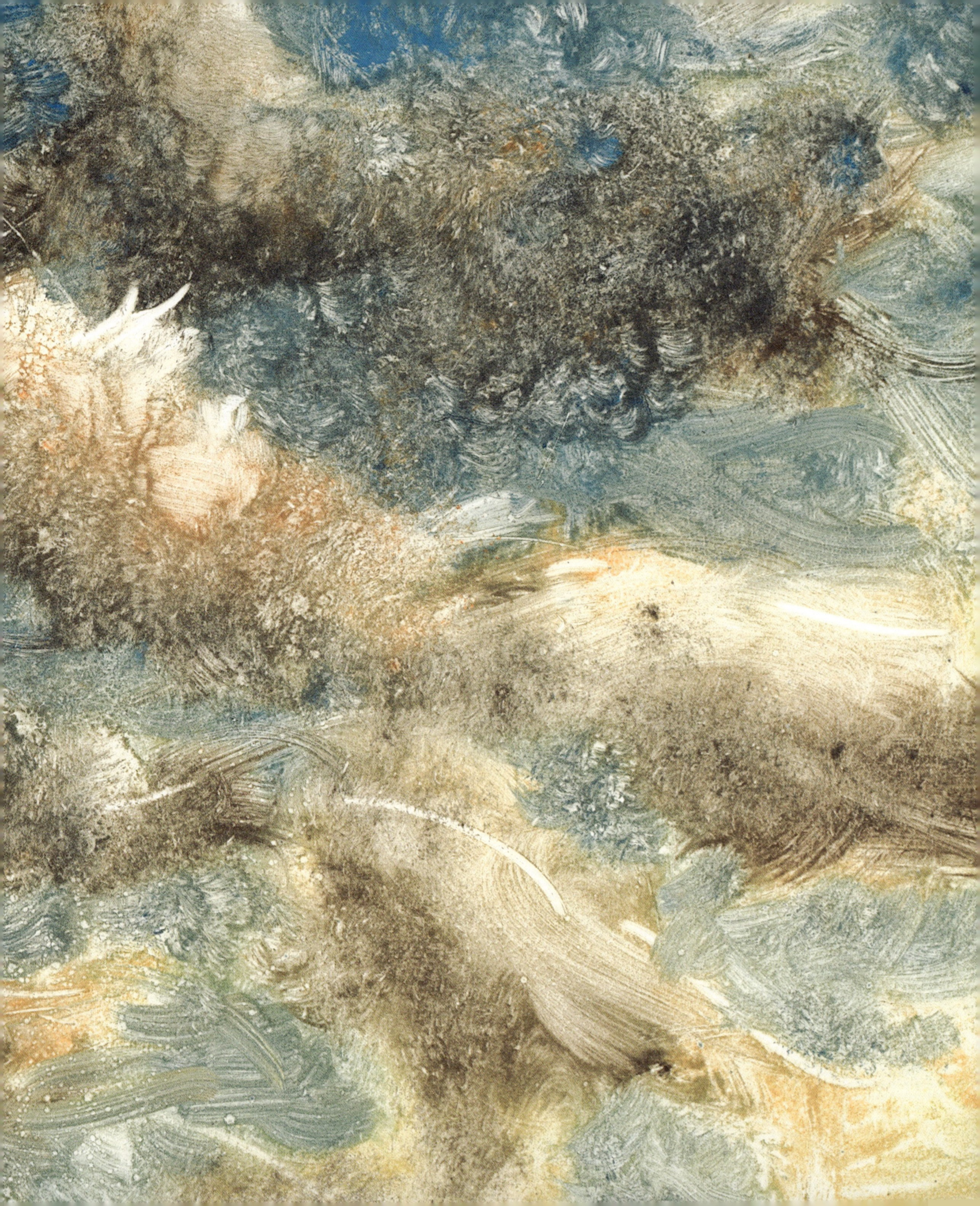

Biography

Born in Hampstead, London, in 1943, Bill Jacklin studied graphics at Walthamstow School of Art, London (1960–61) before working as a graphic designer at Studio Seven in Holborn (1961–62). In 1962 he returned to Walthamstow to study painting and subsequently went on to the Royal College of Art from 1964 to 1967. Between 1967 and 1975, Jacklin taught at Chelsea School of Art, Hornsey College of Arts and Crafts, the Royal College of Art and at schools in Kent and Surrey. Initially abstract, his work moved towards figuration in the mid-1970s, when it became preoccupied with the effects of light and movement.

Jacklin was awarded an Arts Council bursary in 1975, a few years after his first two solo exhibitions at the Upper Gallery and at Nigel Greenwood in London. His work continued to be exhibited in one-man shows throughout the 1970s in London and later in the 1980s with Marlborough Fine Art, London, and Marlborough Gallery, New York. He also participated in numerous group exhibitions internationally from the early 1970s.

Moving to New York in 1985, Bill Jacklin has concentrated on painting portraits of the city in all its guises, from large-scale compositions of crowds in flux to intimate moments in Seurat-like etchings. Jacklin has undertaken many commissions, notably from the Bank of England, the Ivy Restaurant, De Beers and the Metropolitan Washington Airports Authority for the North Terminal of Washington National Airport.

He was elected a Royal Academician in 1991 and in 1993 was Official Artist-in-Residence for the British Council in Hong Kong. He was elected a Fellow of the Royal Society of Painters and Printmakers in 2004. Jacklin presently lives and works in Bristol, Rhode Island.

Solo Exhibitions

1970 Royal College of Art, Upper Gallery, London
Nigel Greenwood, London
1971 Nigel Greenwood, London
1973 Hester van Royen Gallery, London
1975 Nigel Greenwood, London
1977 Hester van Royen Gallery, London
1980 Marlborough Fine Art, London
1983 Marlborough Fine Art, London
1985 Marlborough Gallery, New York
1987 Marlborough Gallery, New York
1988 Marlborough Fine Art, London
1990 Marlborough Gallery, New York
1992 Marlborough Fine Art, London
'Urban Portraits, New York 1986–1992', Museum of Modern Art, Oxford; travelled to Consorcio da Cidade de Santiago – Museo do Pobo Galego, Santiago de Compostela (until 1993)
1994 University of Northumbria at Newcastle, Newcastle upon Tyne
London Print Workshop, London
Marlborough Graphics, London
1995 'Urban Portraits: Hong Kong 1993–95', Hong Kong Arts Centre, Hong Kong
'New Monotypes and Etchings', Marlborough Graphics, London
1997 'New Monotypes and Etchings', Skovridder Gallery, Oslo
'New York City: The Collective Image 1996–97', Marlborough Gallery, New York
'New York City: The Collective Image 1996–97', Marlborough Fine Art and Graphics, London
1998 'New York City: The Connected Image 1997–99', Marlborough Gallery, New York
2000 'Bill Jacklin. Silhouettes and Shadows: New York City', Marlborough Fine Art, London
2002 'Central Park, New York City: Recent Paintings and Monoprints', Marlborough Gallery, New York
2003 'Bill Jacklin: Recent Monotypes', Marlborough Gallery, New York
2004 'Bill Jacklin: Recent Monotypes', Galería Marlborough, Madrid
'Bill Jacklin: A Venetian Affair: Painting and Monotypes', Marlborough Fine Art, London
2005 'Bill Jacklin: New York Skaters: Paintings and Monotypes', Marlborough Fine Art, London
2007 'Bill Jacklin: People and Places', Marlborough Gallery, New York
'Bill Jacklin: People and Places, New Monotypes', Marlborough Graphics, London

2008 'Bill Jacklin: Paintings, Prints and Monotypes', University Gallery, Newcastle

2008–09 'Bill Jacklin: People and Places II: Paintings and Prints', Marlborough Fine Art, London, and Marlborough Monaco, April–June

2009 'Bill Jacklin: People and Places II', Marlborough Fine Art, London

2011 'Bill Jacklin RA, The Lightness of Being', Brook Gallery, Devon

2012 'Bill Jacklin, New Monotypes', Bohun Gallery, Henley-on-Thames
'Bill Jacklin, Recent Work, New York', Marlborough Gallery, New York

2013 'Bill Jacklin, Paintings, Pastels and Prints', Marlborough Fine Art, London

2014 'Bill Jacklin, New York Paintings', Marlborough Gallery, New York

2016 'Bill Jacklin, Paintings and Monotypes', Marlborough Fine Art, London
'Bill Jacklin, RA, A Graphic Artist 1961–2016', Royal Academy of Arts, London

2017 'Bill Jacklin 1986 to 2017 Paintings', Marlborough Gallery, New York

2018 'Bill Jacklin Monotypes', Marlborough Gallery, New York

2019 'Bill Jacklin Paintings and Monotypes', Marlborough Fine Art, London

2022 'Illustrations from *Cressida's Dream*', Ordovas Gallery, London

2023 'Bill Jacklin: Towards the Light', Marlborough Fine Art, London

Group Exhibitions

1967 'Young Contemporaries', London

1970 'John Moore's Exhibition 7', Liverpool
'Contemporary Drawings', The Museum of Modern Art, New York

1971 'Recent Acquisitions', Victoria and Albert Museum, London
'Recent Acquisitions', Tate Gallery, London
'Contemporary Art Society – Recent Acquisitions', R.C.A. Galleries, London

1972 'Contemporary Drawings', The Museum of Modern Art, New York
'Third International Print Biennial', Bradford
'Tokyo Print Biennial', Museum of Modern Art, Tokyo
'Drawings', Museum of Modern Art, Oxford

1973 'English Painting Today', Musée d'Art Moderne, Paris

1974 'Xe Biennale Internationale d'Art', British Council Exhibition, Menton

1975 'Contemporary British Drawings', British Council Exhibition, São Paulo; travelled throughout South America

1977 'Artists at Curwen', Tate Gallery, London
'British Painting 1952–1977', Royal Academy of Arts, London
'Works on Paper – Gifts to Public Galleries 1972–1977', Contemporary Art Society, Diploma Galleries, Royal Academy of Arts, London
'Arts Council: Recent Acquisitions', Hayward Gallery, London
'10 Years of Graphics', Ibis Gallery, Leamington Spa

1978 'Contemporary Mezzotints', Williams College Museum of Art, Williamstown, Massachusetts

1979 'Contemporary Art', De Beers, London
'British International Print Biennial', Bradford

1981 '16 Artists: The Who Album', Tate Gallery, London

1982 'Thirty-five Artists, Printmaking', Royal College of Art, London; travelling exhibition

1983 'Britain Salutes New York', Marlborough Gallery, New York

1985 'Printmakers at the Royal College of Art', Barbican Art Gallery, London

1986 'Collector's Show', Arkansas Art Center, Little Rock, Arkansas
'The Fondation Veranneman Invites Marlborough', Fondation Veranneman, Kruishoutem

1987 'Urban Visions: The Contemporary Artist and New York', Adelphi University, New York
'Director's Choice', Tampa Museum of Art, Florida
'Artists' Choice', Royal College of Art, Print Department, London

1988 '150th Anniversary Painting Exhibition', Royal College of Art, London
'Birthright – The Mother and Child Exhibition', Alex Reid and Lefevre, London
'L'Europe des grands maîtres: quand ils étaient jeunes', Musée Jacquemart-André, Paris

1989 'The Figure', Arkansas Arts Center, Little Rock, Arkansas

1991 'New Acquisitions: British Drawings', The Metropolitan Museum of Art, New York

1992 'Urban Realities: Contemporary Portraits of New York', Walsh Gallery, Regina A. Quick Center, Fairfield University, Fairfield, Connecticut
'Britain and the São Paulo Biennial 1951–1991', British Council, London
'Group Show', Thomas Gibson Fine Art, London

1993 'Monotypes', Skara Gallery, Norway
'Collector's Exhibition', Arkansas Art Center, Little Rock, Arkansas

1996 'New Acquisitions', The Metropolitan Museum of Art, New York

1997 'CityScapes: A Survey of Urban Landscape', Marlborough Gallery, New York

1998 'L'Ecole de Londres – de Bacon à Bevan', La Fondation Dina Vierny – Musée Maillol, Paris, Auditorio de Galicia, Santiago de Compostela, and Kunsthaus, Vienna
'The Colours Black', Universalmuseum Joanneum, Graz

2000 'Elogio de lo Visible, 27 artistas en torno a la figuración', Galería Marlborough, Madrid, Centro Cultural 'Las Claras', Murcia, Centro Cultural 'Casa del Cordón', Burgos, and Centro de la Cultura del Rioja, Logroño

2000 'Paintings/Peintures', Marlborough Gallery, New York, and Marlborough, Monte Carlo (inaugural exhibition)

2001 'Art Transplant: British Artists in New York', British Consul-General's Residence, New York

2003 'La Fête', Le Bellevue, Biarritz, and Museo Valenciano de la Ilustración y la Modernidad, Valencia

2003–04 'Picasso to Warhol, Master Prints 1964–2003', Zamek Ujazdowski, Warsaw, and National Museum, Warsaw

2004 'New York, New York', Galería Marlborough, Madrid, September–October, and CajaGranada Fundación, Puerta Real, November–December

2008–09 'The Curwen Studio 50th Anniversary 1958–2008', Goodison Room, Tate Britain, London

2015 'Metropolis, Paintings of Contemporary Urban Landscape', Edward Tyler Nahem, New York

2016–19 Summer Exhibition, Royal Academy of Arts, London

2017 'Be Magnificent, Walthamstow School of Art 1957 to 1967', William Morris Gallery, London

2018–19 'Monotypes', Mezzanine Gallery, The Metropolitan Museum of Art, New York

2022–23 Summer Exhibition, Royal Academy of Arts, London

Selected Commissions

1988 *Futures Market*, commissioned by the Bank of England, London
The Ivy, commissioned by the Ivy Restaurant, London

1993 *The Park*, tapestry, commissioned by De Beers, London, completed 1995

1994 *The Rink*, commissioned by the Metropolitan Washington Airports Authority as part of the Architectural Enhancement Program at the new North Terminal for Washington National Airport; César Pelli and Associates, Design Architect; Leo A. Daly Company, Architect of Record

1995 *Bar Centrale*, commissioned by Orsino Restaurant, London

2000 *After the Event I*, commissioned by the Print Club of New York

2003 *Target Benchmarks Central Park*, commissioned by the Central Park Conservancy for a benefit auction

Selected Bibliography

1971 John Russell, 'One Man's Marks', *The Sunday Times*, 19 December

1972 Richard Cork, review in *Evening Standard*, 6 January
Penelope Marcus, *The Tate Gallery Report 1970–72*, London, p. 128

1973 Edward Lucie-Smith, *English Painting Today*, exh. cat., Musée d'Art Moderne, Paris

1974 M. Sandiford, 'Introduction', in *Six Jeunes Artistes Anglais*, exh. cat., Xe Biennale Internationale d'Art, Menton, pp. 359–63

1975 Norbert Lynton, *Contemporary British Drawings*, exh. cat., British Council, London

1980 Edward Lucie-Smith, *Art International*, vol. XXXIII, no. 10, March–April

1983 John Russell Taylor, 'Transcending All the Easy Formulas', *The Times*, 8 November

1985 John Russell, *The New York Times*, 5 April
John Russell Taylor, essay in *Bill Jacklin: Recent Work: New York Paintings, Pastels and Drawings*, exh. cat., Marlborough Gallery, New York
Carter Ratcliff, 'An Introspective View' The Philips Industries Collection, Dayton, Ohio

1988 Robert Rosenblum, 'Urban Portraits', in *Bill Jacklin: Urban Portraits*, exh. cat., Marlborough Fine Art, London
Robert Rosenblum, 'Scenes from Urban Life', *Observer Magazine*, 15 May
John Russell Taylor, 'Irresistible Logic of Adventure', *The Times*, 31 May
Brian Sewell, 'The Rebel in Reverse', *Evening Standard*, 3 June
Larry Berryman, 'Urban Portraits', *Arts Review*, 3 June
Sarah Kent, 'Art: Bill Jacklin', *Time Out*, 8–15 June
Sarah Kent, *Pictures by Living British Artists*, exh. cat., Bank of England, London

1989 Larry Berryman, 'Bill Jacklin: Urban Portraits', *Independent*, 6 June

1990 *L'Europe des grands maîtres: quand ils étaient jeunes*, exh. cat., Musée Jacquemart-André, Paris
Edward Lucie-Smith, *Art in the Eighties*, London

1990 John Kobal, *Bill Jacklin*, exh. cat., Marlborough Gallery, New York

1992 Grace Glueck, *New York: The Painted City*, New York
Bill Jacklin, Urban Portraits: Coney Island Series, exh. cat., Marlborough Fine Art, London
Roger Bevan, 'Jacklin at Marlborough and Oxford's MoMA', *The Art Newspaper*, no. 22, November
Anthony O'Heara, 'Bill Jacklin', *Modern Painters*, Winter
David Elliott, John Yau and Nick Cohn, *Bill Jacklin: Urban Portraits, New York 1986–1992*, exh. cat., Museum of Modern Art, Oxford

1993 Albino Mallo, 'Bill Jacklin quiere pintar la luz que hay en Galicia', *El Correo Gallego*, 21 January

1995 Richard Noyce, 'Interview with Bill Jacklin', *Art Line Magazine*, Summer
Hilary Binks, 'Bill Jacklin's Hong Kong', *Window Magazine*, 20 January

1997 John Russell Taylor, *Bill Jacklin*, London
Robin Muir, 'An Englishman in New York', *Independent Magazine*, 29 March
Roger Bevan, 'London Diary: Bill Jacklin Skater', *The Art Newspaper*, no. 70, May
Tracy O'Shaughnessy, 'A Product of his Environment: The Evolution of a Painter', *Republican American*, 11 May
John Russell Taylor, review of *Bill Jacklin*, *Big Issue*, 12 May
John Russell Taylor, 'Bill Jacklin Monograph', *London Magazine*, June–July

1999 Phoebe Hoban, *Bill Jacklin: New York City, The Connected Image 1997–99*, exh. cat., Marlborough Gallery, New York

2000 Jill Lloyd, 'Silhouettes and Shadows, New York City', in *Bill Jacklin. Silhouettes and Shadows: New York City*, exh. cat., Marlborough Fine Art, London

2001 Irving Sandler, *Art Transplant: British Artists in New York*, exh. cat., British Consul-General's Residence, New York

2003 *La Fête*, exh. cat., Le Bellevue, Biarritz

2004 Mary Rose Beaumont, *Bill Jacklin: A Venetian Affair: Paintings and Monotypes*, exh. cat., Marlborough Fine Art, London

2006 John Russell Taylor, 'Crowd Pleaser', *RA Magazine*, no. 84, Autumn
Ihor Holubizky, 'Bill Jacklin: The Art of Being There', in *The Past Is Forgiven: Herman Levy and Josef Herman*, exh. cat., McMaster Museum of Art, Ontario

2007 Jill Lloyd, *Bill Jacklin: People and Places: Recent Paintings*, exh. cat., Marlborough Gallery, New York

2008 Steve Pill, 'Bill Jacklin RA City Dwelling', *Artists & Illustrators*, May

2009 Michael Peppiatt, *Bill Jacklin: People and Places II: Paintings and Monotypes*, exh. cat., Marlborough Fine Art, London, and Marlborough, Monaco

2012 Margaret Priest, 'A Stranger in New York. A Recollection, a Reawakening and a Revelation', in *Bill Jacklin: Recent Work/New York*, exh. cat., Marlborough Gallery, New York

2013 Ihor Holubizky, *Bill Jacklin: Paintings, Pastels and Prints*, exh. cat., Marlborough Fine Art, London

2017 Eric Bryant, 'Bill Jacklin: Life as an Intuitive Conceptualist', in *Bill Jacklin, 1986 to 2017, Paintings*, exh. cat., Marlborough Gallery, New York

2019 Bill Jacklin, 'A Sense of Place', in *Bill Jacklin: Paintings and Monotypes 2019*, exh. cat., Marlborough Fine Art, London

2021 Bill Jacklin (illustrator), Simon Astaire (author), *Cressida's Dream*, Ordovas Gallery, London

Film, Television, Radio

1980 Edward Lucie-Smith, 'Critics' Choice', BBC Radio 4, 4 June
1988 Marina Vaizey, Anthony Curtis, Adam Mars-Jones and John Wilders, 'Critics' Forum', BBC Radio 4
1989 'Washington Square at Night, Painted Tales', Canning Factory Productions, Channel 4
1992 Tina O'Donnell, 'Bill Jacklin in New York', Tina Eden Productions Video, New York
1994 'Making Marks, Bill Jacklin in Hong Kong', British Council Hong Kong Educational Film
1998 'Washington National Airport: The New Terminal', promotional film (interview with Bill Jacklin), Viewfinder Productions

Selected Public Collections

Arkansas Arts Center, Little Rock, Arkansas
Arts Council England, London
Arts Council of Ireland, Dublin
Art Gallery of New South Wales, Sydney
Ashmolean Museum, Oxford
Bayley Art Museum, University of Virginia, Charlottesville, Virginia
British Council, London
The British Museum, London
Brooklyn Museum of Art, Brooklyn, New York
City Art Gallery, Bradford
Contemporary Art Society, London
Fitzwilliam Museum, Cambridge
Fondation Veranneman, Kruishoutem
Government Art Collection, England
Houghton Library, Harvard College, The Harvard Theatre Collection
Hunterian Art Gallery, Glasgow
Isle of Man Arts Council, Douglas
Kemper Museum of Contemporary Art, Kansas City, Missouri
The Library of Congress, Anglo American Acquisitions Division, Washington DC
The Metropolitan Museum of Art, New York
The Morgan Library & Museum, New York
Museum Boijmans-van-Beuningen, Rotterdam
Museum of Fine Arts, the Brian Montgomery Collection, Budapest
The Museum of Modern Art, New York
National Army Museum, London
National Portrait Gallery, Smithsonian Institution, Washington DC
The New York Public Library of the Performing Arts, Billy Rose Theatre Division, New York
Palmer Museum of Art, Pennsylvania State University
Portland Museum of Art, Oregon
The Queen's Gallery (RA Portfolio), London
Royal Academy of Arts, London
Tampa Museum of Art, Florida
Tate, London
Thyssen-Bornemisza Foundation, Villa Favorita, Castagnola
University of Alberta Art and Artifact Collection, Edmonton
University of Guelph, Ontario
University of Leicester
University of Northumbria at Newcastle, Newcastle upon Tyne
Victoria and Albert Museum, London
Yale Center for British Art, New Haven, Connecticut
Zimmerli Art Museum, Rutgers University, New Brunswick, New Jersey

Selected Corporate Collections

The Bank of England, London
Cathay Pacific, London and Frankfurt
De Beers, London
Deutsche Morgan Grenfell, London
Gartmore plc, London
Goldman Sachs, London
McCrory Corporation, New York
Midland Bank, London
Philips Industries, Dayton, Ohio
Texaco Properties, San Ramon, California

Photographic Acknowledgements

Every attempt has been made to trace photographic acknowledgements. We apologise for any inadvertent infringement and invite appropriate rights-holders to contact us.

Index of Works Illustrated